KING'S ROAD™

THE LONG WAY HOME

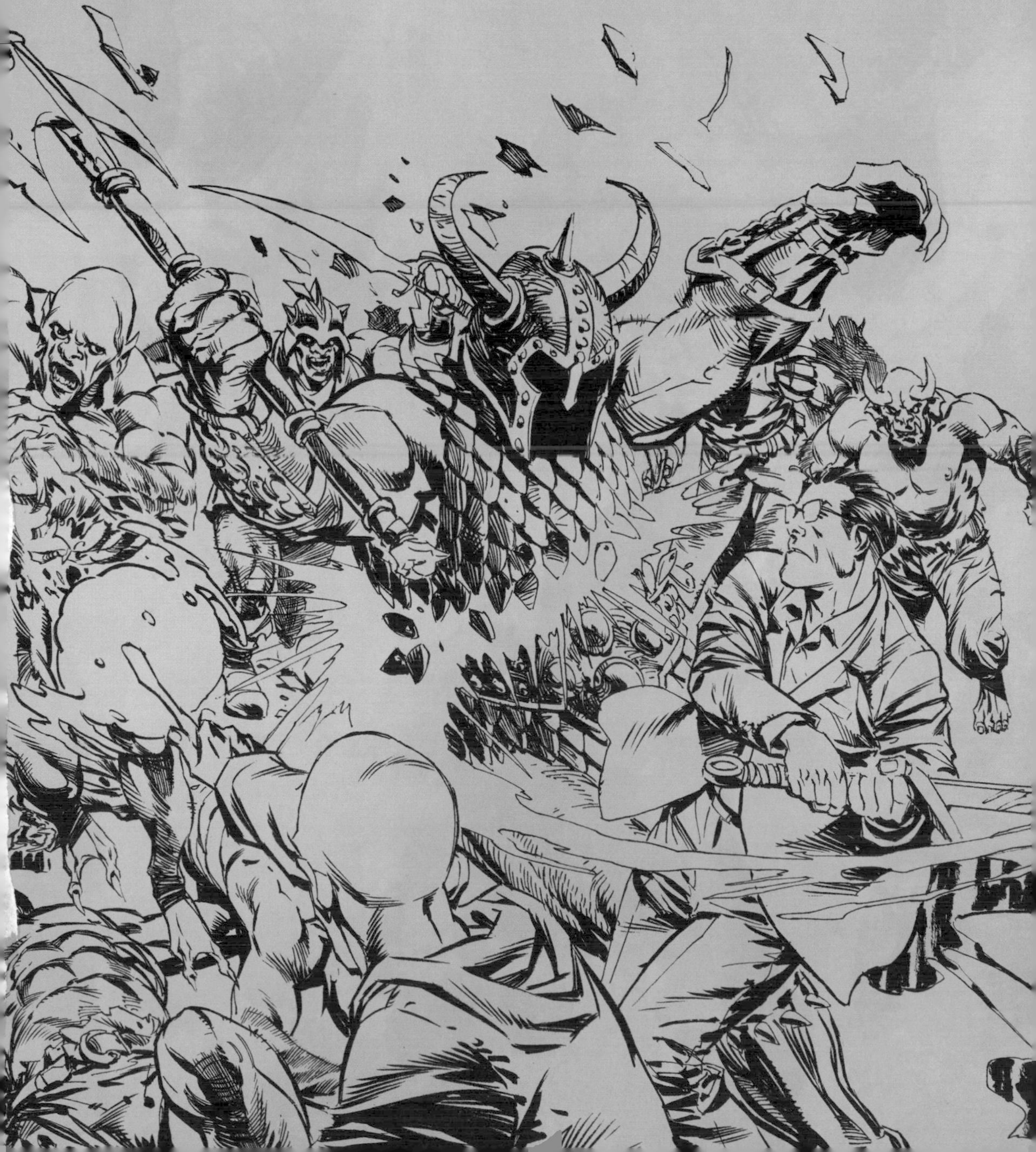

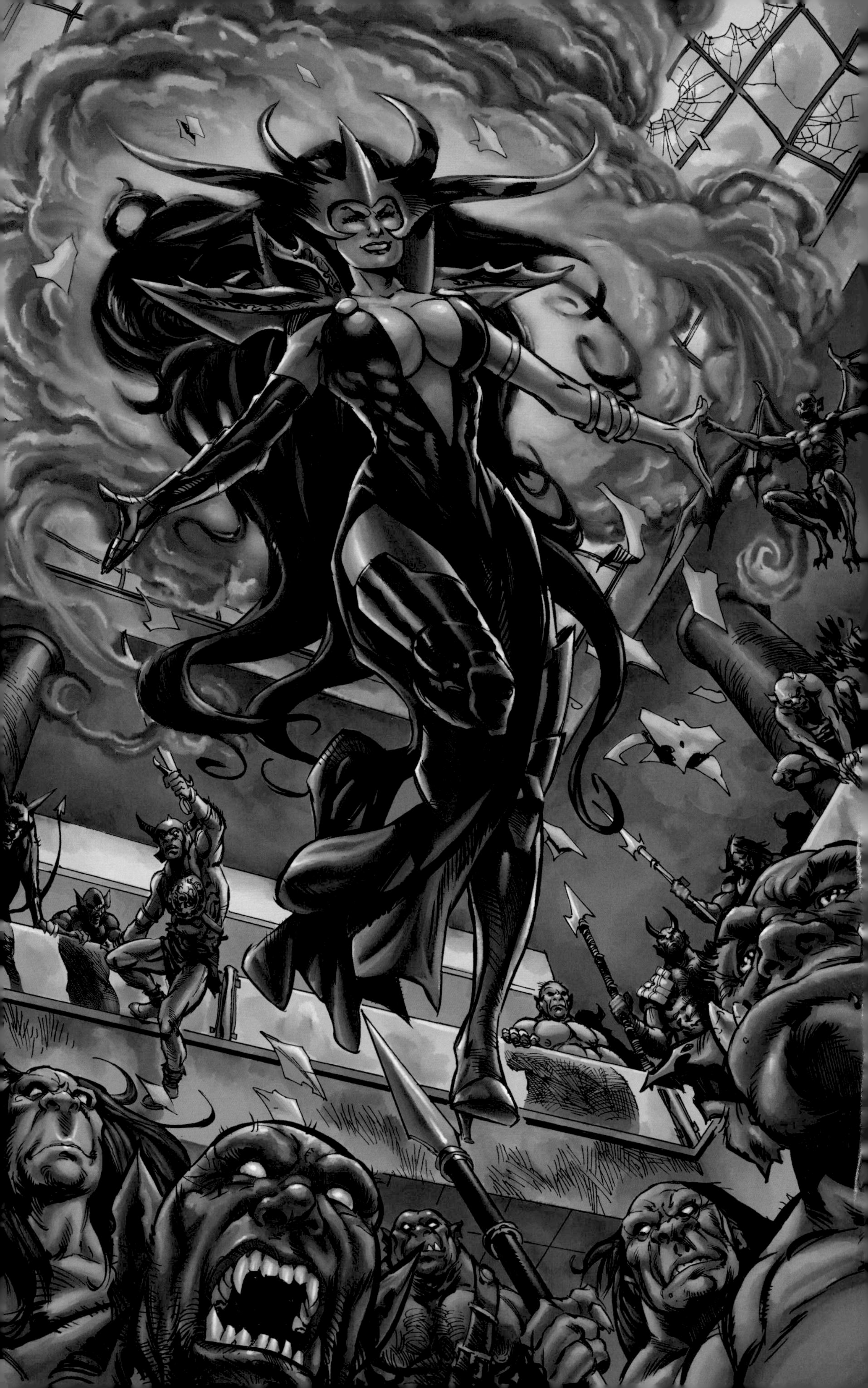

KING'S ROAD

THE LONG WAY HOME

Based on characters originally created by
Peter Hogan and Phil Winslade

Script
PETER HOGAN

Art and Colors
pages 5 to 28
PHIL WINSLADE

Art
pages 29 to 94
STAZ JOHNSON

Colors
pages 29 to 94
DOUGLAS SIROIS

Lettering
STEVE DUTRO

Cover art by STAZ JOHNSON

Cover colors by DOUGLAS SIROIS

DARK HORSE BOOKS

Publisher
MIKE RICHARDSON

Editor
PHILIP R. SIMON

Designer
JACK THOMAS

Digital Art Technician
CHRISTIANNE GOUDREAU

This volume collects issues #1–#3 of the Dark Horse Comics miniseries *King's Road*, published in 2016. Some of the contents of issue #1 were originally serialized in *Dark Horse Presents* Volume 2, #23 through #25, published in 2013.

Published by
Dark Horse Books
A division of Dark Horse Comics, Inc.
10956 SE Main Street
Milwaukie, OR 97222

DarkHorse.com

International Licensing: (503) 905-2377

To find a comics shop in your area, call the
Comic Shop Locator Service toll-free at 1-888-266-4226

First edition: August 2016
ISBN 978-1-61655-961-8

1 3 5 7 9 10 8 6 4 2

Printed in China

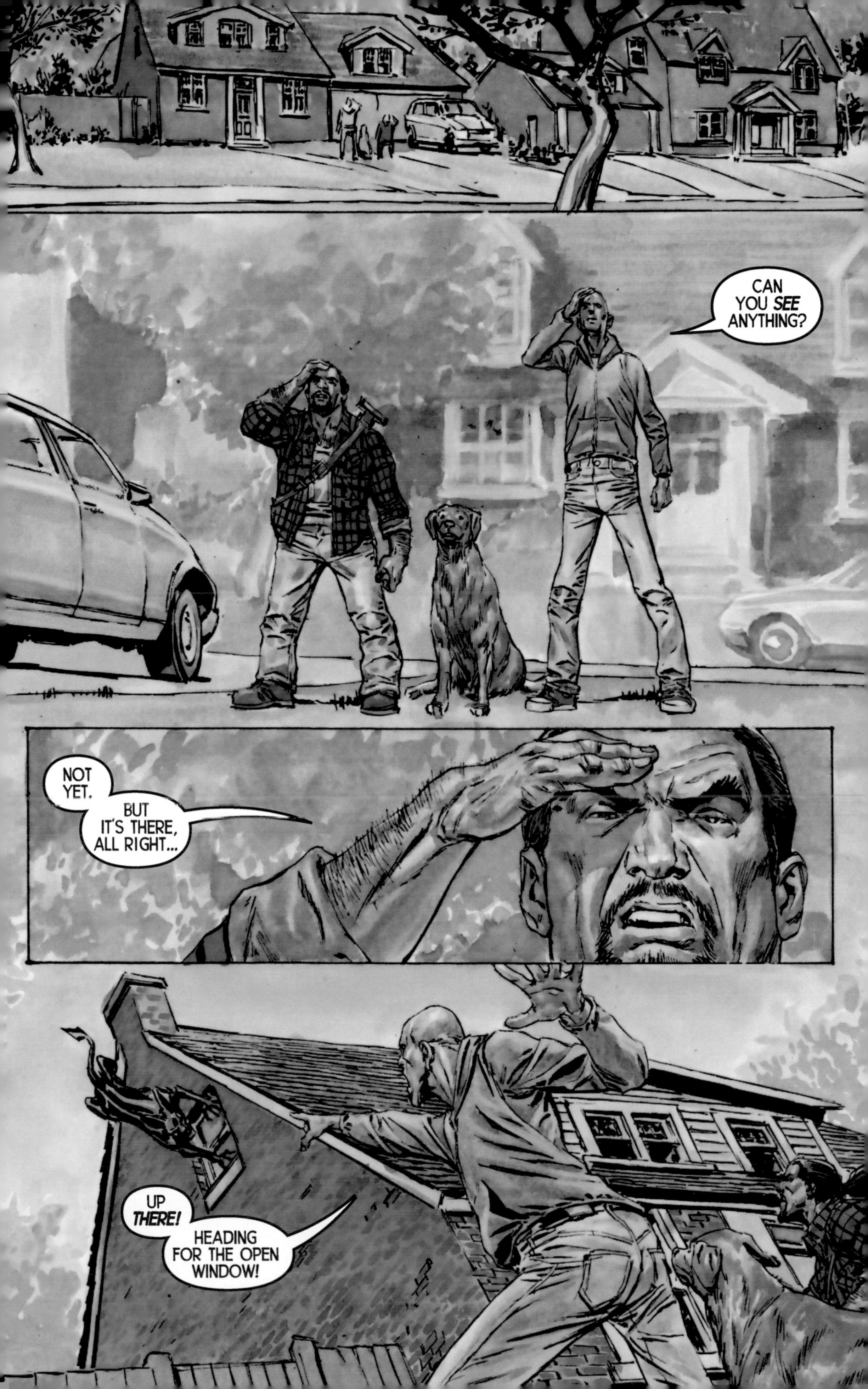
CAN YOU SEE ANYTHING?
NOT YET.
BUT IT'S THERE, ALL RIGHT...
UP THERE!
HEADING FOR THE OPEN WINDOW!

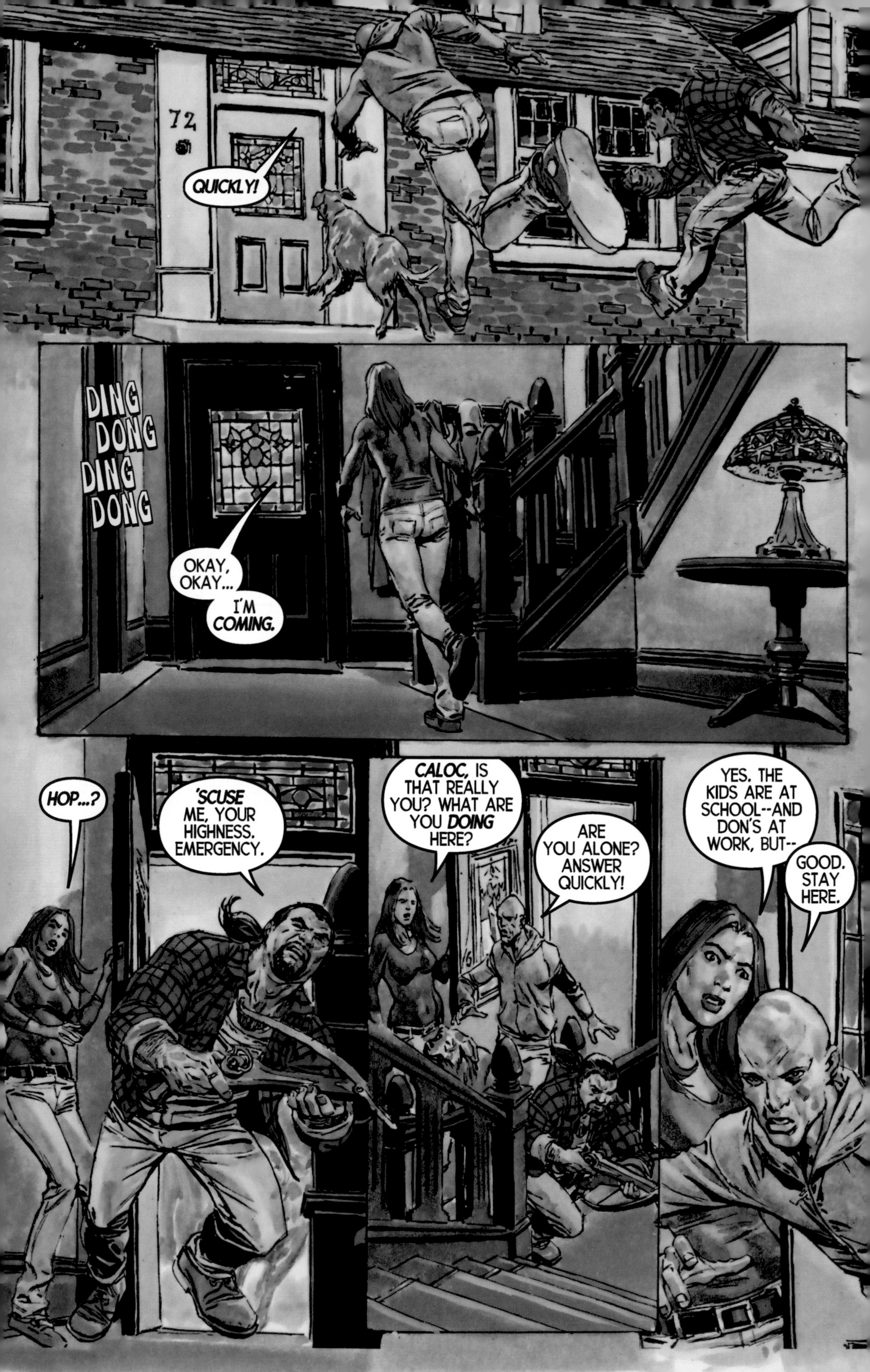

72
QUICKLY!
DING DONG DING DONG
OKAY, OKAY...
I'M COMING.
HOP...?
'SCUSE ME, YOUR HIGHNESS. EMERGENCY.
CALOC, IS THAT REALLY YOU? WHAT ARE YOU DOING HERE?
ARE YOU ALONE? ANSWER QUICKLY!
YES. THE KIDS ARE AT SCHOOL--AND DON'S AT WORK, BUT--
GOOD. STAY HERE.

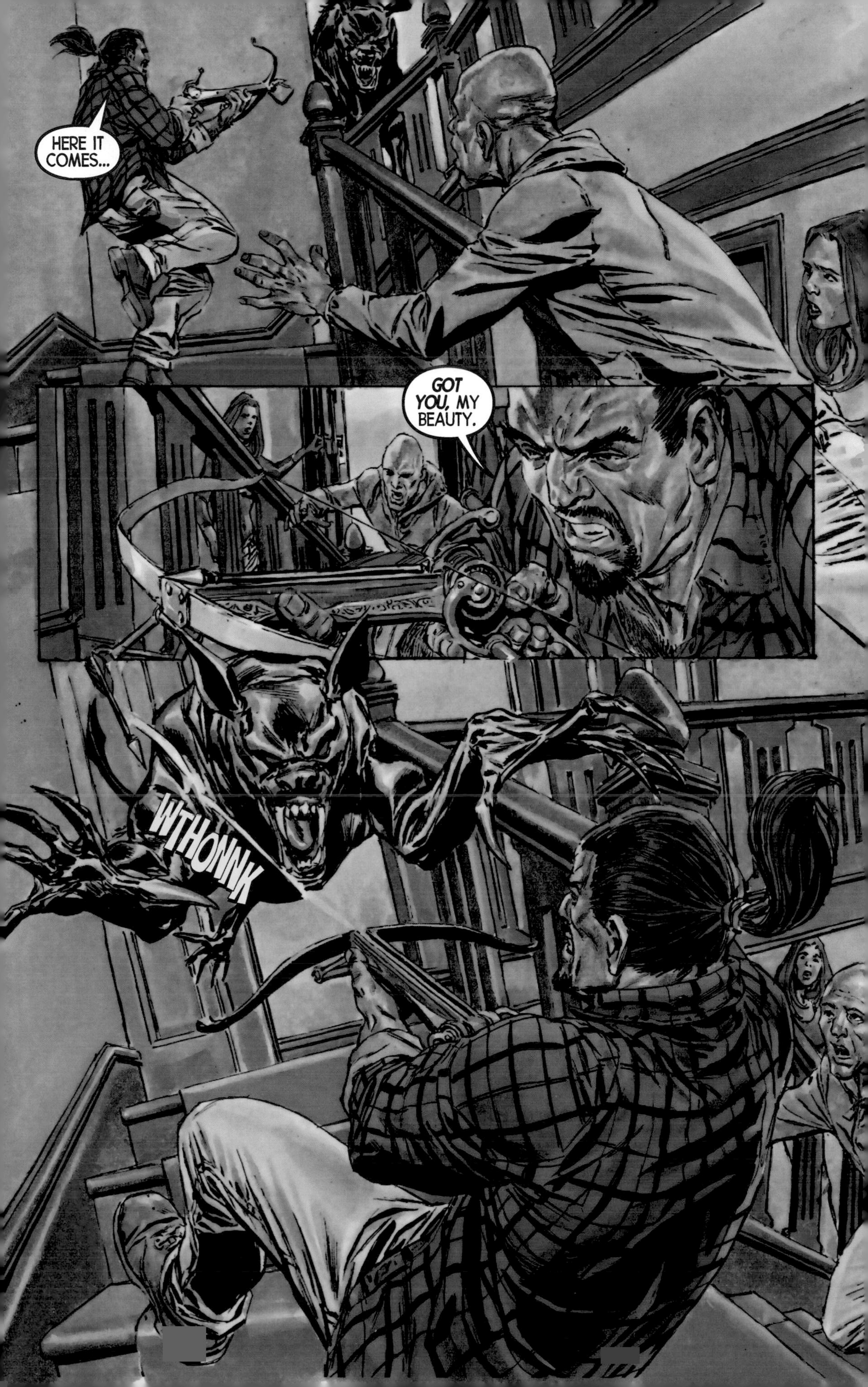
HERE IT COMES...
GOT YOU, MY BEAUTY.
WTHONNK

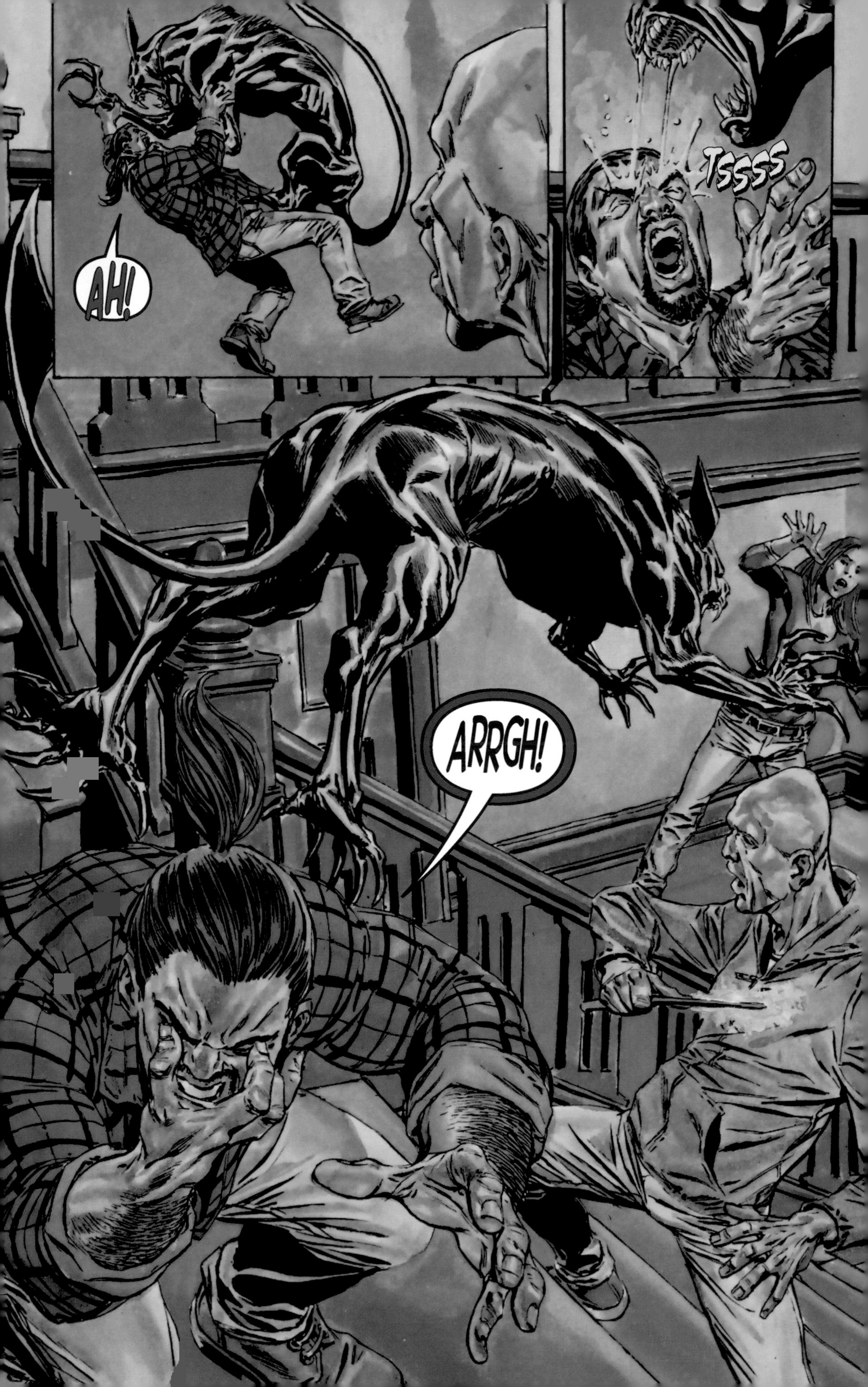
AH!
TSSSS
ARRGH!

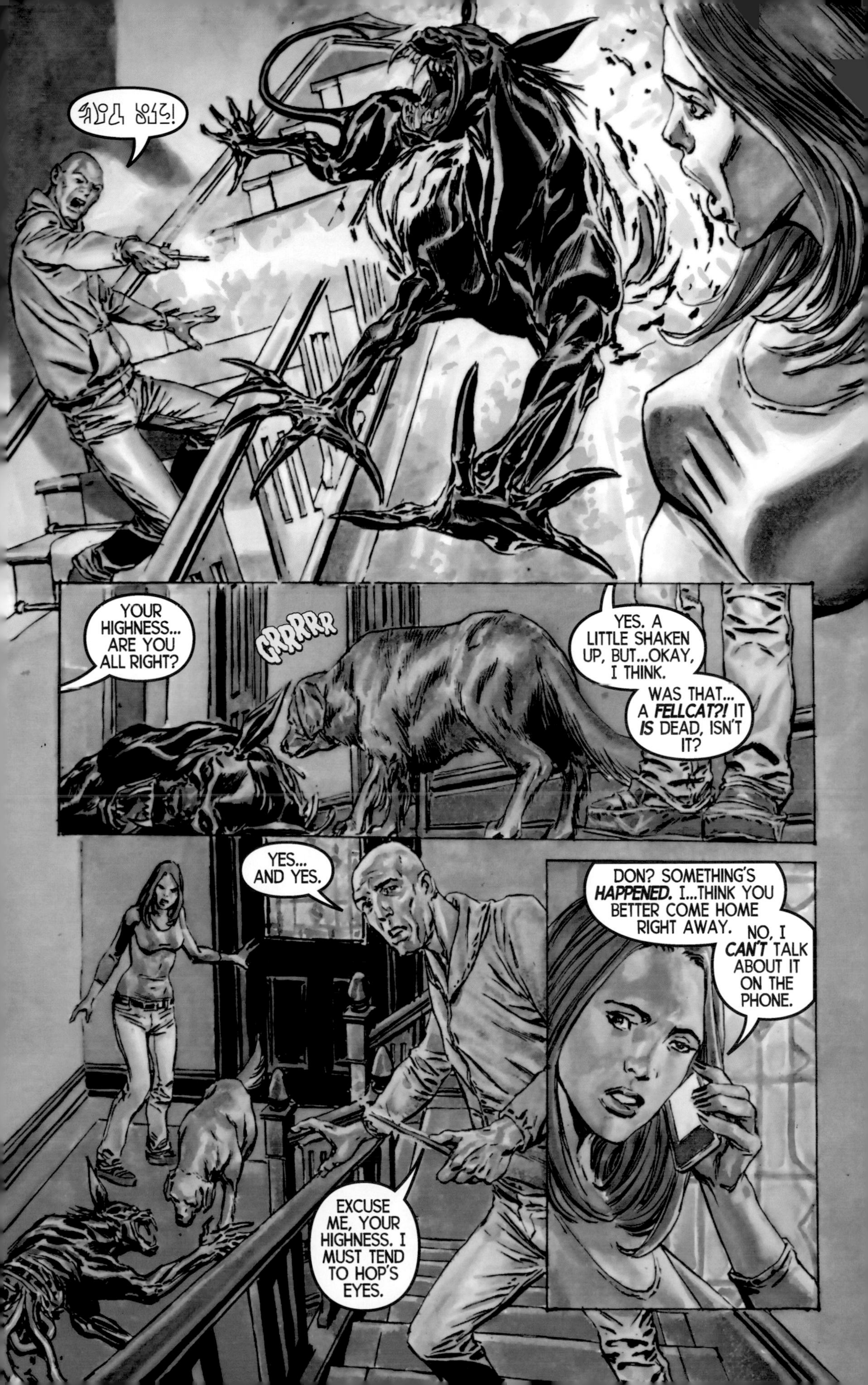
YOUR HIGHNESS... ARE YOU ALL RIGHT?
GRRRRR
YES. A LITTLE SHAKEN UP, BUT...OKAY, I THINK.
WAS THAT... A FELLCAT?! IT IS DEAD, ISN'T IT?
YES... AND YES.
EXCUSE ME, YOUR HIGHNESS. I MUST TEND TO HOP'S EYES.
DON? SOMETHING'S HAPPENED. I...THINK YOU BETTER COME HOME RIGHT AWAY.
NO, I CAN'T TALK ABOUT IT ON THE PHONE.

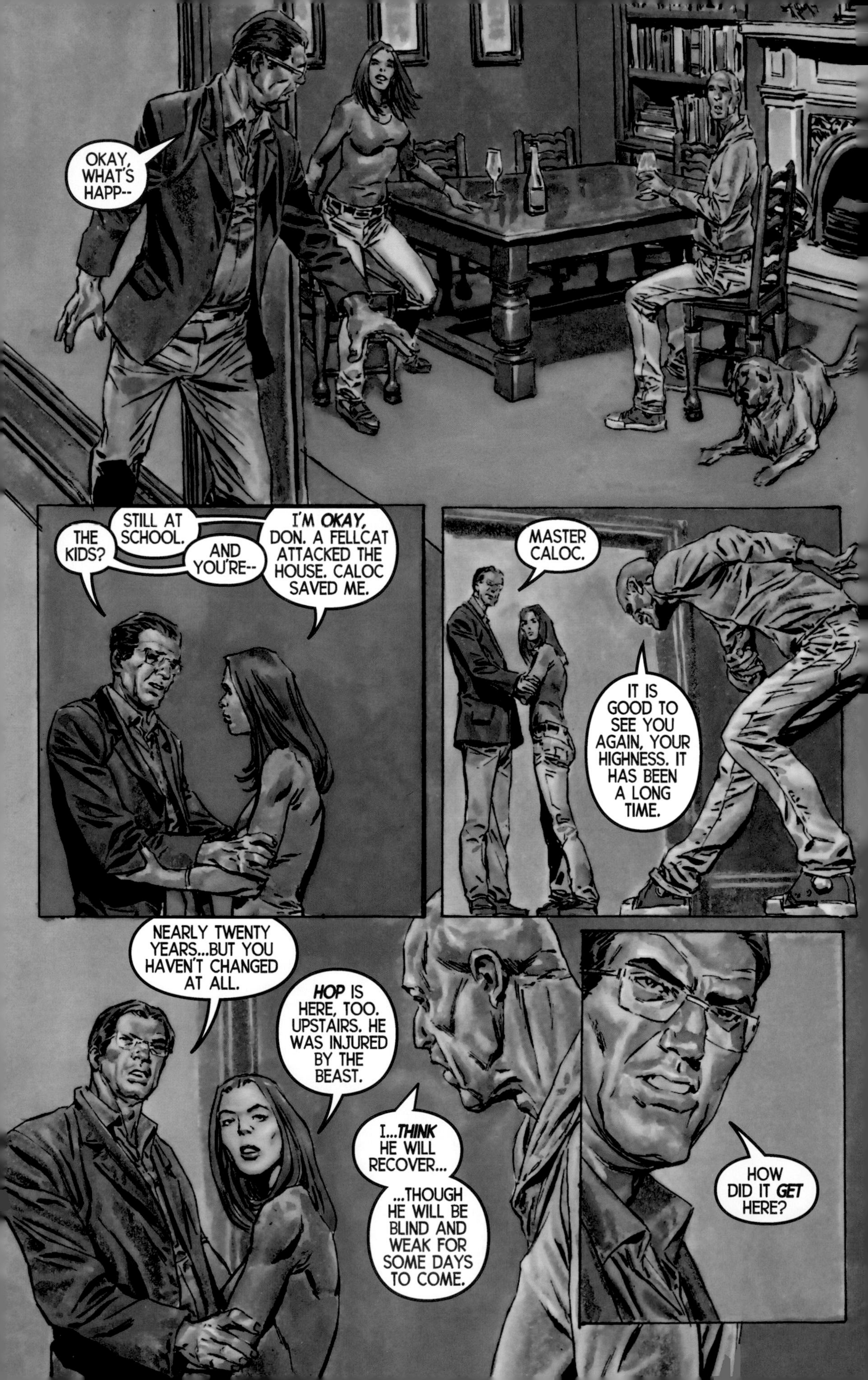
OKAY, WHAT'S HAPP--
THE KIDS?
STILL AT SCHOOL.
AND YOU'RE--
I'M *OKAY,* DON. A FELLCAT ATTACKED THE HOUSE. CALOC SAVED ME.
MASTER CALOC.
IT IS GOOD TO SEE YOU AGAIN, YOUR HIGHNESS. IT HAS BEEN A LONG TIME.
NEARLY TWENTY YEARS...BUT YOU HAVEN'T CHANGED AT ALL.
HOP IS HERE, TOO. UPSTAIRS. HE WAS INJURED BY THE BEAST.
I...*THINK* HE WILL RECOVER...
...THOUGH HE WILL BE BLIND AND WEAK FOR SOME DAYS TO COME.
HOW DID IT *GET* HERE?

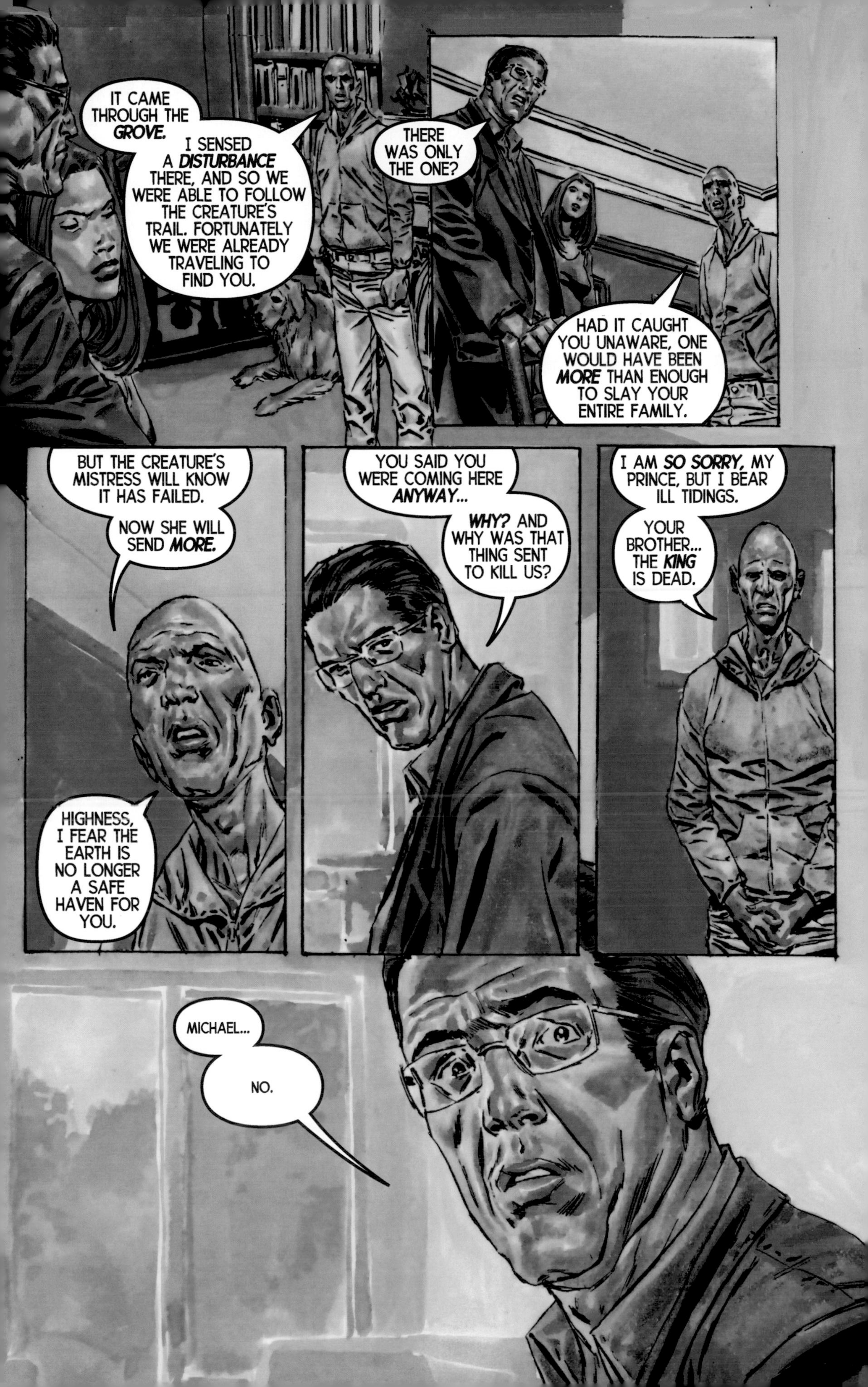
IT CAME THROUGH THE GROVE.
I SENSED A DISTURBANCE THERE, AND SO WE WERE ABLE TO FOLLOW THE CREATURE'S TRAIL. FORTUNATELY WE WERE ALREADY TRAVELING TO FIND YOU.
THERE WAS ONLY THE ONE?
HAD IT CAUGHT YOU UNAWARE, ONE WOULD HAVE BEEN MORE THAN ENOUGH TO SLAY YOUR ENTIRE FAMILY.
BUT THE CREATURE'S MISTRESS WILL KNOW IT HAS FAILED.
NOW SHE WILL SEND MORE.
HIGHNESS, I FEAR THE EARTH IS NO LONGER A SAFE HAVEN FOR YOU.
YOU SAID YOU WERE COMING HERE ANYWAY...
WHY? AND WHY WAS THAT THING SENT TO KILL US?
I AM SO SORRY, MY PRINCE, BUT I BEAR ILL TIDINGS.
YOUR BROTHER... THE KING IS DEAD.
MICHAEL...
NO.

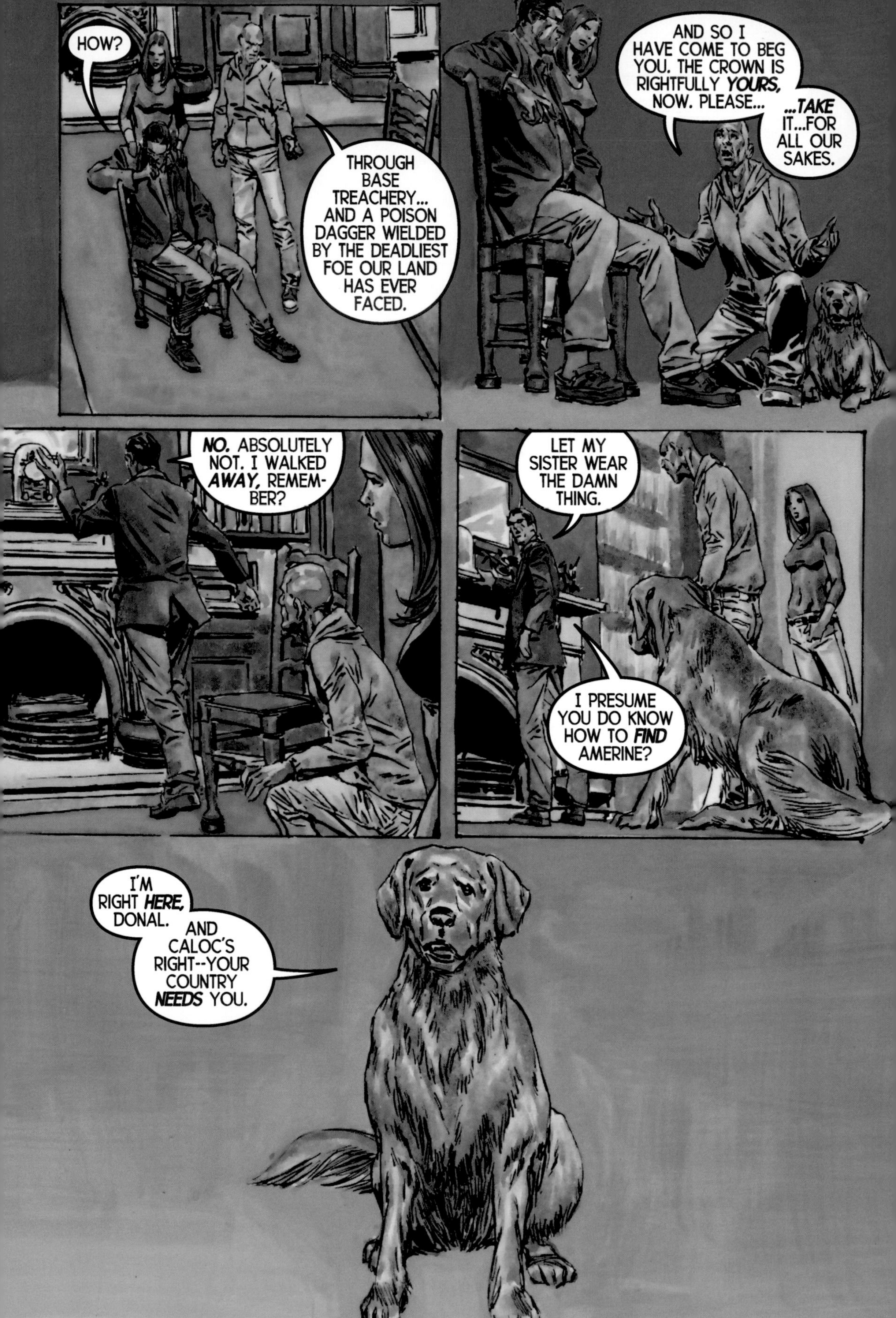
HOW?
THROUGH BASE TREACHERY... AND A POISON DAGGER WIELDED BY THE DEADLIEST FOE OUR LAND HAS EVER FACED.
AND SO I HAVE COME TO BEG YOU. THE CROWN IS RIGHTFULLY YOURS, NOW. PLEASE...
...TAKE IT...FOR ALL OUR SAKES.
NO. ABSOLUTELY NOT. I WALKED AWAY, REMEMBER?
LET MY SISTER WEAR THE DAMN THING.
I PRESUME YOU DO KNOW HOW TO FIND AMERINE?
I'M RIGHT HERE, DONAL.
AND CALOC'S RIGHT--YOUR COUNTRY NEEDS YOU.

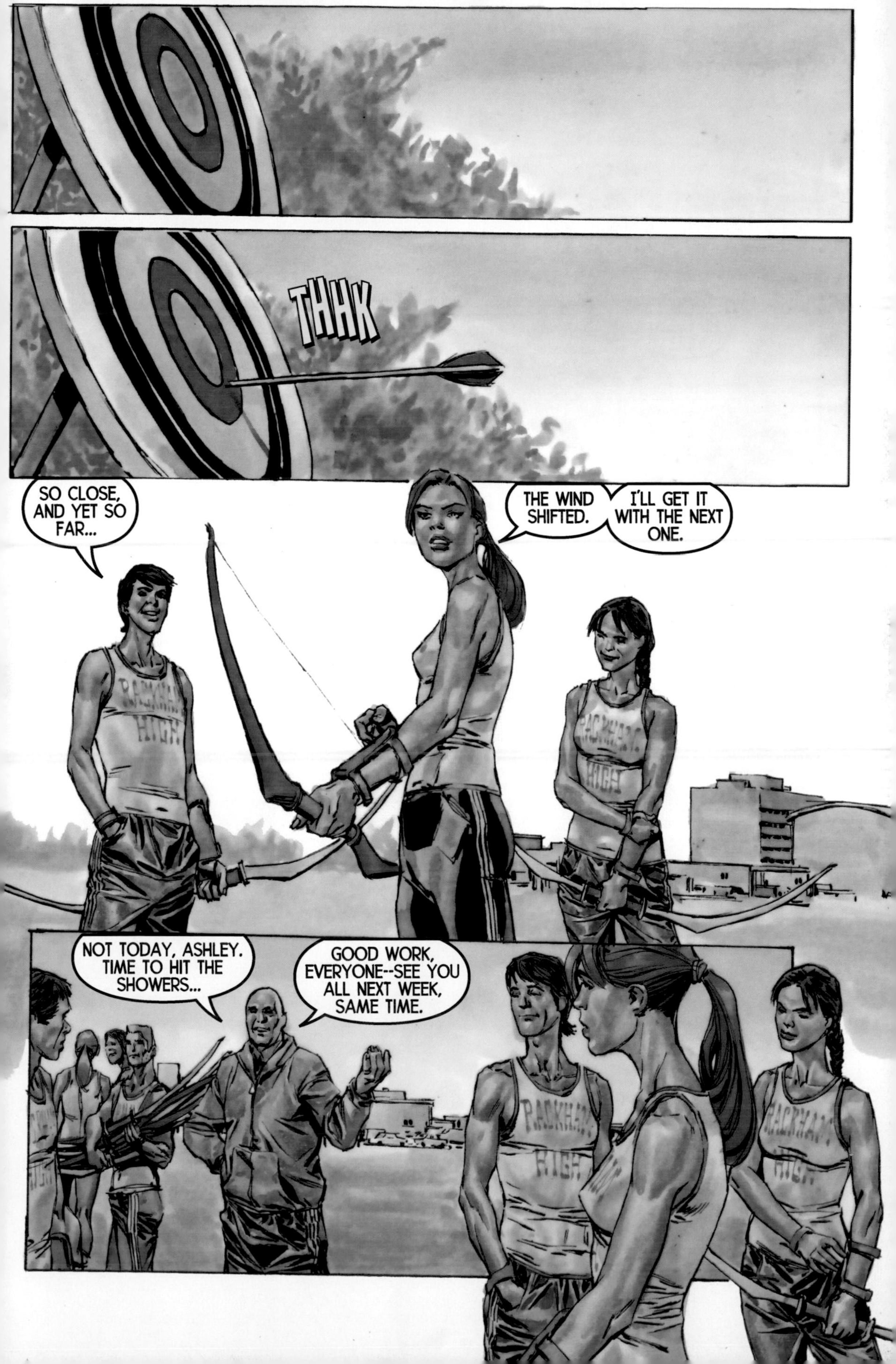
THHK
SO CLOSE, AND YET SO FAR...
THE WIND SHIFTED.
I'LL GET IT WITH THE NEXT ONE.
RACKHAM HIGH
NOT TODAY, ASHLEY. TIME TO HIT THE SHOWERS...
GOOD WORK, EVERYONE--SEE YOU ALL NEXT WEEK, SAME TIME.

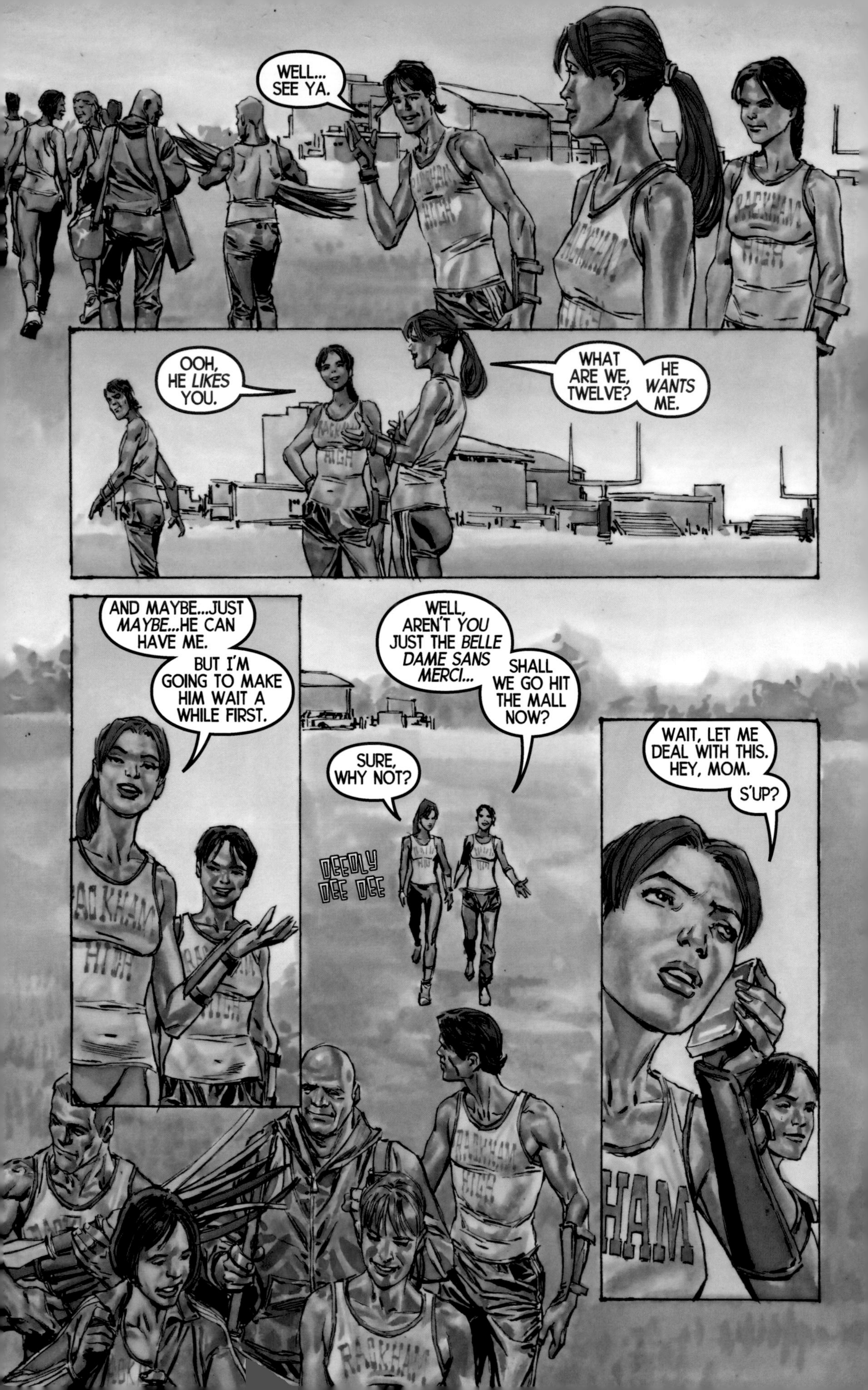
WELL... SEE YA.
OOH, HE LIKES YOU.
WHAT ARE WE, TWELVE?
HE WANTS ME.
AND MAYBE...JUST MAYBE...HE CAN HAVE ME.
BUT I'M GOING TO MAKE HIM WAIT A WHILE FIRST.
WELL, AREN'T YOU JUST THE BELLE DAME SANS MERCI...
SHALL WE GO HIT THE MALL NOW?
SURE, WHY NOT?
DEEDLY DEE DEE
WAIT, LET ME DEAL WITH THIS. HEY, MOM.
S'UP?

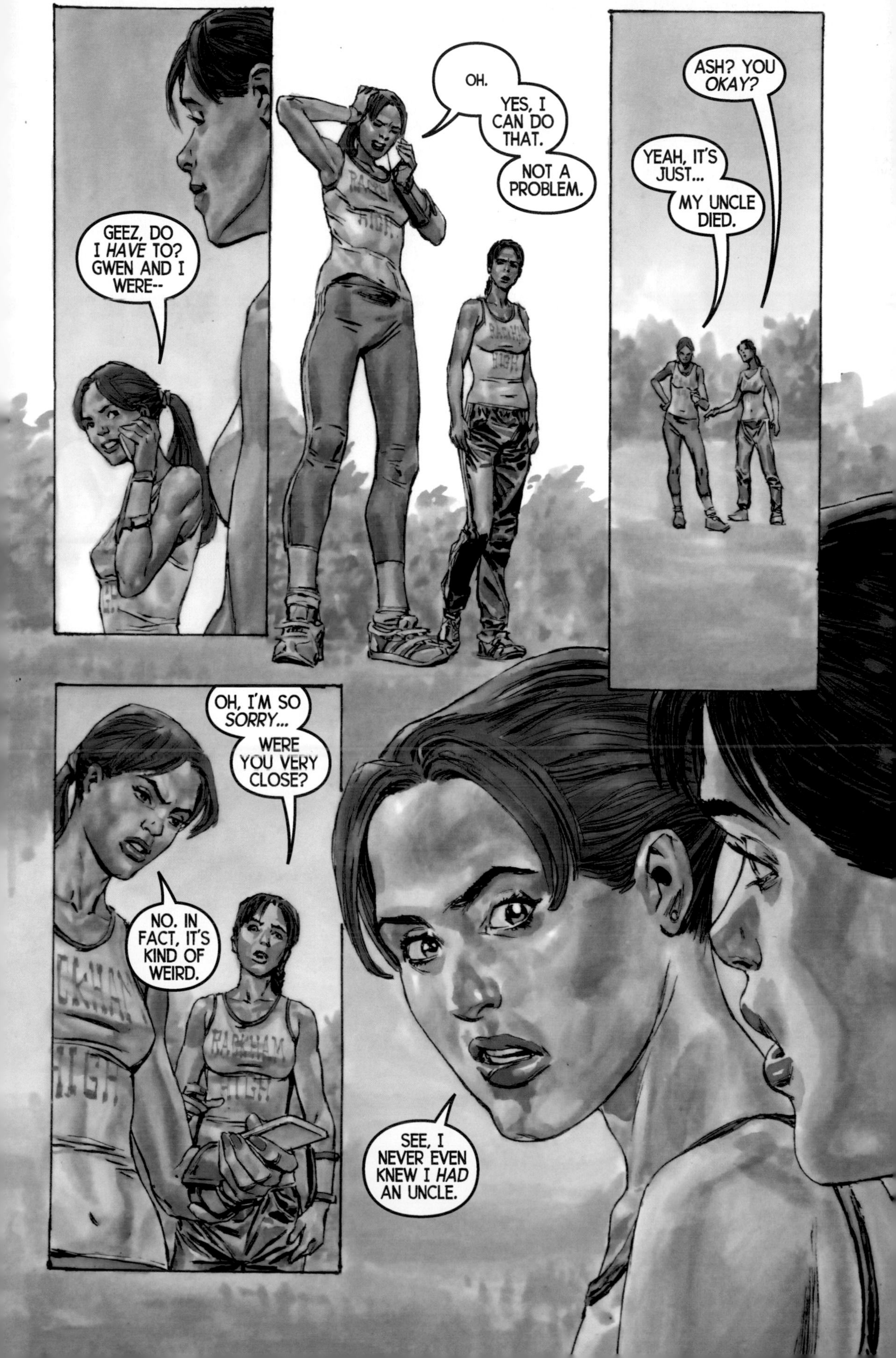
GEEZ, DO I HAVE TO? GWEN AND I WERE--
OH.
YES, I CAN DO THAT.
NOT A PROBLEM.
ASH? YOU OKAY?
YEAH, IT'S JUST...
MY UNCLE DIED.
OH, I'M SO SORRY...
WERE YOU VERY CLOSE?
NO. IN FACT, IT'S KIND OF WEIRD.
SEE, I NEVER EVEN KNEW I HAD AN UNCLE.

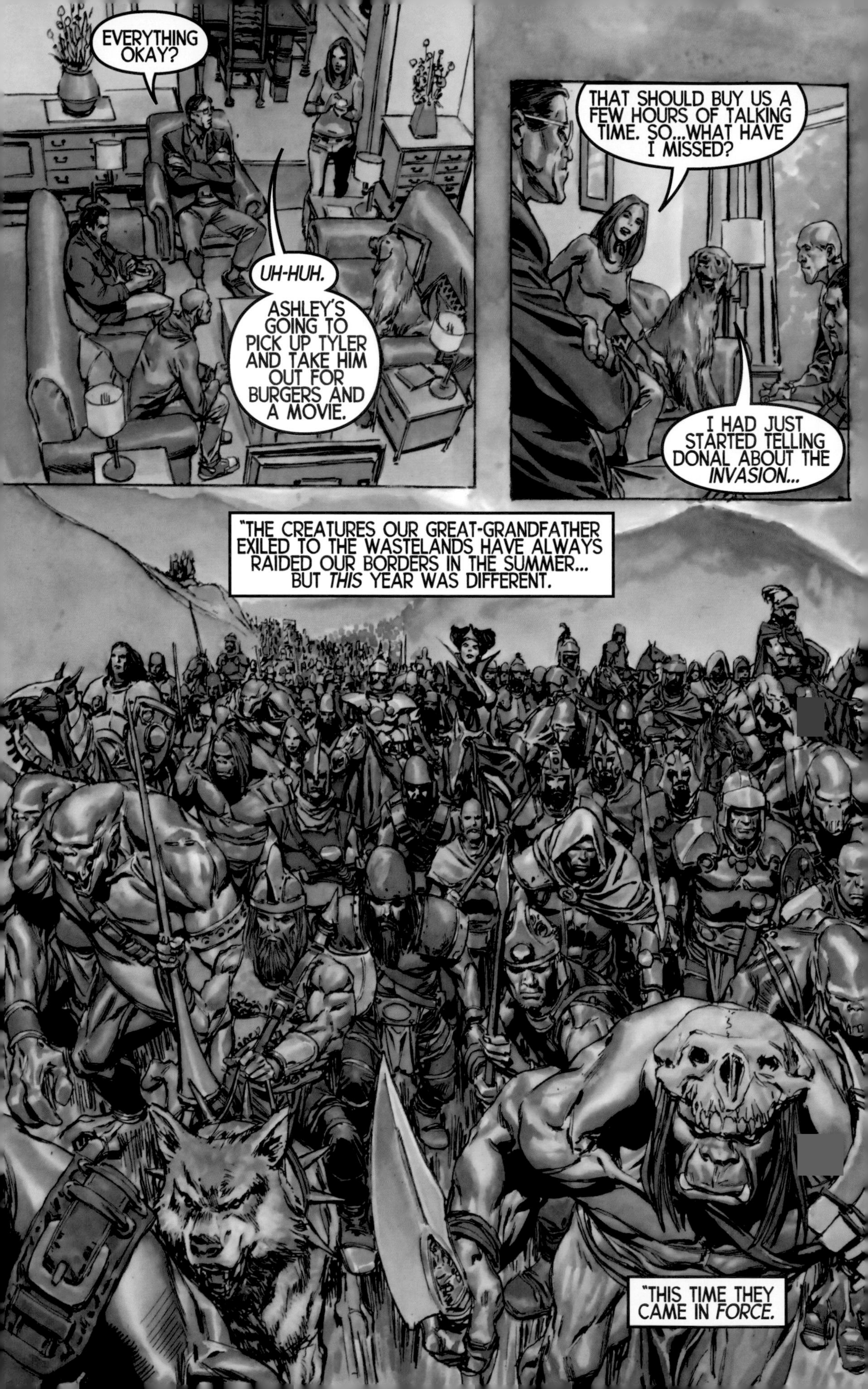
EVERYTHING OKAY?
UH-HUH.
ASHLEY'S GOING TO PICK UP TYLER AND TAKE HIM OUT FOR BURGERS AND A MOVIE.
THAT SHOULD BUY US A FEW HOURS OF TALKING TIME. SO...WHAT HAVE I MISSED?
I HAD JUST STARTED TELLING DONAL ABOUT THE *INVASION*...
"THE CREATURES OUR GREAT-GRANDFATHER EXILED TO THE WASTELANDS HAVE ALWAYS RAIDED OUR BORDERS IN THE SUMMER... BUT *THIS* YEAR WAS DIFFERENT.
"THIS TIME THEY CAME IN *FORCE*.

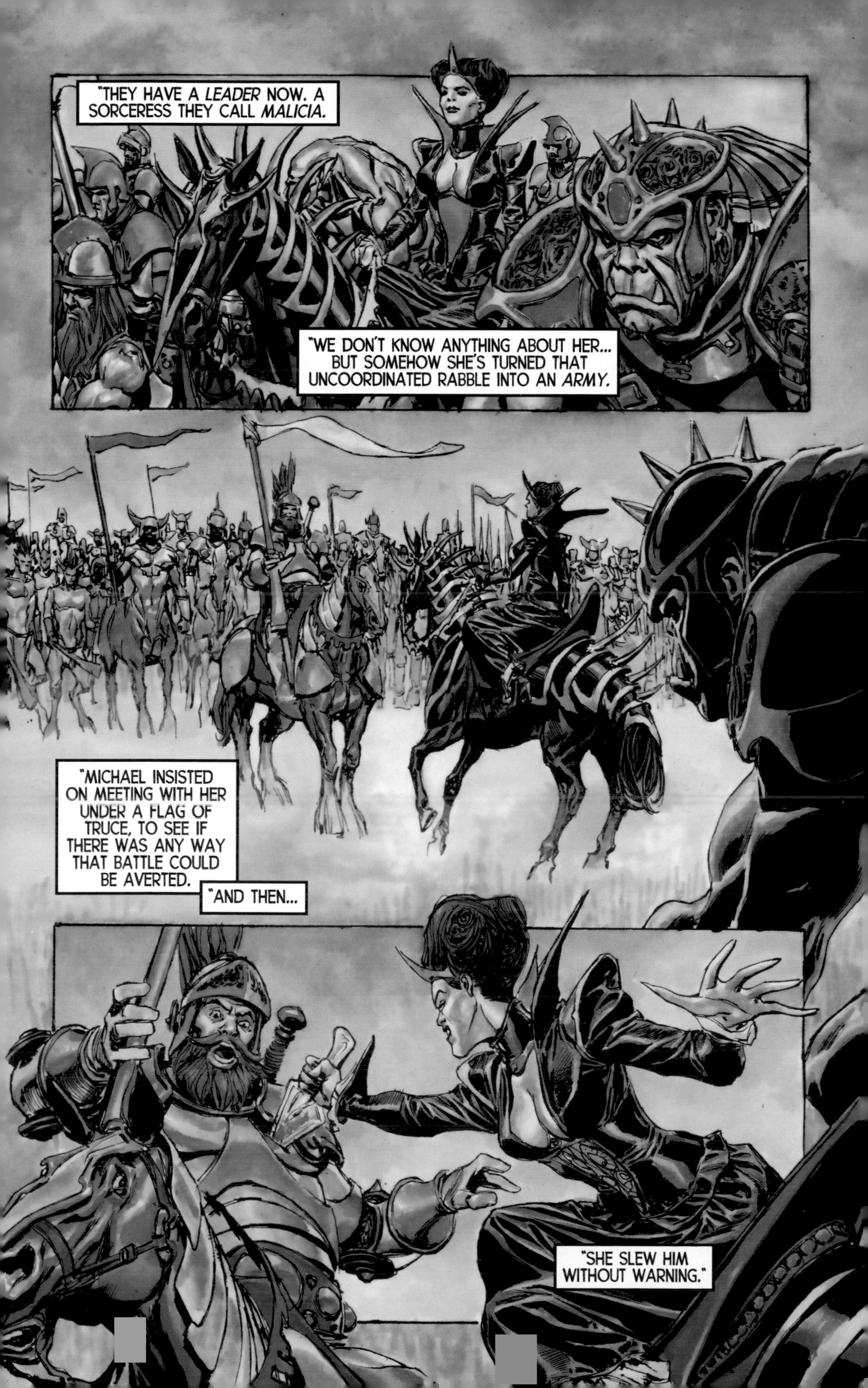
"THEY HAVE A *LEADER* NOW. A SORCERESS THEY CALL *MALICIA.*
"WE DON'T KNOW ANYTHING ABOUT HER... BUT SOMEHOW SHE'S TURNED THAT UNCOORDINATED RABBLE INTO AN *ARMY.*
"MICHAEL INSISTED ON MEETING WITH HER UNDER A FLAG OF TRUCE, TO SEE IF THERE WAS ANY WAY THAT BATTLE COULD BE AVERTED.
"AND THEN...
"SHE SLEW HIM WITHOUT WARNING."

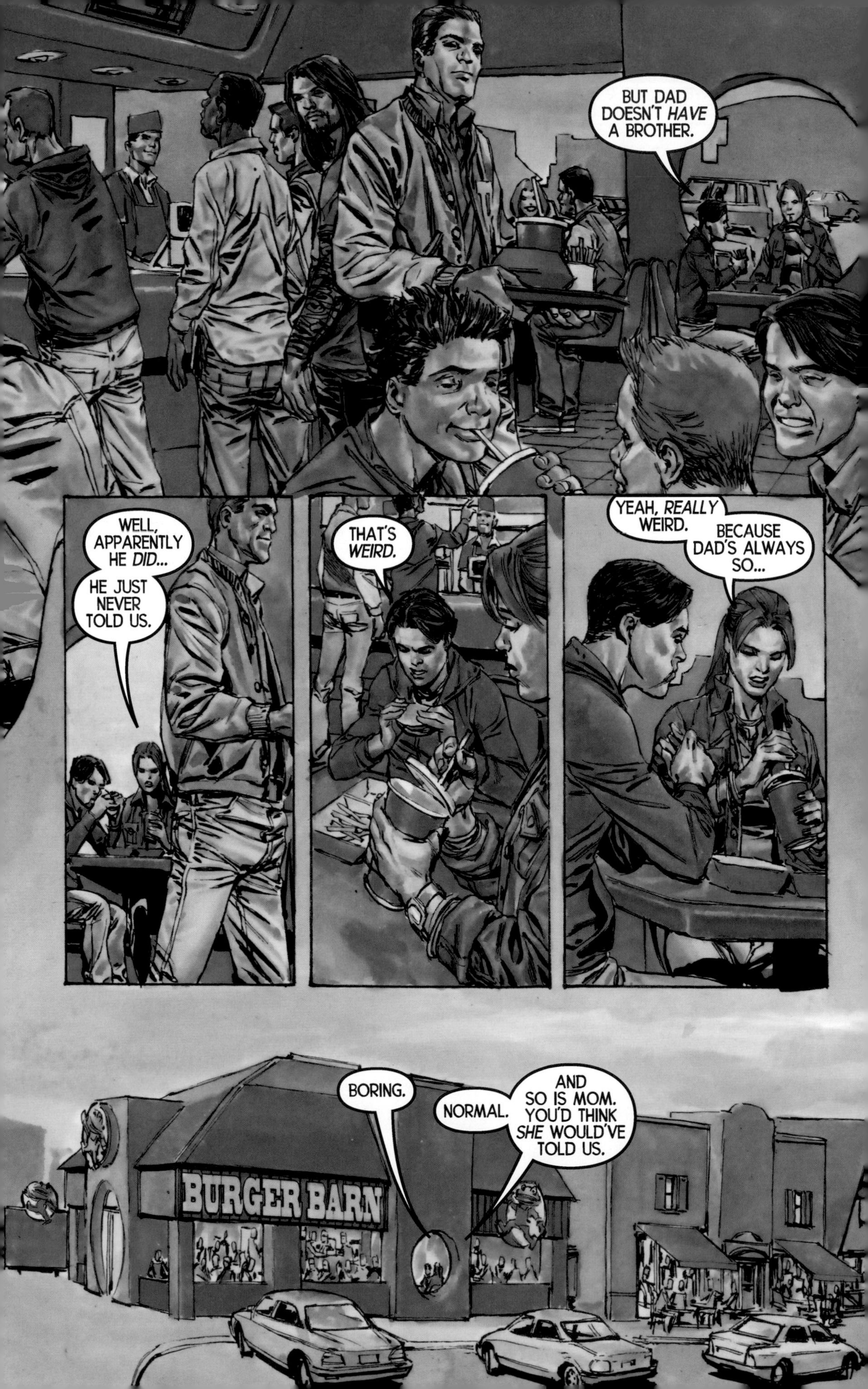
BUT DAD DOESN'T *HAVE* A BROTHER.
WELL, APPARENTLY HE *DID*...
HE JUST NEVER TOLD US.
THAT'S *WEIRD.*
YEAH, *REALLY* WEIRD.
BECAUSE DAD'S ALWAYS SO...
BORING.
NORMAL.
AND SO IS MOM. YOU'D THINK *SHE* WOULD'VE TOLD US.
BURGER BARN

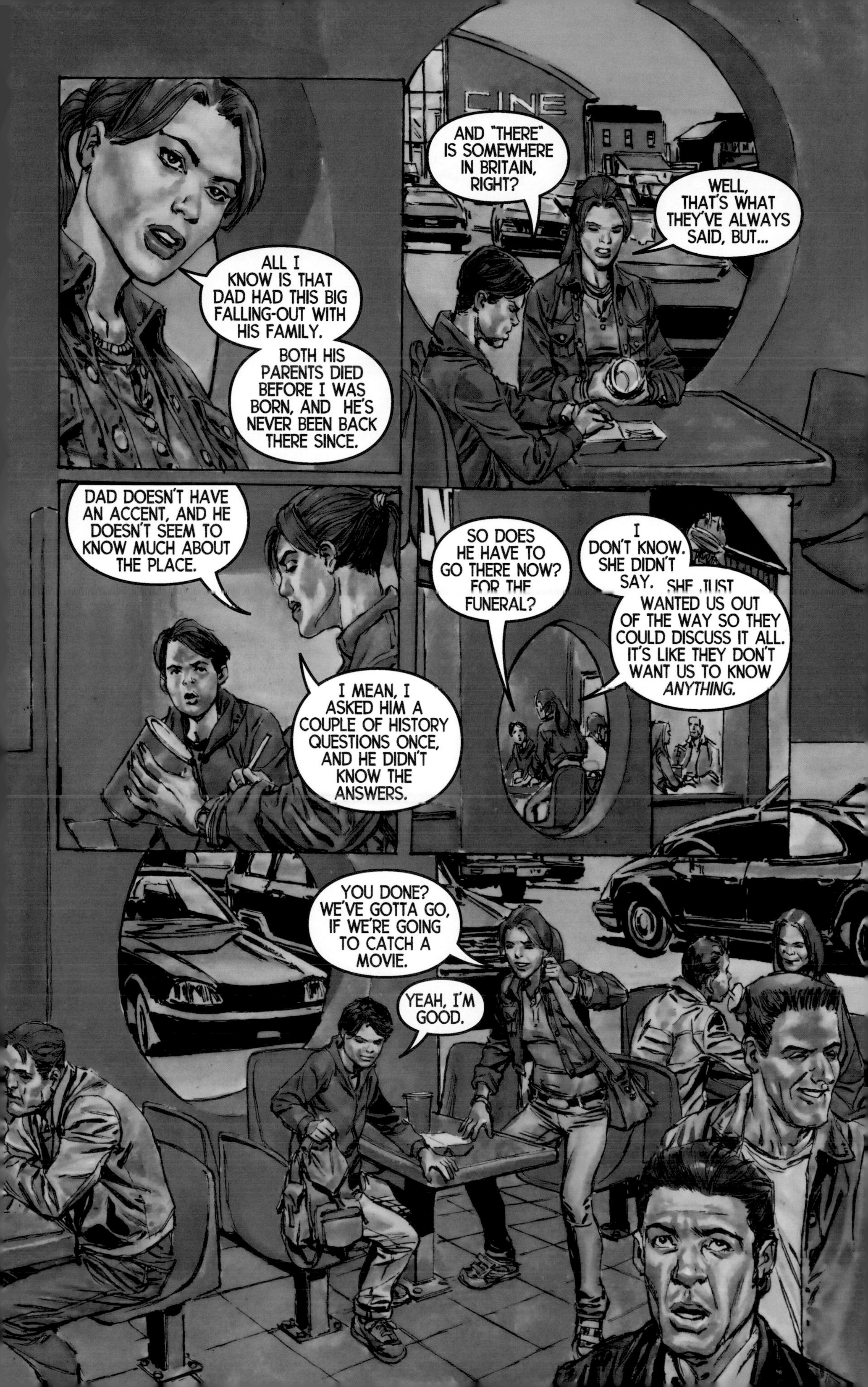
ALL I KNOW IS THAT DAD HAD THIS BIG FALLING-OUT WITH HIS FAMILY.
BOTH HIS PARENTS DIED BEFORE I WAS BORN, AND HE'S NEVER BEEN BACK THERE SINCE.
CINE
AND "THERE" IS SOMEWHERE IN BRITAIN, RIGHT?
WELL, THAT'S WHAT THEY'VE ALWAYS SAID, BUT...
DAD DOESN'T HAVE AN ACCENT, AND HE DOESN'T SEEM TO KNOW MUCH ABOUT THE PLACE.
I MEAN, I ASKED HIM A COUPLE OF HISTORY QUESTIONS ONCE, AND HE DIDN'T KNOW THE ANSWERS.
SO DOES HE HAVE TO GO THERE NOW? FOR THE FUNERAL?
I DON'T KNOW. SHE DIDN'T SAY.
SHE JUST WANTED US OUT OF THE WAY SO THEY COULD DISCUSS IT ALL. IT'S LIKE THEY DON'T WANT US TO KNOW *ANYTHING.*
YOU DONE? WE'VE GOTTA GO, IF WE'RE GOING TO CATCH A MOVIE.
YEAH, I'M GOOD.

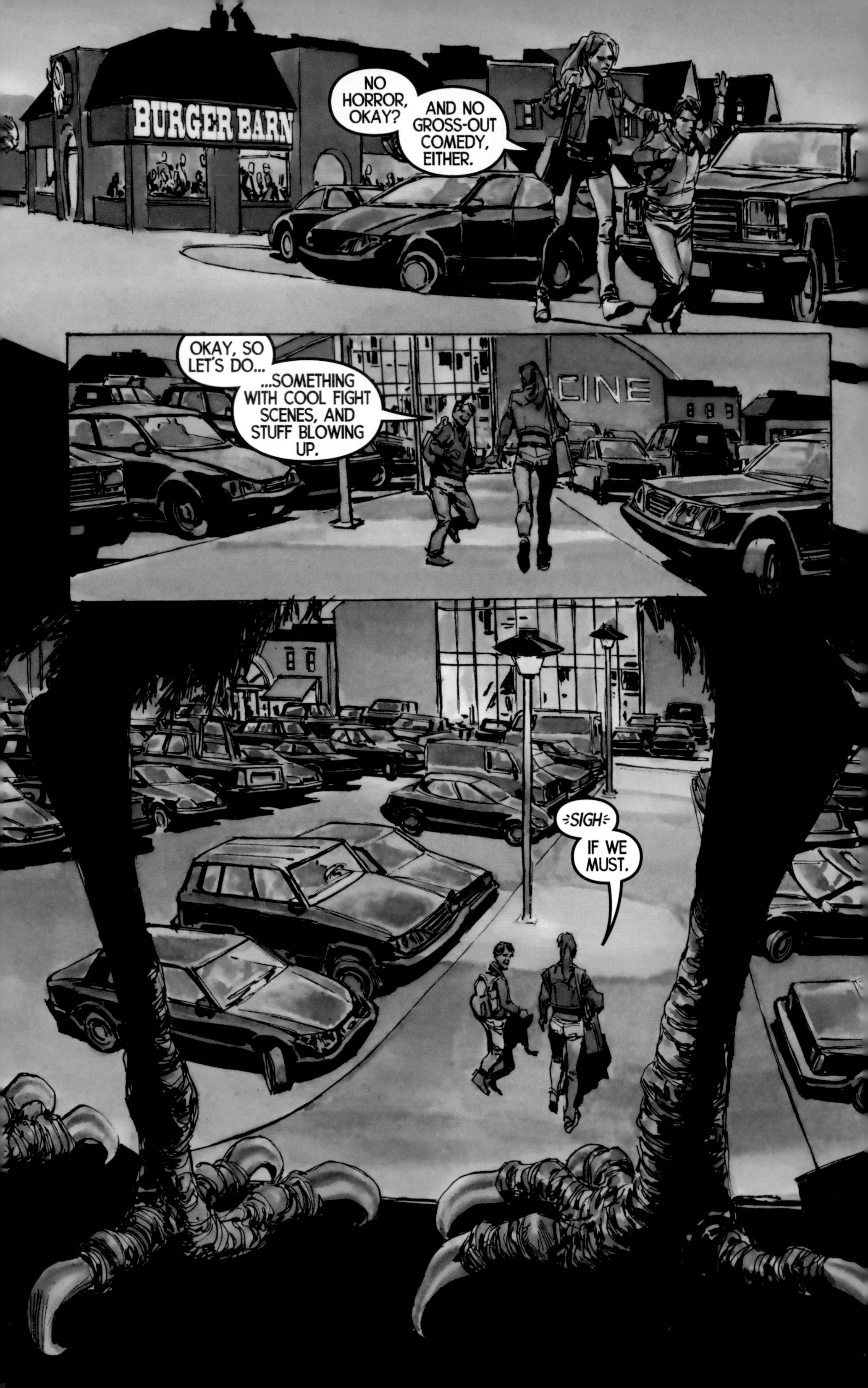
BURGER BARN
NO HORROR, OKAY?
AND NO GROSS-OUT COMEDY, EITHER.
OKAY, SO LET'S DO...
...SOMETHING WITH COOL FIGHT SCENES, AND STUFF BLOWING UP.
CINE
=SIGH=
IF WE MUST.

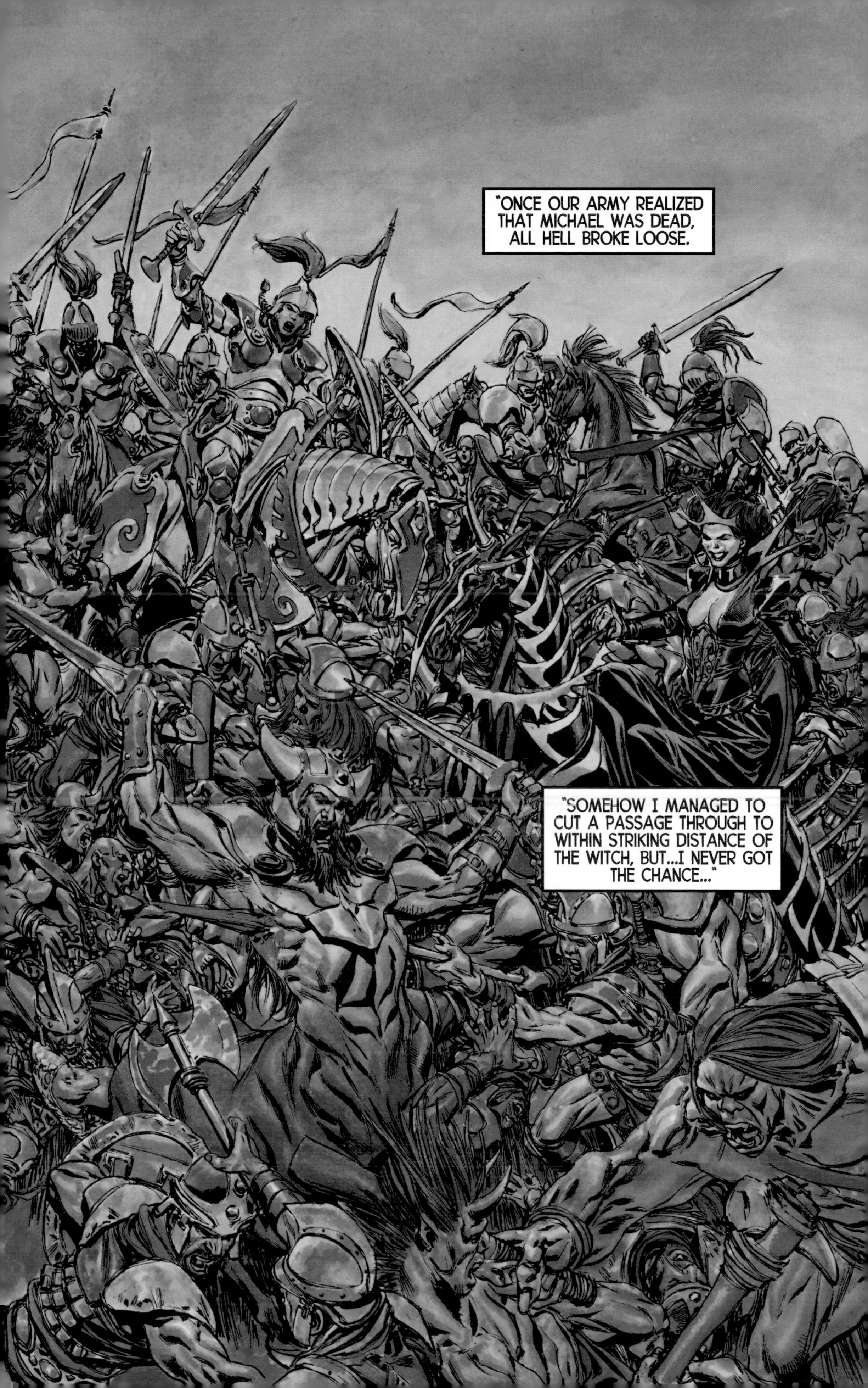
"ONCE OUR ARMY REALIZED THAT MICHAEL WAS DEAD, ALL HELL BROKE LOOSE.
"SOMEHOW I MANAGED TO CUT A PASSAGE THROUGH TO WITHIN STRIKING DISTANCE OF THE WITCH, BUT...I NEVER GOT THE CHANCE..."

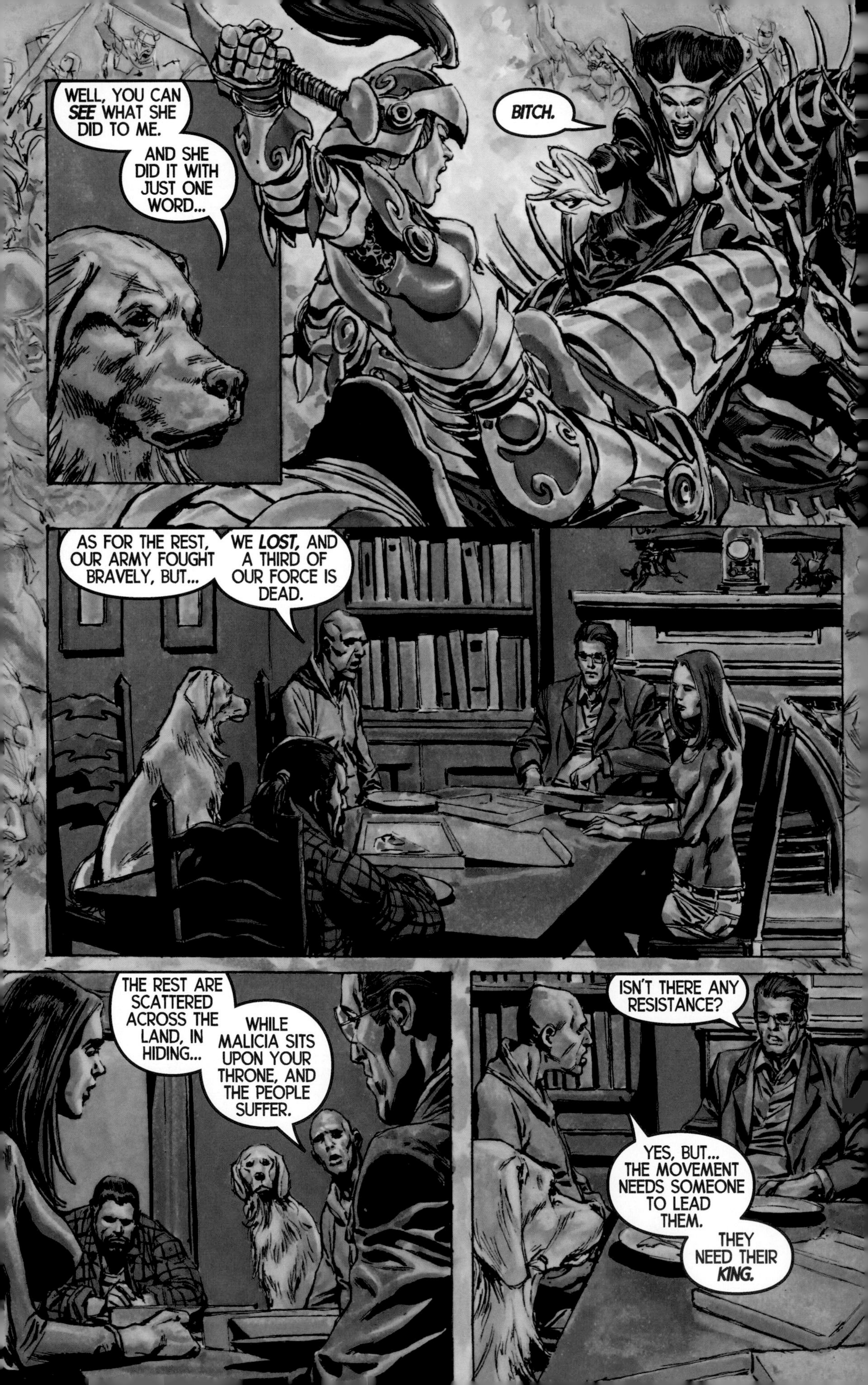
WELL, YOU CAN SEE WHAT SHE DID TO ME.
AND SHE DID IT WITH JUST ONE WORD...
BITCH.
AS FOR THE REST, OUR ARMY FOUGHT BRAVELY, BUT...
WE LOST, AND A THIRD OF OUR FORCE IS DEAD.
THE REST ARE SCATTERED ACROSS THE LAND, IN HIDING...
WHILE MALICIA SITS UPON YOUR THRONE, AND THE PEOPLE SUFFER.
ISN'T THERE ANY RESISTANCE?
YES, BUT... THE MOVEMENT NEEDS SOMEONE TO LEAD THEM.
THEY NEED THEIR KING.

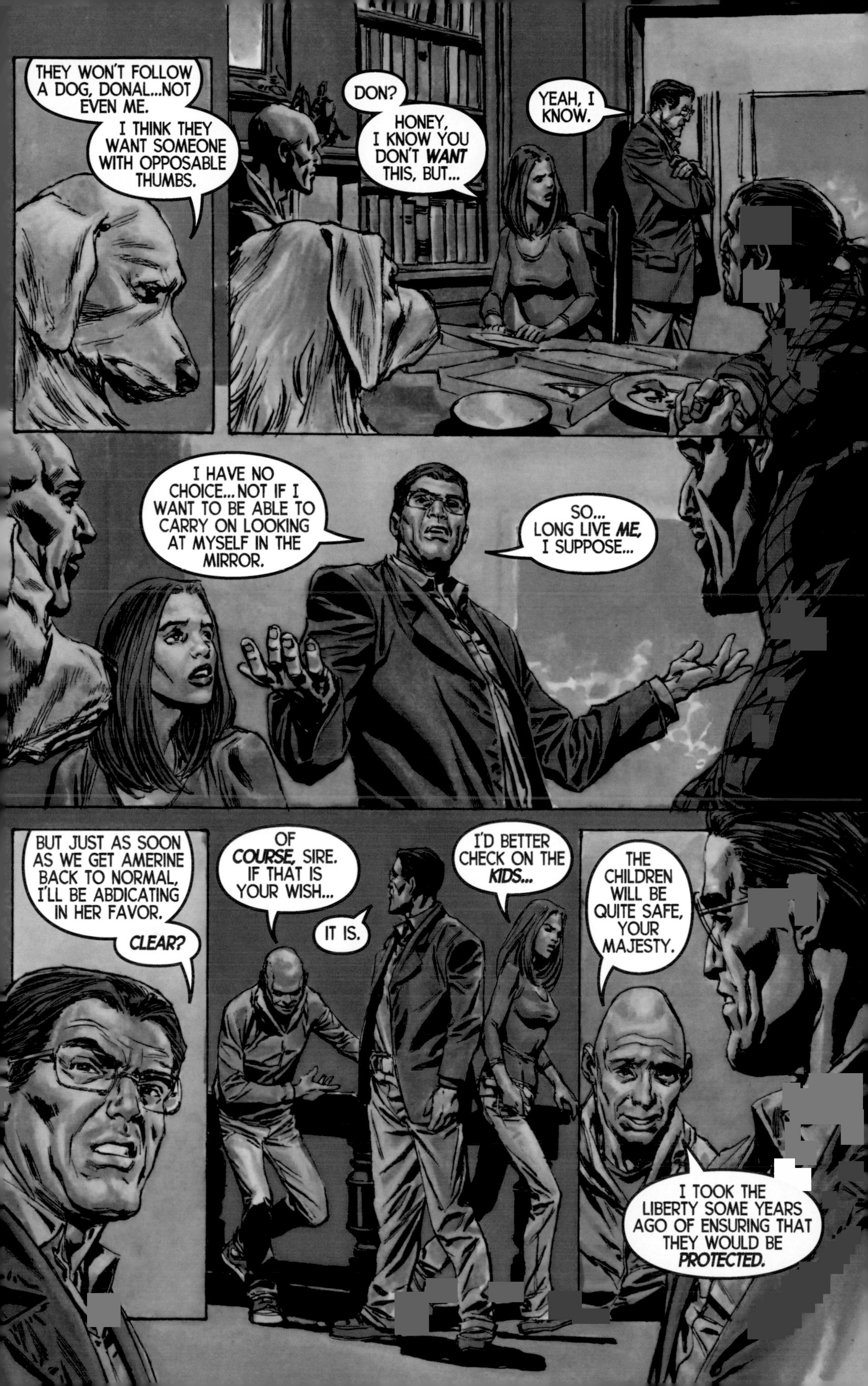
THEY WON'T FOLLOW A DOG, DONAL...NOT EVEN ME.
I THINK THEY WANT SOMEONE WITH OPPOSABLE THUMBS.
DON?
HONEY, I KNOW YOU DON'T *WANT* THIS, BUT...
YEAH, I KNOW.
I HAVE NO CHOICE...NOT IF I WANT TO BE ABLE TO CARRY ON LOOKING AT MYSELF IN THE MIRROR.
SO... LONG LIVE *ME,* I SUPPOSE...
BUT JUST AS SOON AS WE GET AMERINE BACK TO NORMAL, I'LL BE ABDICATING IN HER FAVOR.
CLEAR?
OF *COURSE,* SIRE. IF THAT IS YOUR WISH...
IT IS.
I'D BETTER CHECK ON THE *KIDS...*
THE CHILDREN WILL BE QUITE SAFE, YOUR MAJESTY.
I TOOK THE LIBERTY SOME YEARS AGO OF ENSURING THAT THEY WOULD BE *PROTECTED.*

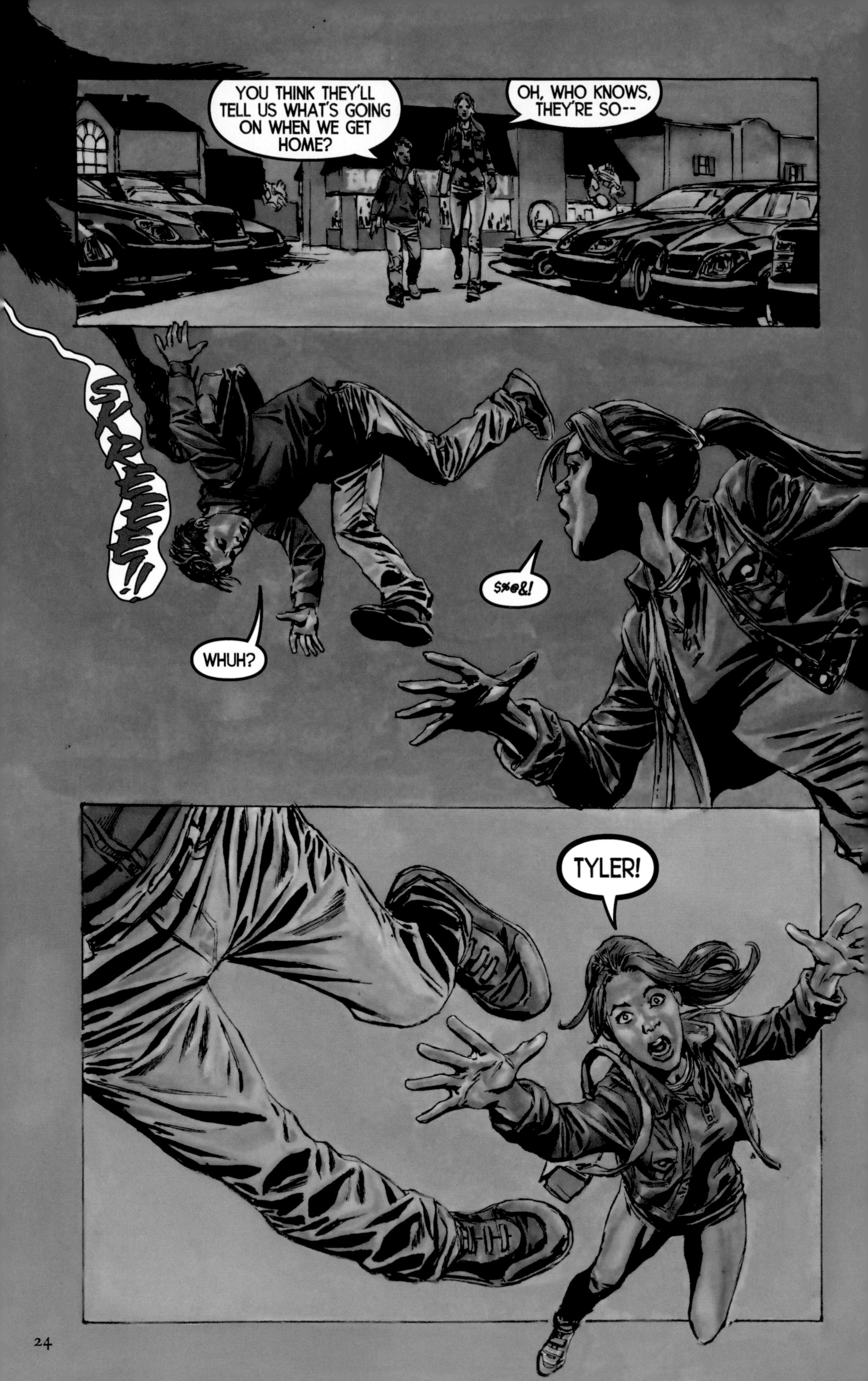
YOU THINK THEY'LL TELL US WHAT'S GOING ON WHEN WE GET HOME?
OH, WHO KNOWS, THEY'RE SO--
SKREEEE!!
WHUH?
$%@&!
TYLER!

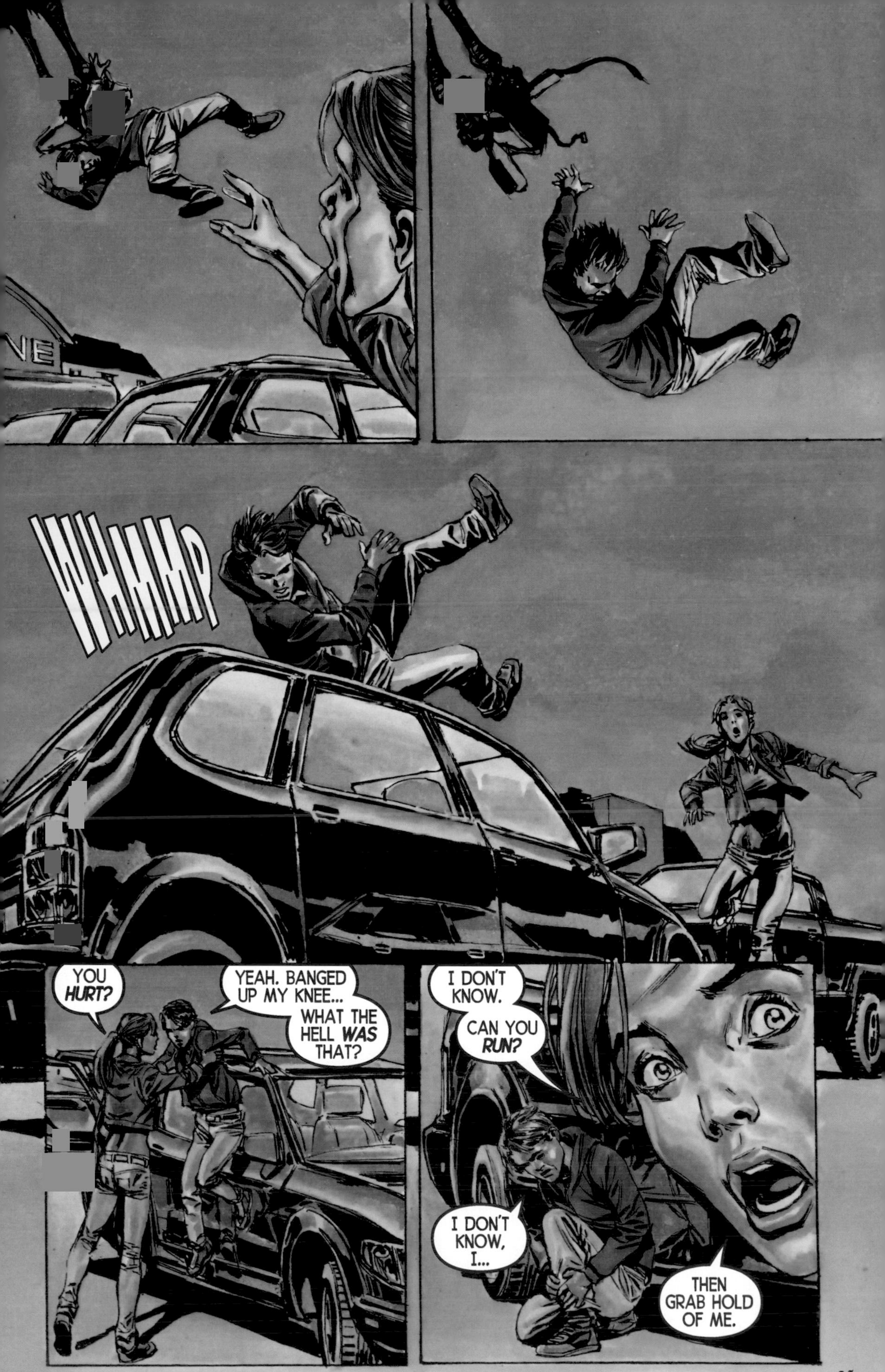
WHMMP
YOU HURT?
YEAH. BANGED UP MY KNEE...
WHAT THE HELL WAS THAT?
I DON'T KNOW.
CAN YOU RUN?
I DON'T KNOW, I...
THEN GRAB HOLD OF ME.

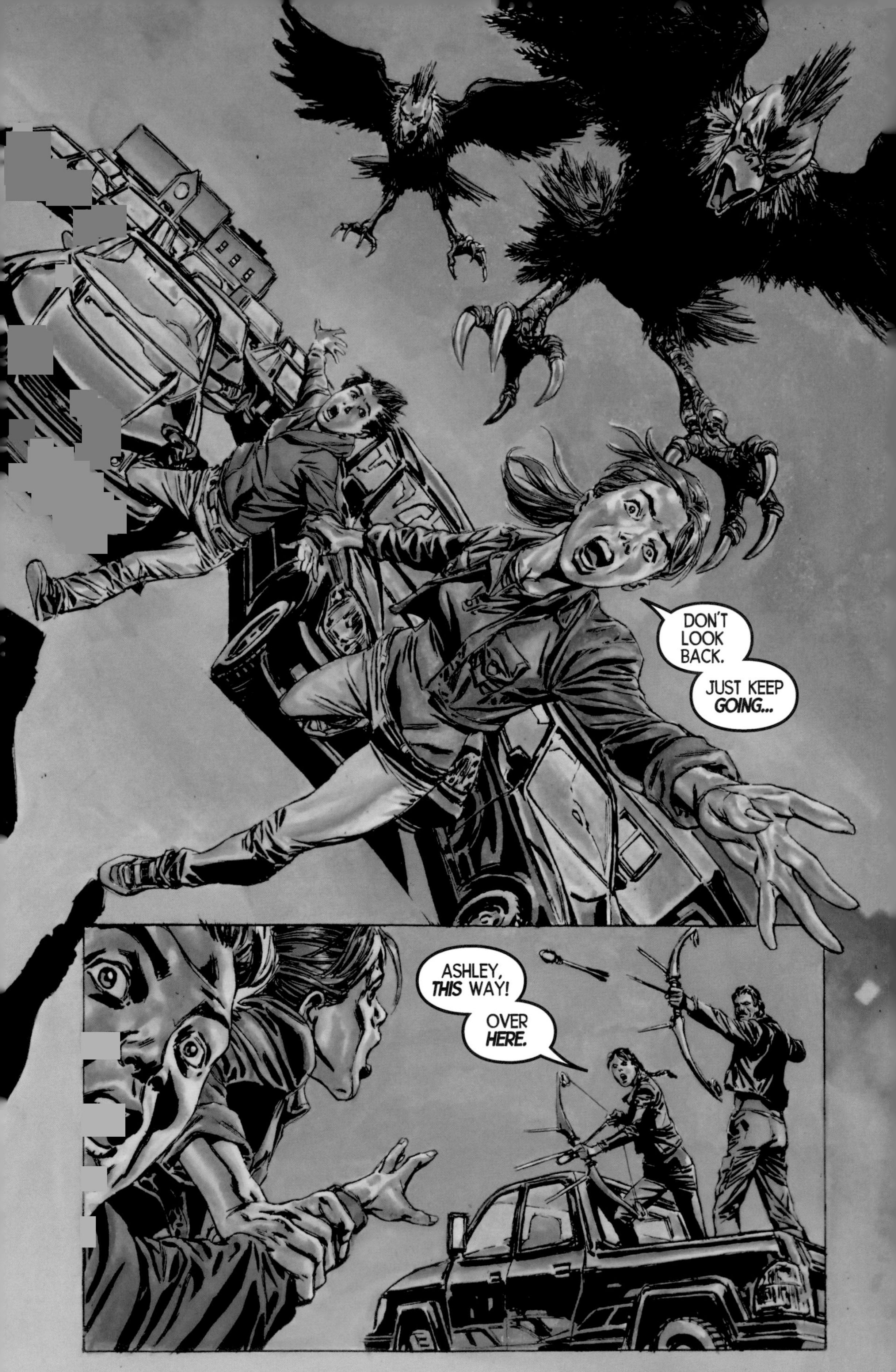
DON'T LOOK BACK.
JUST KEEP GOING...
ASHLEY, THIS WAY!
OVER HERE.

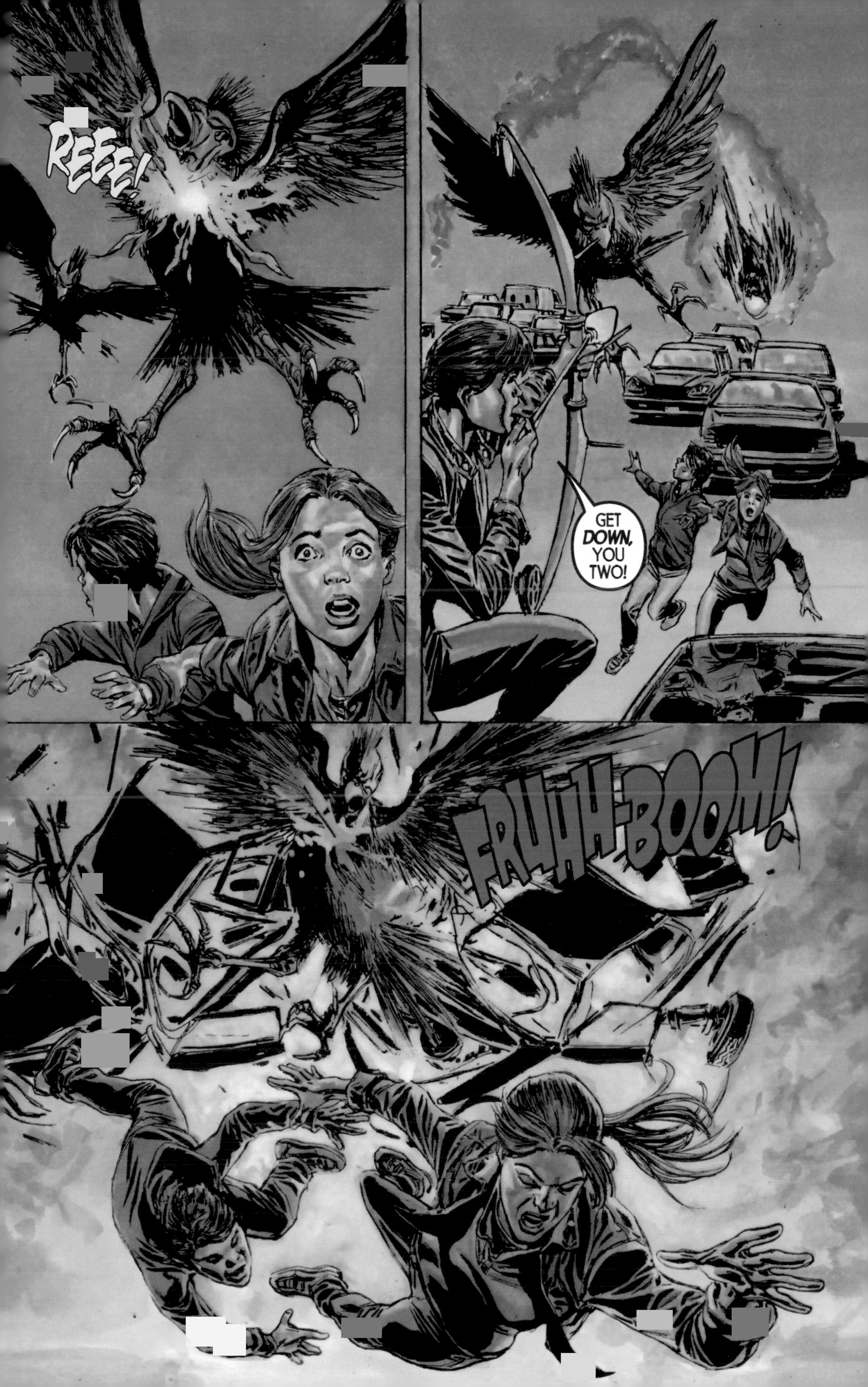
REEEE!
GET DOWN, YOU TWO!
FRUHH-BOOM!

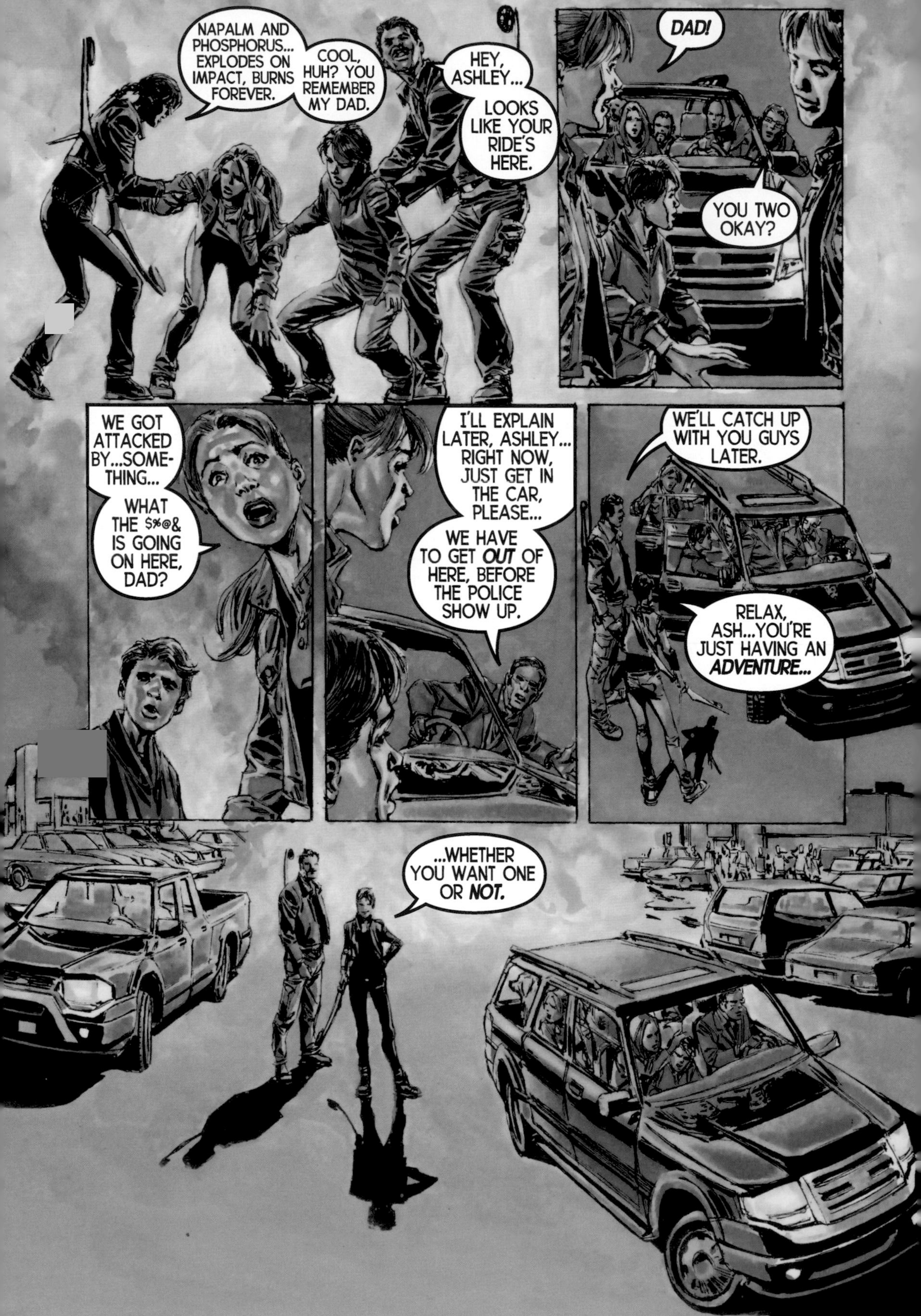
NAPALM AND PHOSPHORUS... EXPLODES ON IMPACT, BURNS FOREVER.
COOL, HUH? YOU REMEMBER MY DAD.
HEY, ASHLEY...
LOOKS LIKE YOUR RIDE'S HERE.
DAD!
YOU TWO OKAY?
WE GOT ATTACKED BY...SOME-THING...
WHAT THE $%@& IS GOING ON HERE, DAD?
I'LL EXPLAIN LATER, ASHLEY... RIGHT NOW, JUST GET IN THE CAR, PLEASE...
WE HAVE TO GET OUT OF HERE, BEFORE THE POLICE SHOW UP.
WE'LL CATCH UP WITH YOU GUYS LATER.
RELAX, ASH...YOU'RE JUST HAVING AN ADVENTURE...
...WHETHER YOU WANT ONE OR NOT.

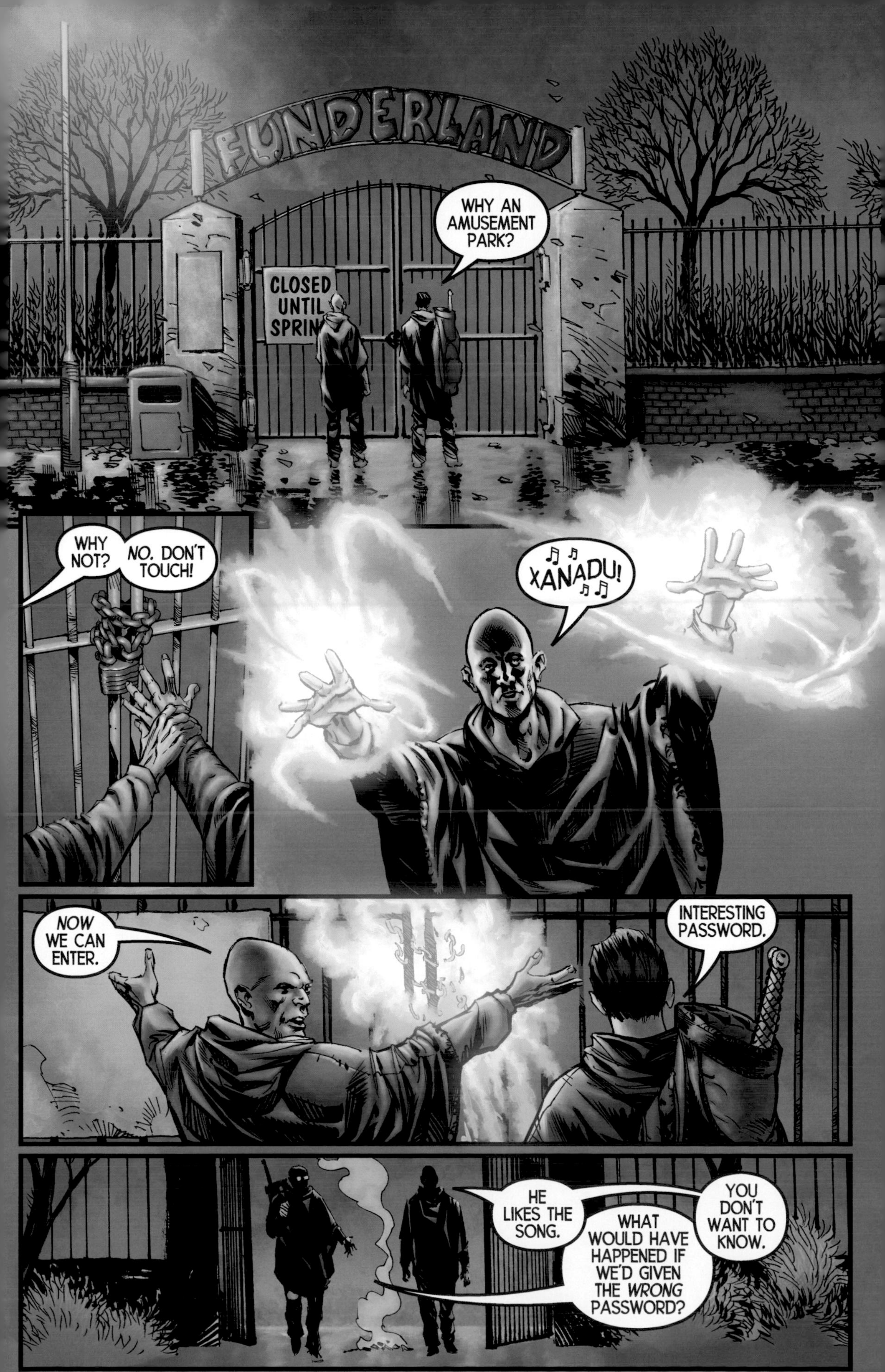
FUNDERLAND
CLOSED UNTIL SPRIN
WHY AN AMUSEMENT PARK?
WHY NOT?
NO. DON'T TOUCH!
♫ ♫ XANADU! ♫ ♫
NOW WE CAN ENTER.
INTERESTING PASSWORD.
HE LIKES THE SONG.
WHAT WOULD HAVE HAPPENED IF WE'D GIVEN THE *WRONG* PASSWORD?
YOU DON'T WANT TO KNOW.

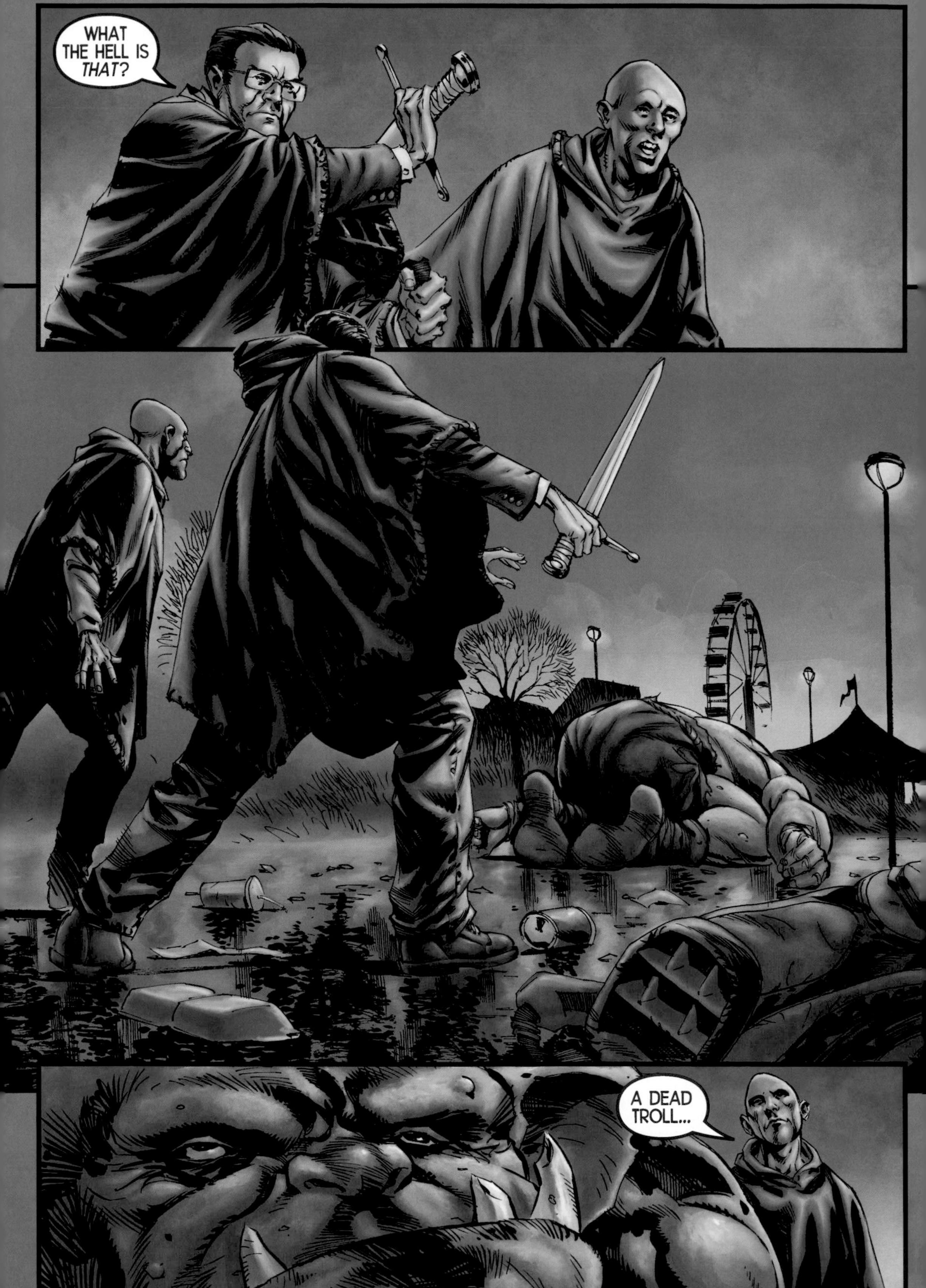
WHAT THE HELL IS *THAT*?
A DEAD TROLL...

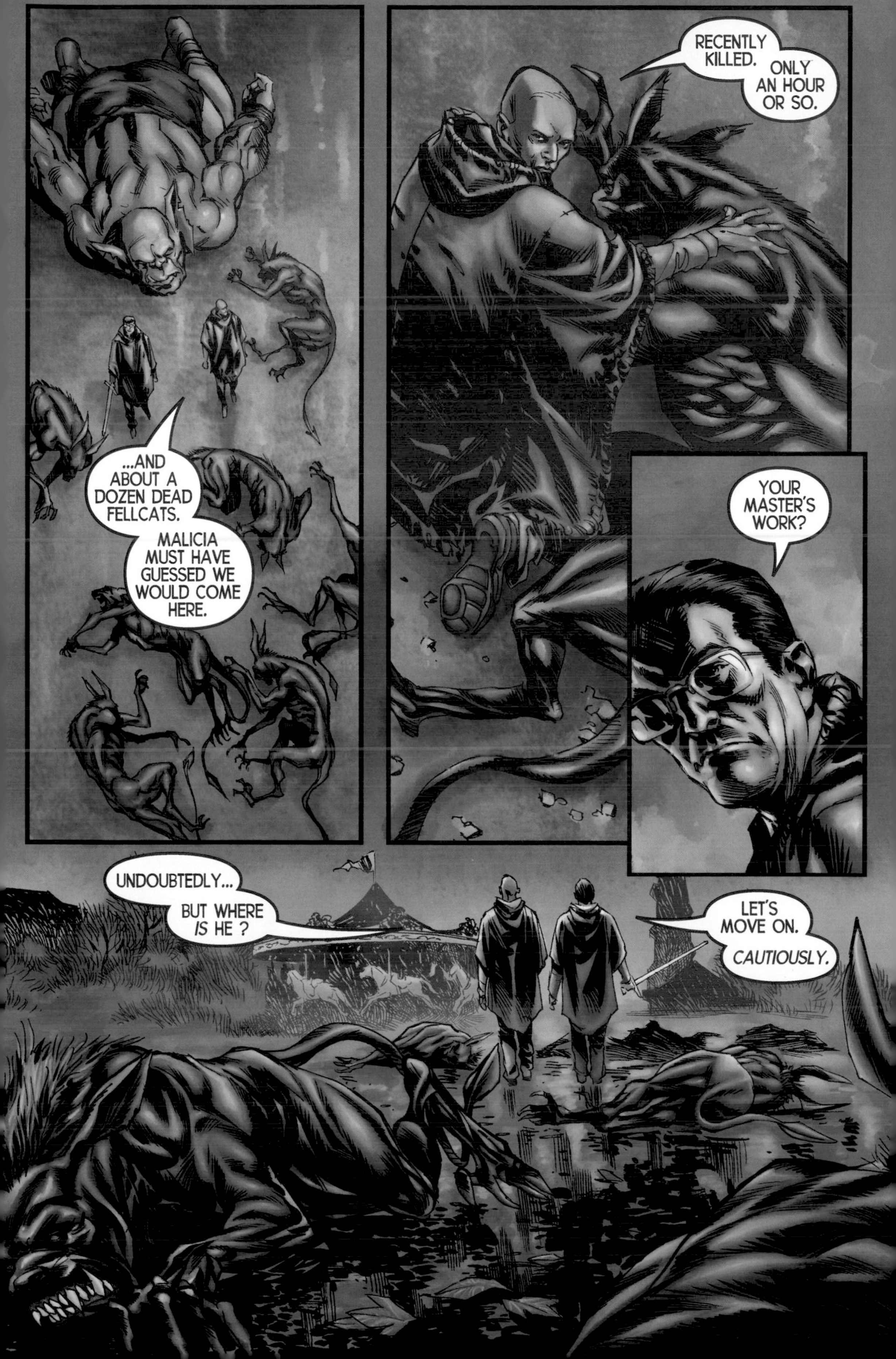
...AND ABOUT A DOZEN DEAD FELLCATS.
MALICIA MUST HAVE GUESSED WE WOULD COME HERE.
RECENTLY KILLED.
ONLY AN HOUR OR SO.
YOUR MASTER'S WORK?
UNDOUBTEDLY...
BUT WHERE *IS* HE ?
LET'S MOVE ON.
CAUTIOUSLY.

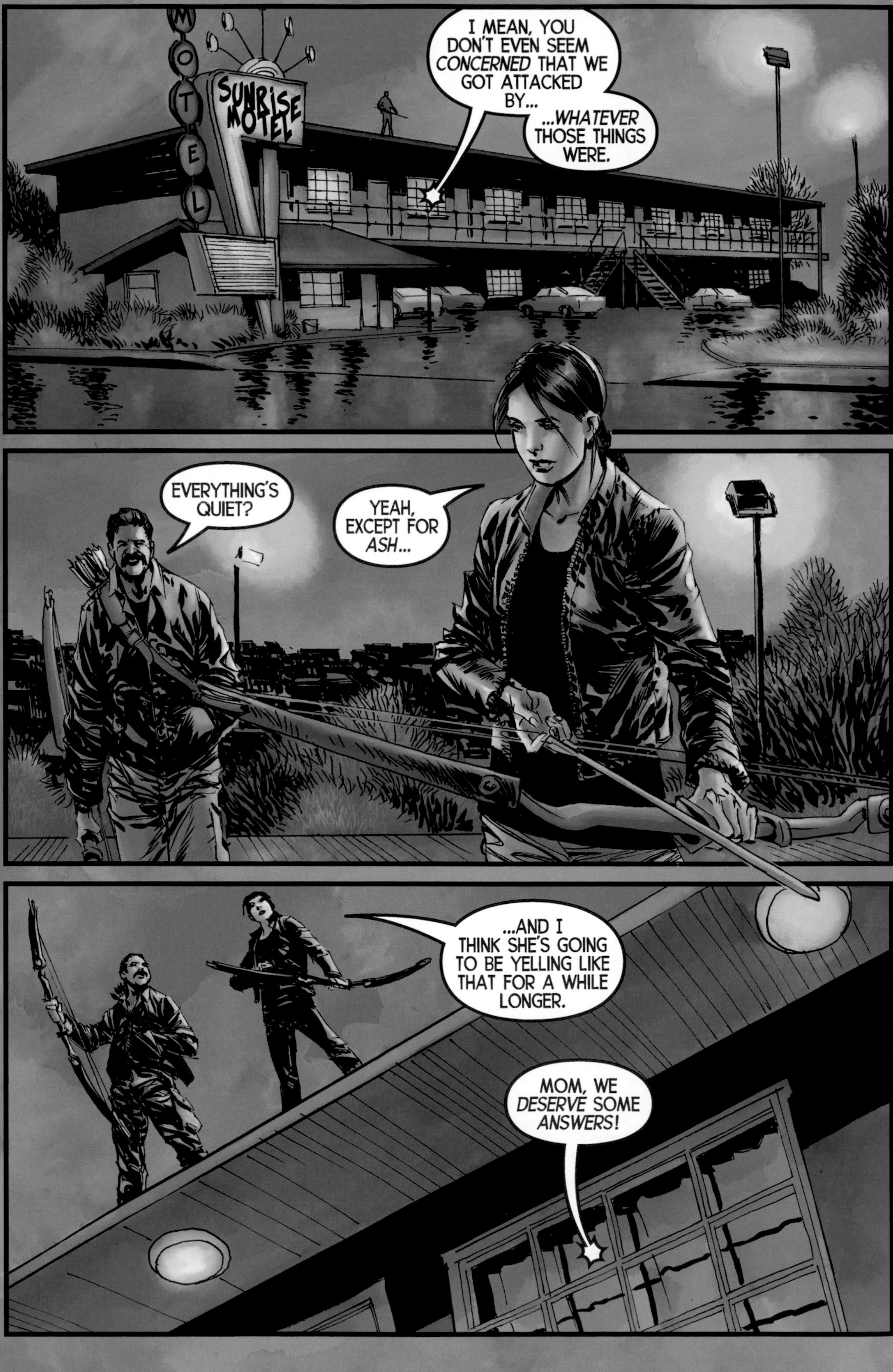
SUNRISE MOTEL
MOTEL
I MEAN, YOU DON'T EVEN SEEM *CONCERNED* THAT WE GOT ATTACKED BY...
...*WHATEVER* THOSE THINGS WERE.
EVERYTHING'S QUIET?
YEAH, EXCEPT FOR *ASH*...
...AND I THINK SHE'S GOING TO BE YELLING LIKE THAT FOR A WHILE LONGER.
MOM, WE *DESERVE* SOME *ANSWERS*!

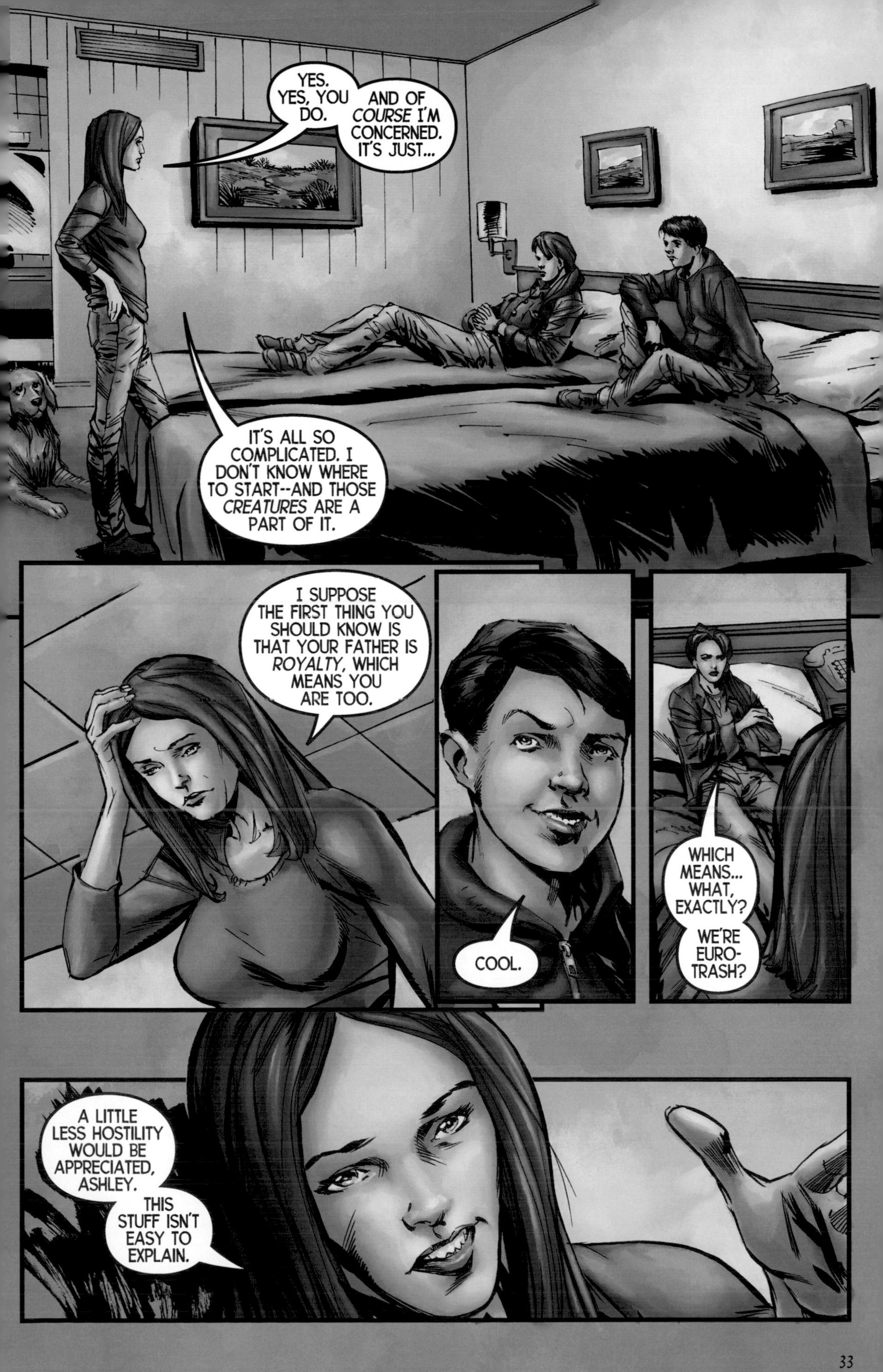
YES. YES, YOU DO.
AND OF *COURSE* I'M CONCERNED. IT'S JUST...
IT'S ALL SO COMPLICATED. I DON'T KNOW WHERE TO START--AND THOSE *CREATURES* ARE A PART OF IT.
I SUPPOSE THE FIRST THING YOU SHOULD KNOW IS THAT YOUR FATHER IS *ROYALTY*, WHICH MEANS YOU ARE TOO.
COOL.
WHICH MEANS... WHAT, EXACTLY?
WE'RE EURO-TRASH?
A LITTLE LESS HOSTILITY WOULD BE APPRECIATED, ASHLEY.
THIS STUFF ISN'T EASY TO EXPLAIN.

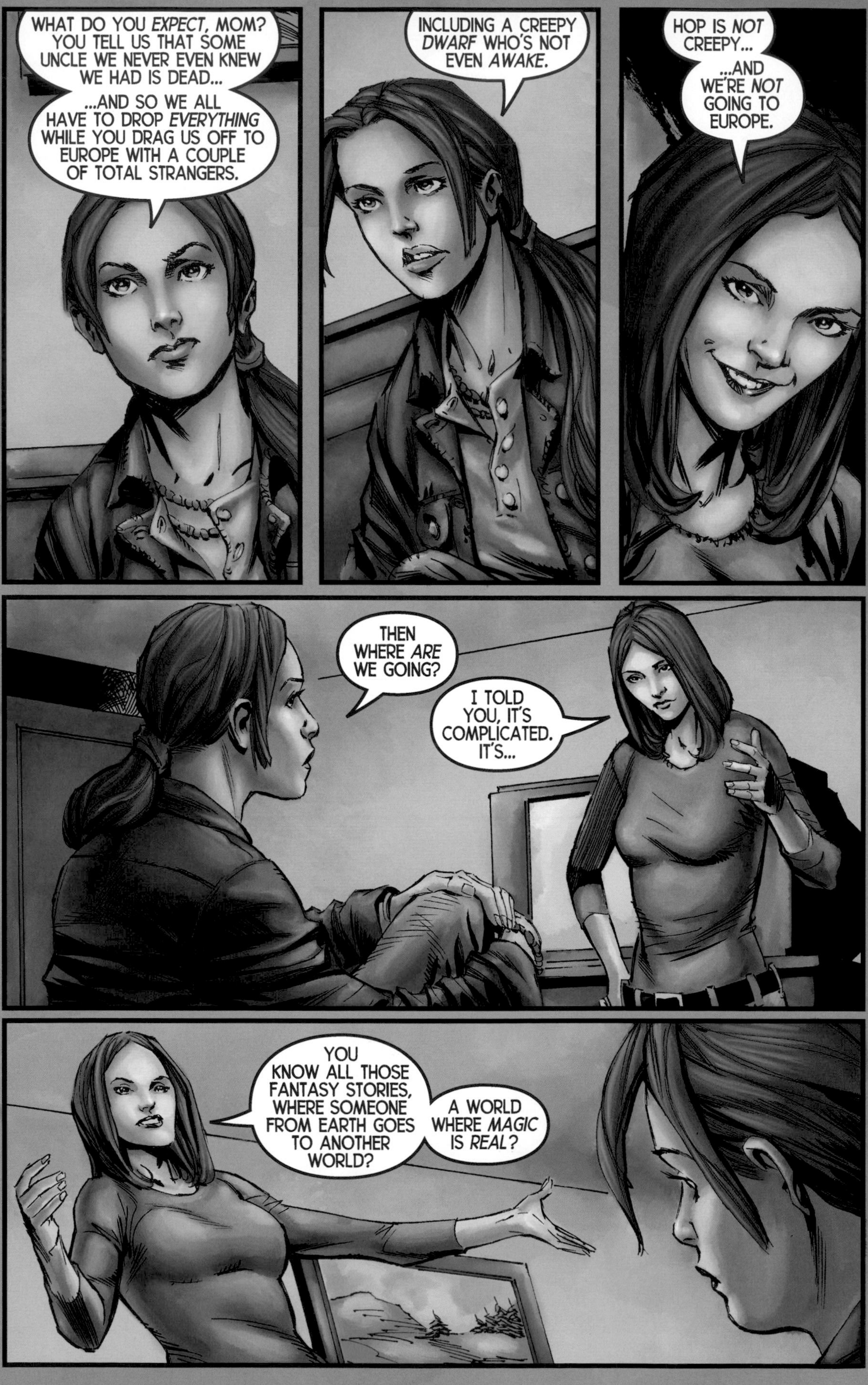
WHAT DO YOU *EXPECT*, MOM? YOU TELL US THAT SOME UNCLE WE NEVER EVEN KNEW WE HAD IS DEAD...
...AND SO WE ALL HAVE TO DROP *EVERYTHING* WHILE YOU DRAG US OFF TO EUROPE WITH A COUPLE OF TOTAL STRANGERS.
INCLUDING A CREEPY *DWARF* WHO'S NOT EVEN *AWAKE*.
HOP IS *NOT* CREEPY...
...AND WE'RE *NOT* GOING TO EUROPE.
THEN WHERE *ARE* WE GOING?
I TOLD YOU, IT'S COMPLICATED. IT'S...
YOU KNOW ALL THOSE FANTASY STORIES, WHERE SOMEONE FROM EARTH GOES TO ANOTHER WORLD?
A WORLD WHERE *MAGIC* IS *REAL*?

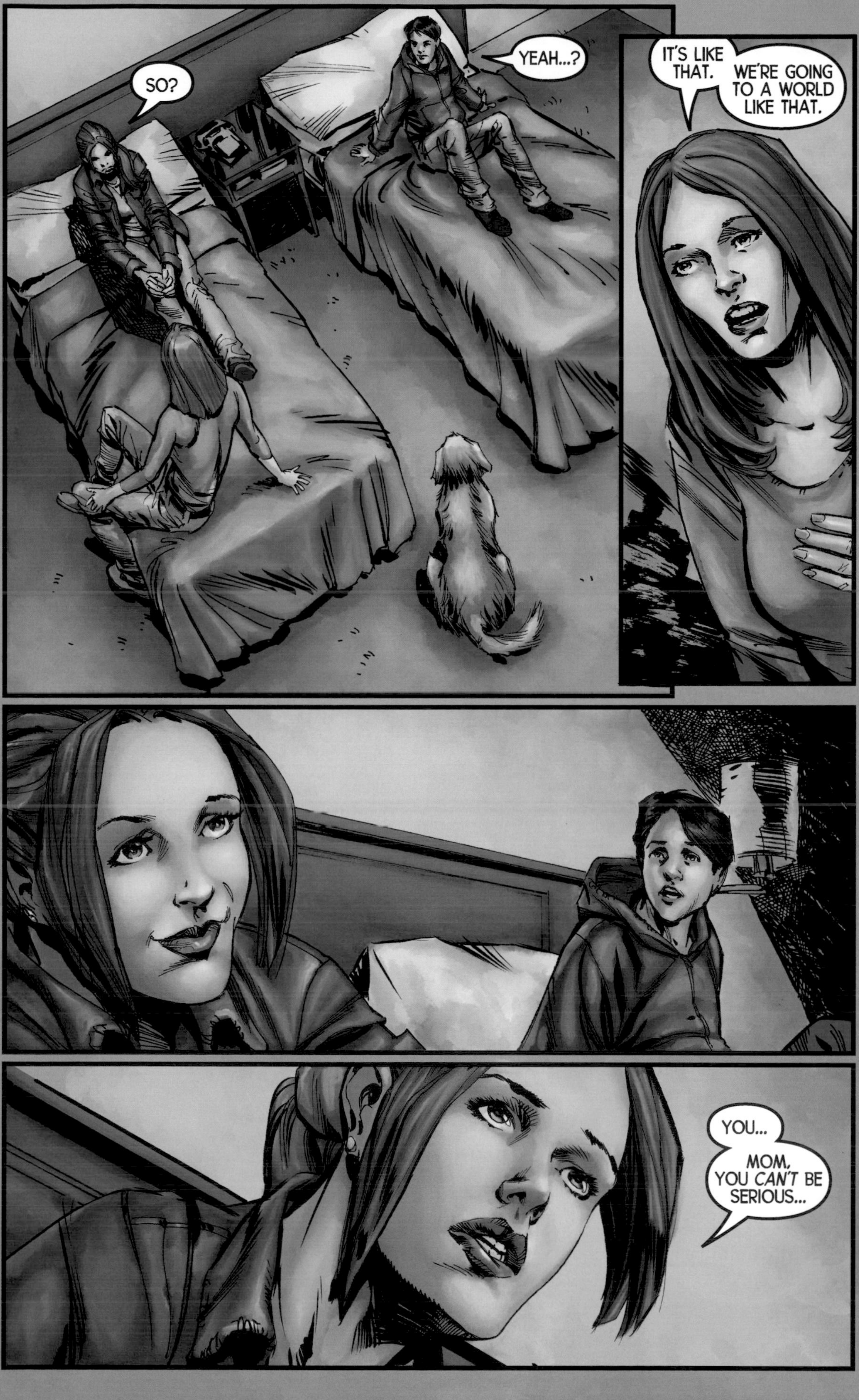
SO?
YEAH...?
IT'S LIKE THAT.
WE'RE GOING TO A WORLD LIKE THAT.
YOU...
MOM, YOU *CAN'T* BE SERIOUS...

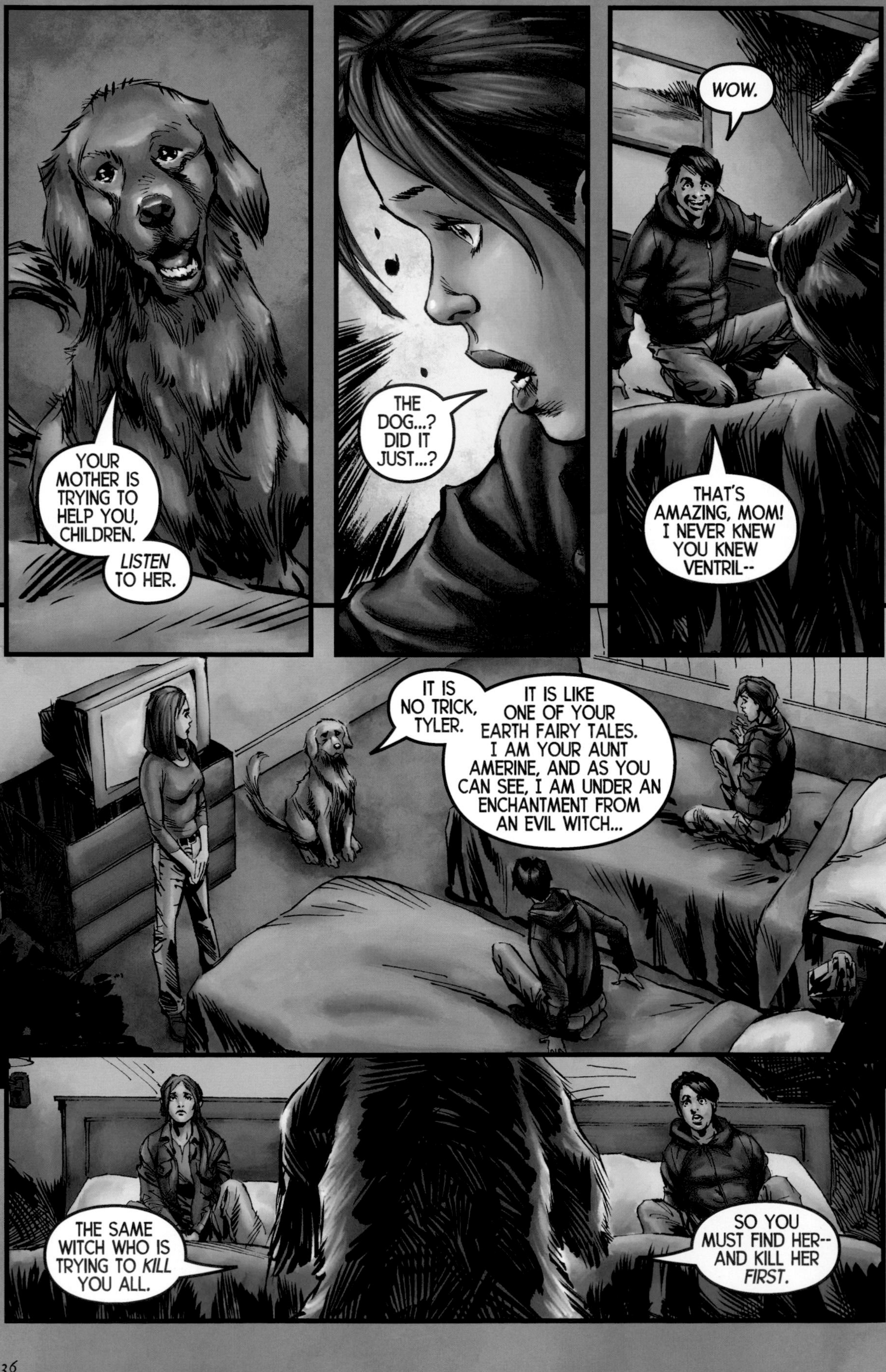
YOUR MOTHER IS TRYING TO HELP YOU, CHILDREN.
LISTEN TO HER.
THE DOG...? DID IT JUST...?
WOW.
THAT'S AMAZING, MOM! I NEVER KNEW YOU KNEW VENTRIL--
IT IS NO TRICK, TYLER.
IT IS LIKE ONE OF YOUR EARTH FAIRY TALES. I AM YOUR AUNT AMERINE, AND AS YOU CAN SEE, I AM UNDER AN ENCHANTMENT FROM AN EVIL WITCH...
THE SAME WITCH WHO IS TRYING TO *KILL* YOU ALL.
SO YOU MUST FIND HER-- AND KILL HER *FIRST*.

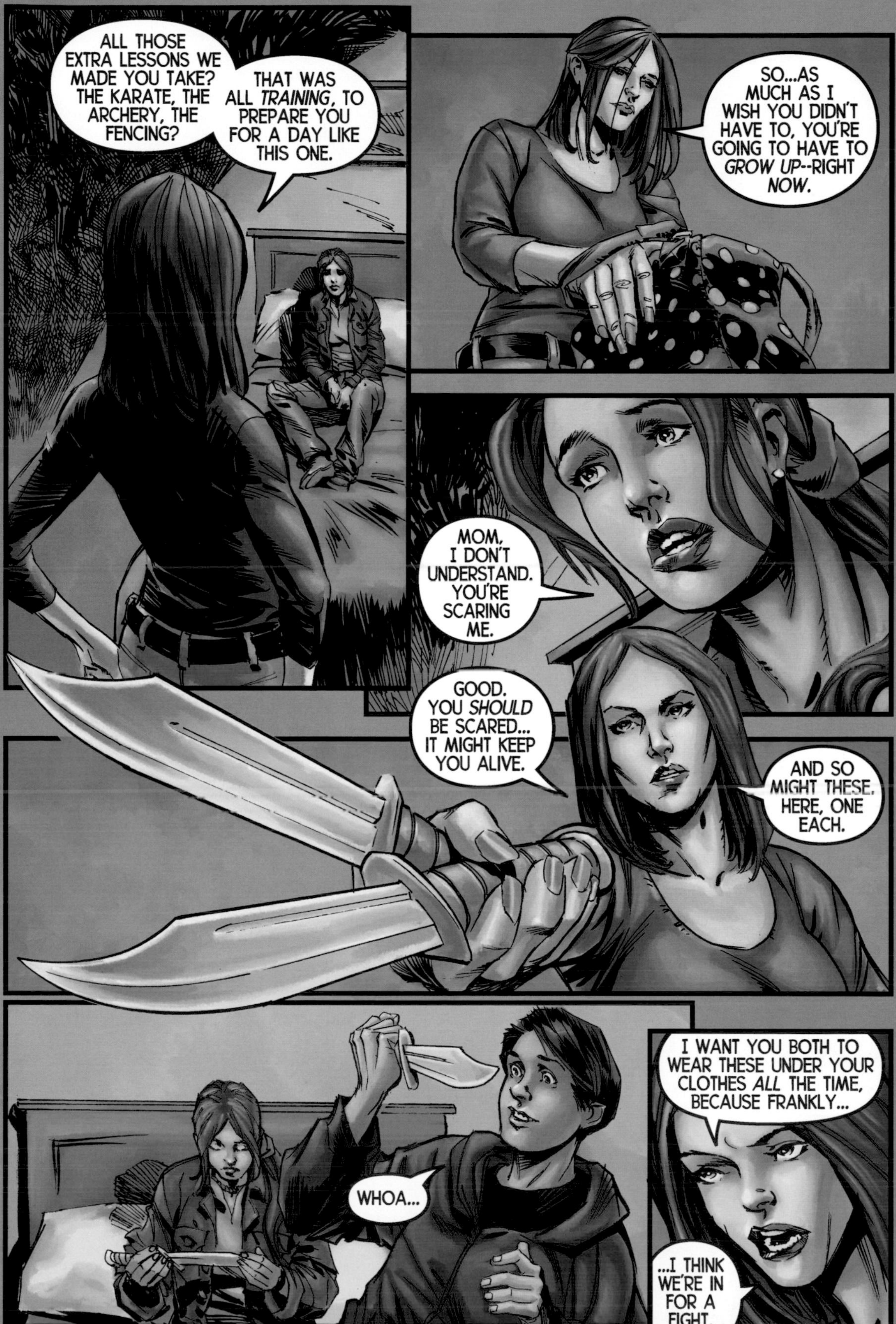
ALL THOSE EXTRA LESSONS WE MADE YOU TAKE? THE KARATE, THE ARCHERY, THE FENCING?
THAT WAS ALL *TRAINING*, TO PREPARE YOU FOR A DAY LIKE THIS ONE.
SO...AS MUCH AS I WISH YOU DIDN'T HAVE TO, YOU'RE GOING TO HAVE TO *GROW UP*--RIGHT *NOW*.
MOM, I DON'T UNDERSTAND. YOU'RE SCARING ME.
GOOD. YOU *SHOULD* BE SCARED... IT MIGHT KEEP YOU ALIVE.
AND SO MIGHT THESE. HERE, ONE EACH.
WHOA...
I WANT YOU BOTH TO WEAR THESE UNDER YOUR CLOTHES *ALL* THE TIME, BECAUSE FRANKLY...
...I THINK WE'RE IN FOR A FIGHT.

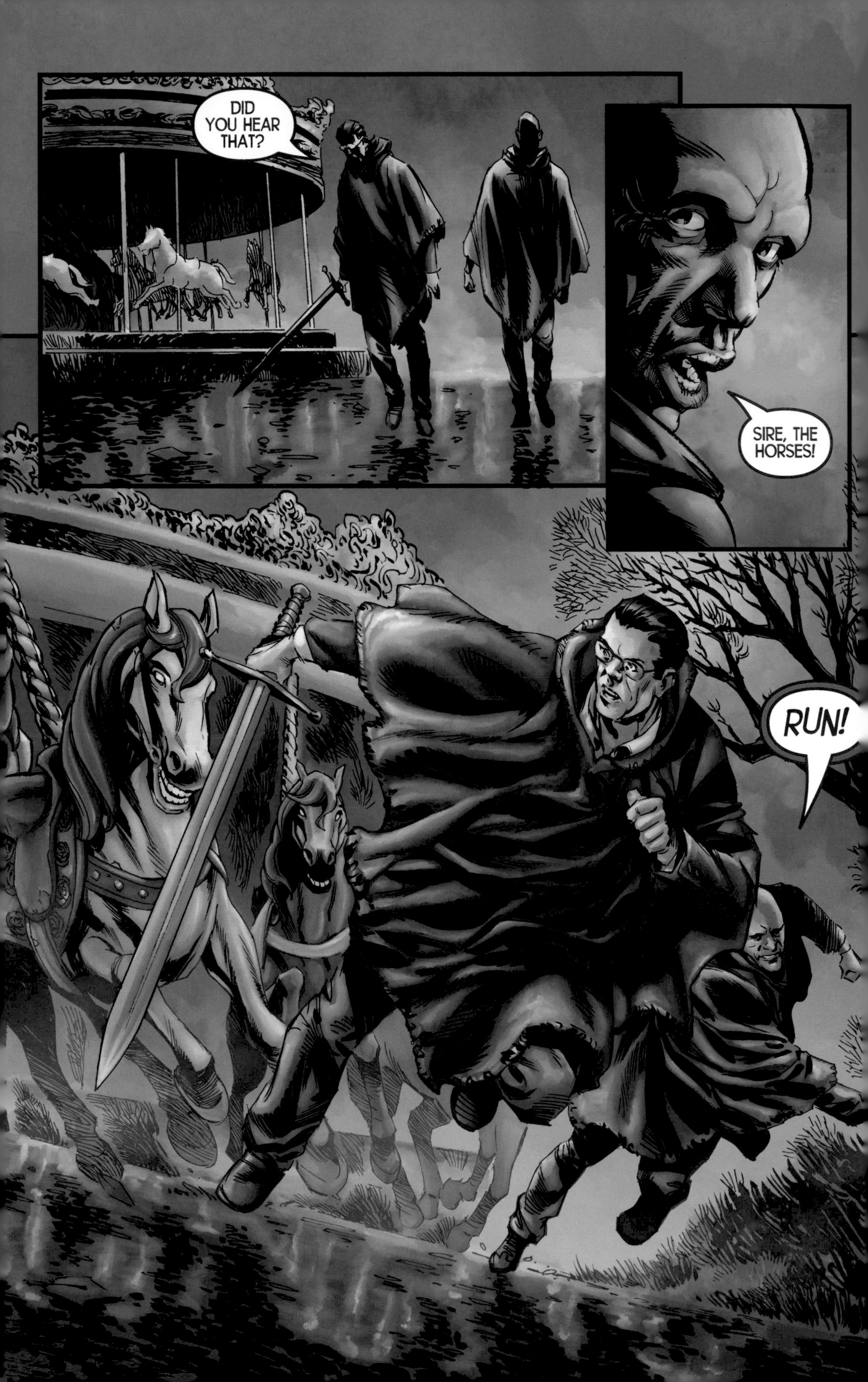
DID YOU HEAR THAT?
SIRE, THE HORSES!
RUN!

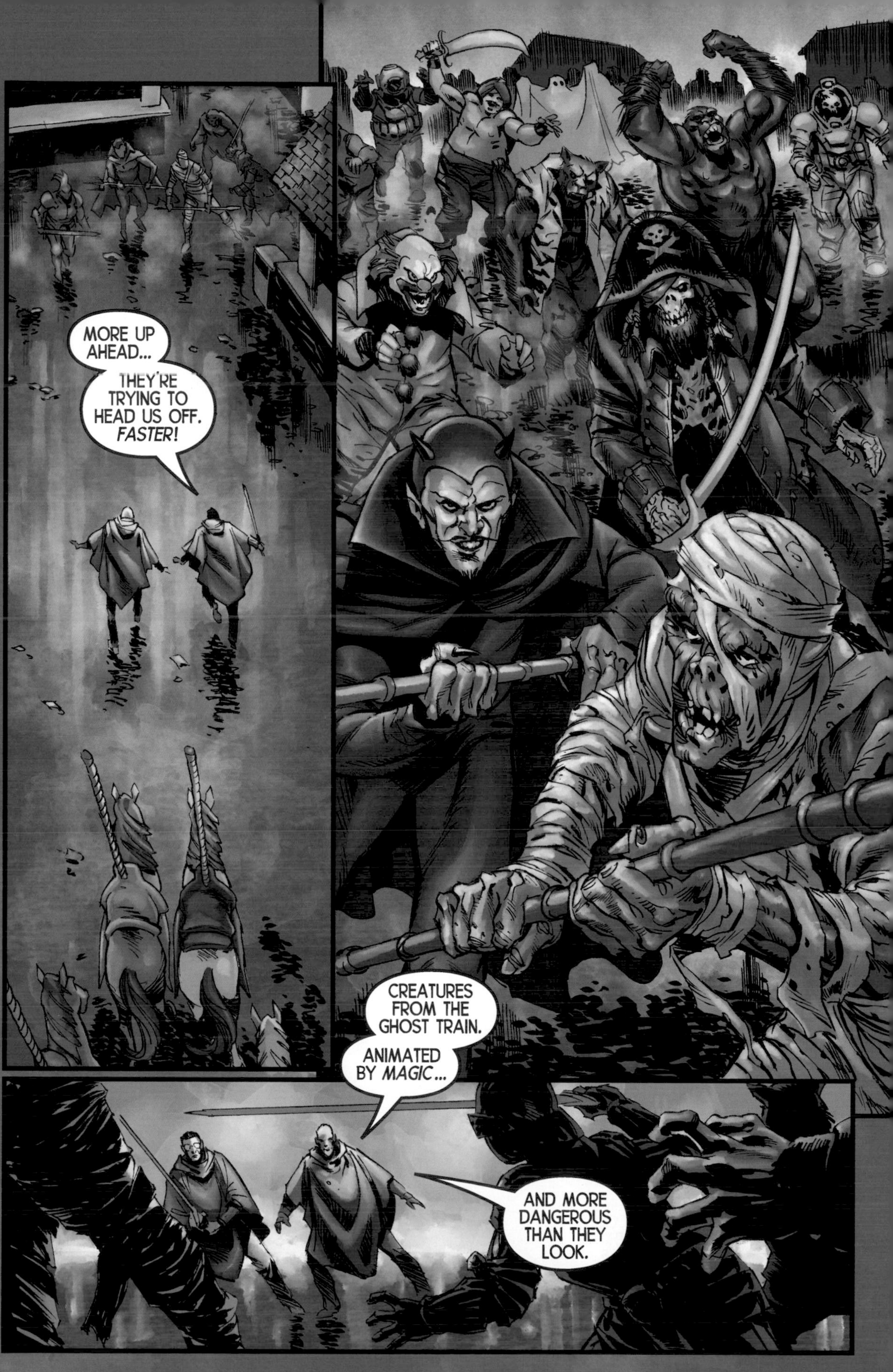
MORE UP AHEAD...
THEY'RE TRYING TO HEAD US OFF. *FASTER*!
CREATURES FROM THE GHOST TRAIN.
ANIMATED BY *MAGIC*...
AND MORE DANGEROUS THAN THEY LOOK.

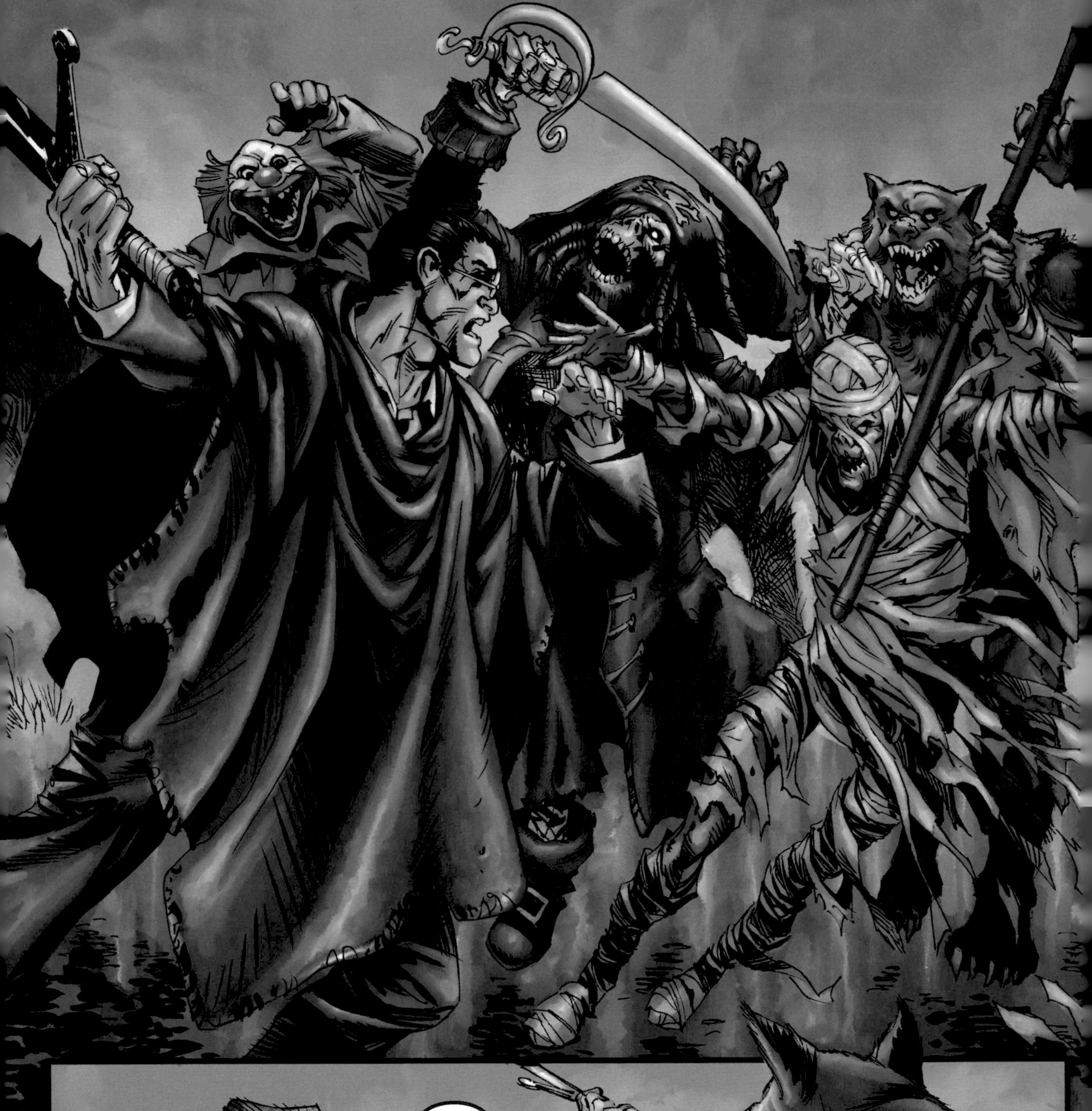

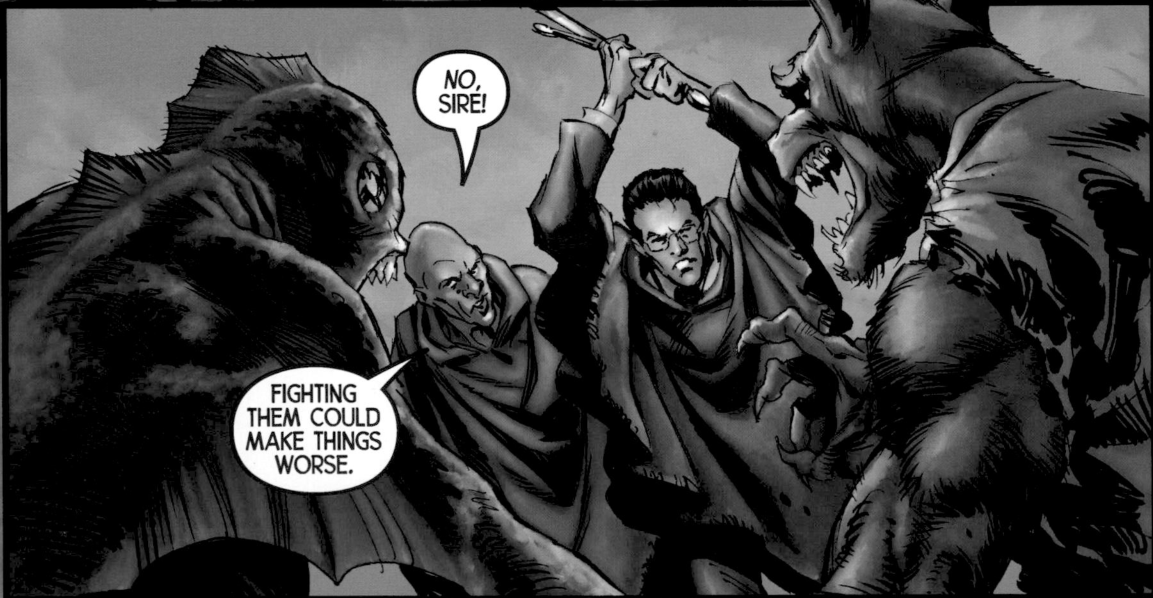
NO, SIRE!
FIGHTING THEM COULD MAKE THINGS WORSE.

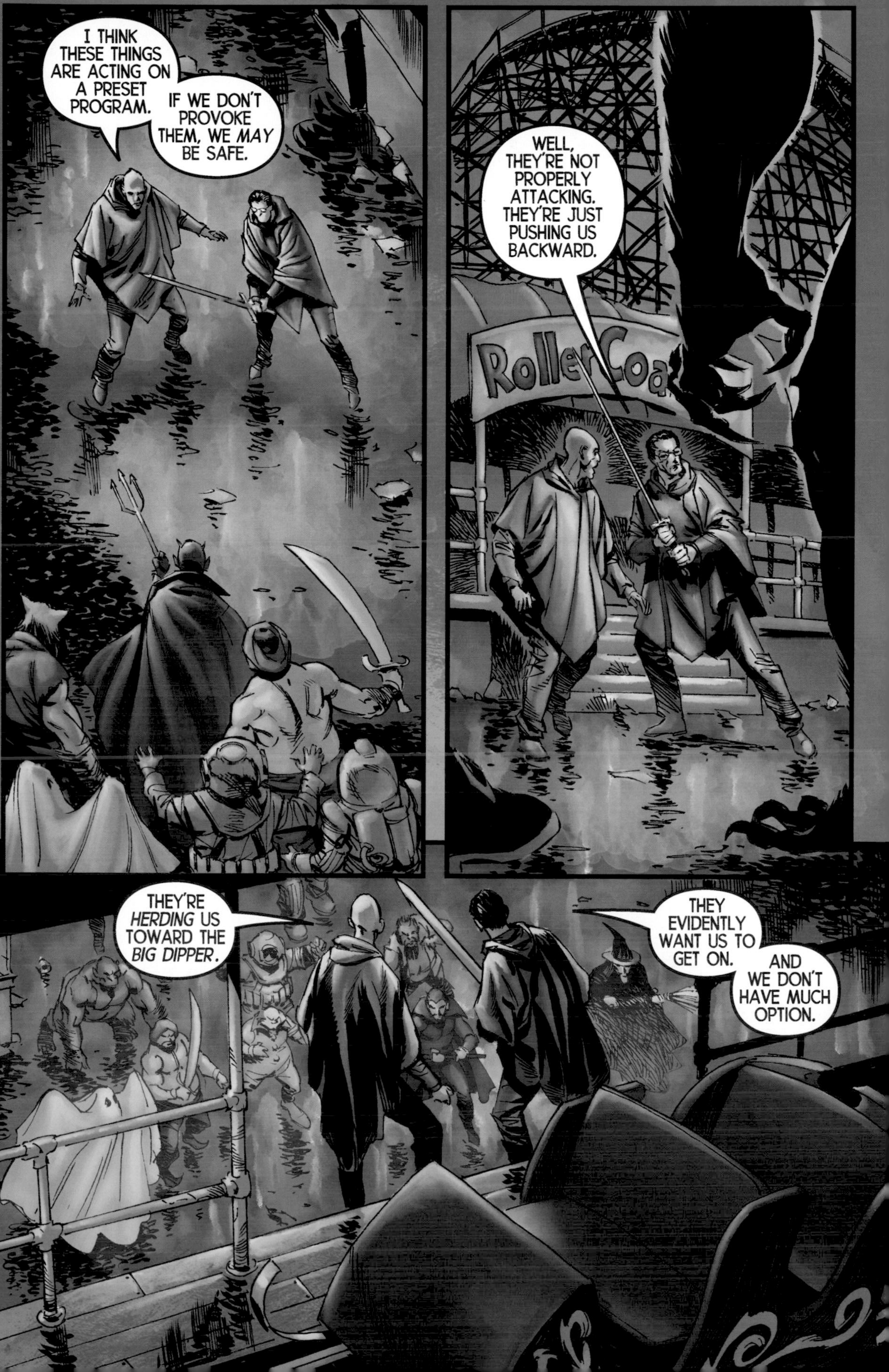
I THINK THESE THINGS ARE ACTING ON A PRESET PROGRAM.
IF WE DON'T PROVOKE THEM, WE *MAY* BE SAFE.
WELL, THEY'RE NOT PROPERLY ATTACKING. THEY'RE JUST PUSHING US BACKWARD.
RollerCoa
THEY'RE *HERDING* US TOWARD THE *BIG DIPPER*.
THEY EVIDENTLY WANT US TO GET ON.
AND WE DON'T HAVE MUCH OPTION.

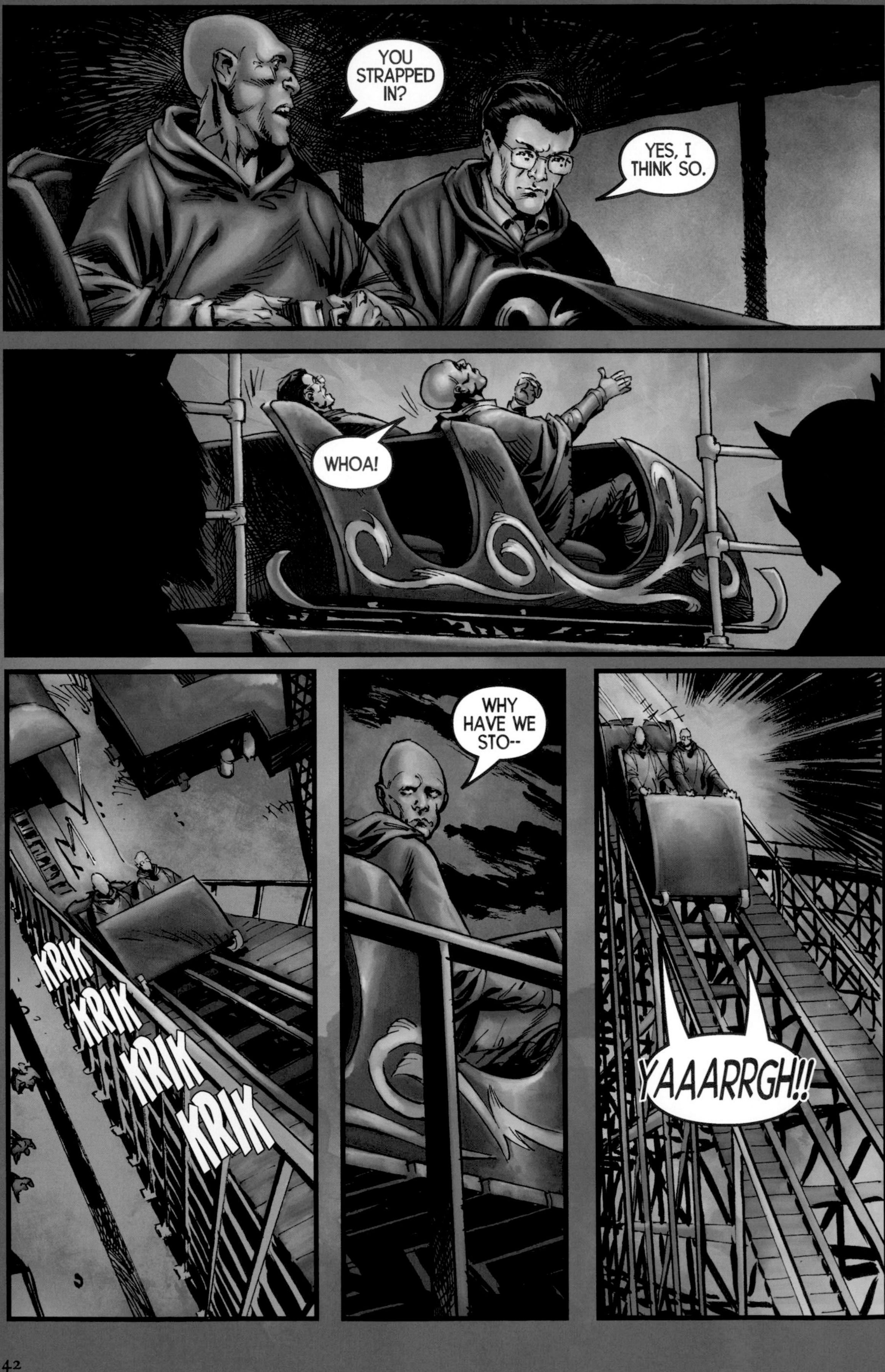
YOU STRAPPED IN?
YES, I THINK SO.
WHOA!
KRIK KRIK KRIK KRIK
WHY HAVE WE STO--
YAAARRGH!!

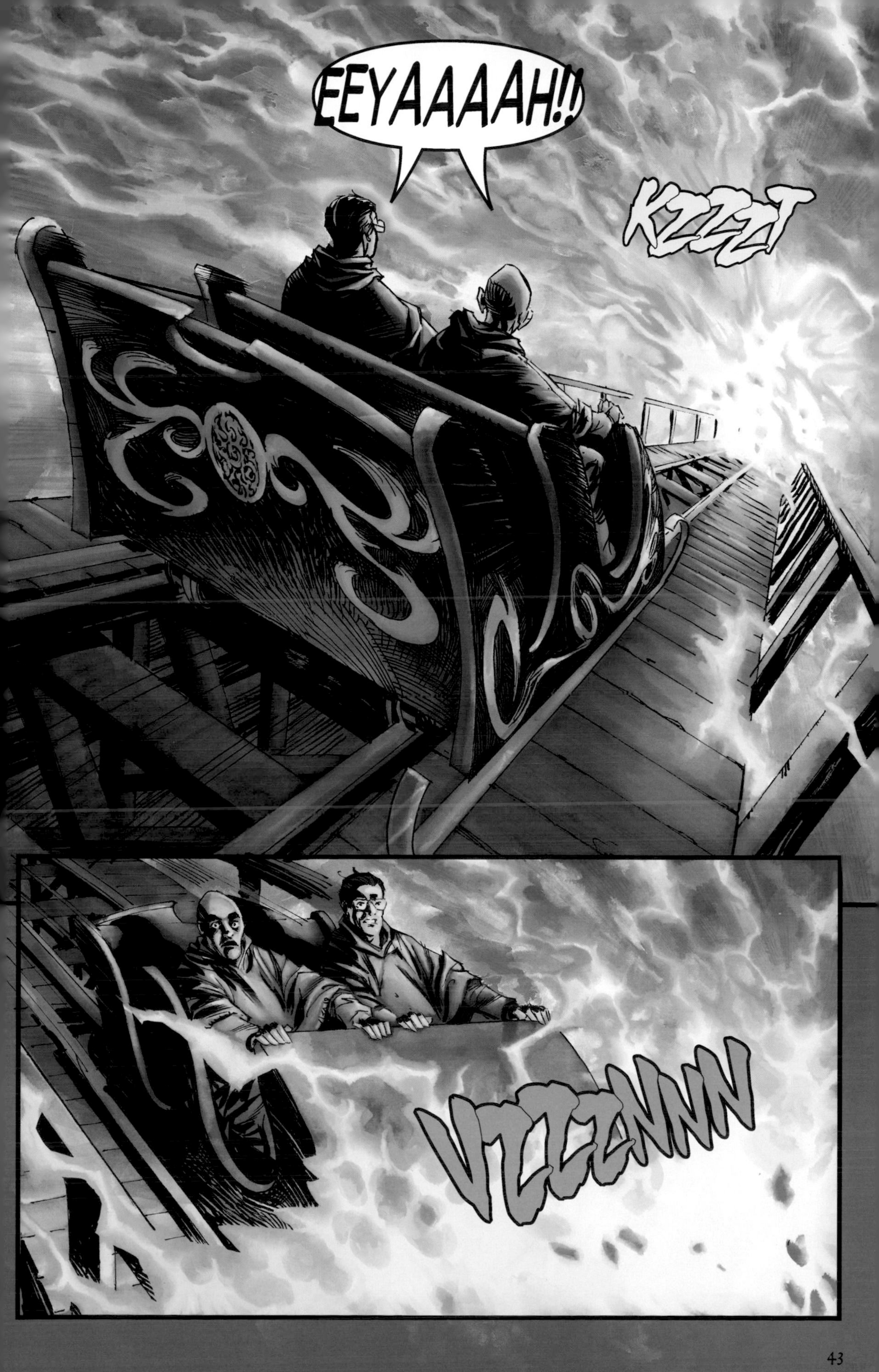
EEYAAAAH!!
KZZZT
VZZZNNN

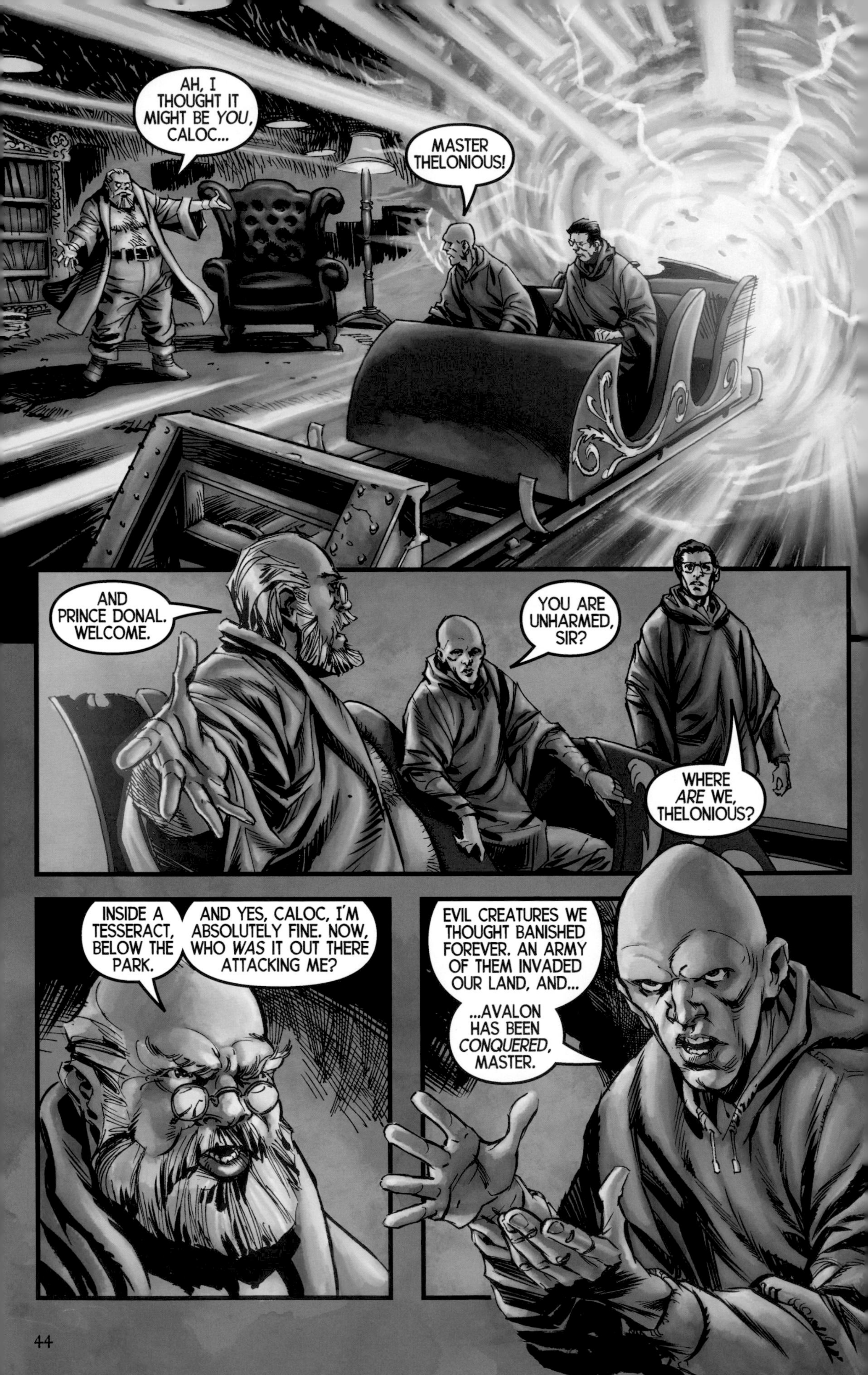
AH, I THOUGHT IT MIGHT BE YOU, CALOC...
MASTER THELONIOUS!
AND PRINCE DONAL. WELCOME.
YOU ARE UNHARMED, SIR?
WHERE ARE WE, THELONIOUS?
INSIDE A TESSERACT, BELOW THE PARK.
AND YES, CALOC, I'M ABSOLUTELY FINE. NOW, WHO WAS IT OUT THERE ATTACKING ME?
EVIL CREATURES WE THOUGHT BANISHED FOREVER. AN ARMY OF THEM INVADED OUR LAND, AND...
...AVALON HAS BEEN CONQUERED, MASTER.

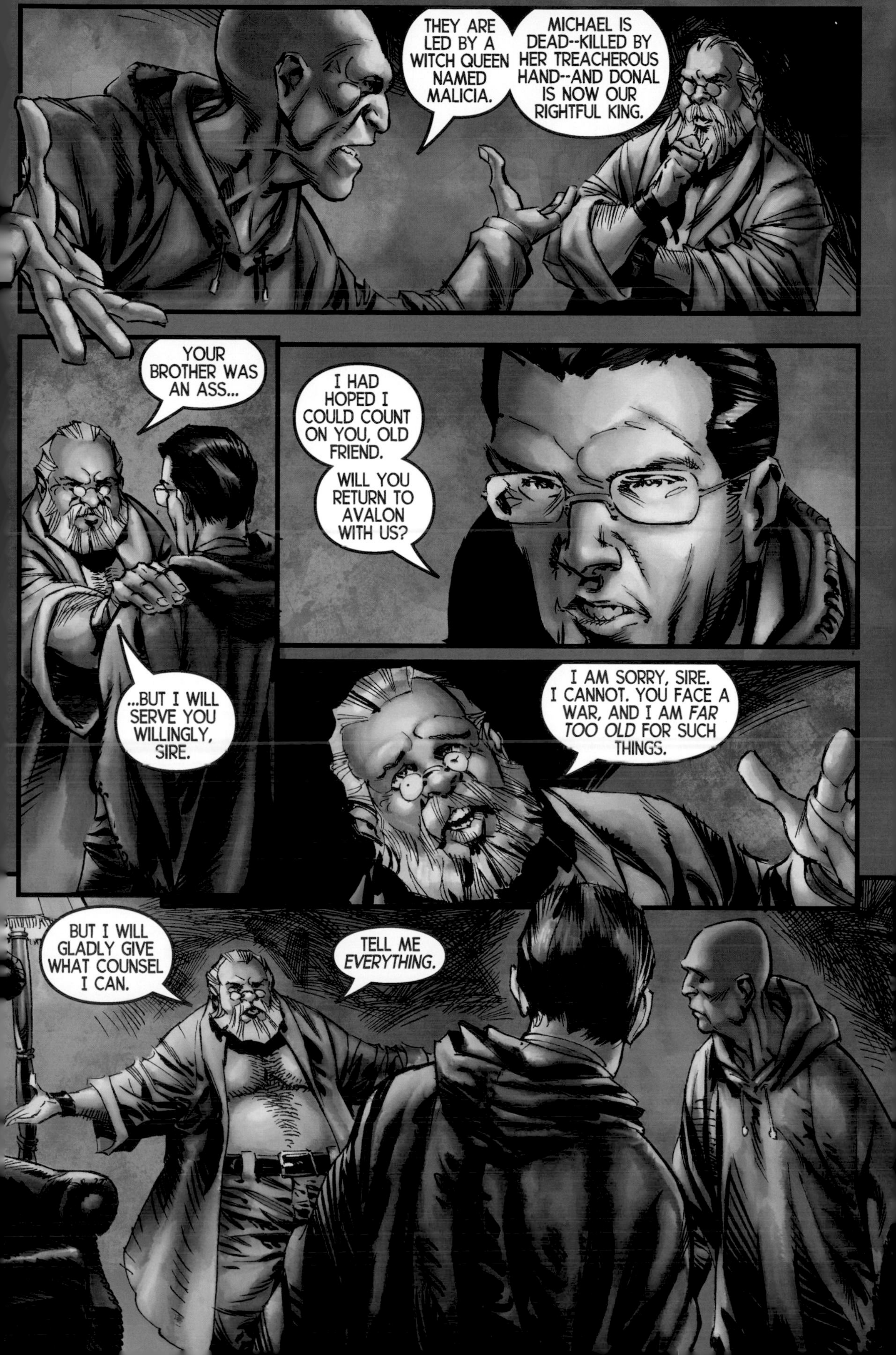
THEY ARE LED BY A WITCH QUEEN NAMED MALICIA.
MICHAEL IS DEAD--KILLED BY HER TREACHEROUS HAND--AND DONAL IS NOW OUR RIGHTFUL KING.
YOUR BROTHER WAS AN ASS...
I HAD HOPED I COULD COUNT ON YOU, OLD FRIEND.
WILL YOU RETURN TO AVALON WITH US?
...BUT I WILL SERVE YOU WILLINGLY, SIRE.
I AM SORRY, SIRE. I CANNOT. YOU FACE A WAR, AND I AM *FAR TOO OLD* FOR SUCH THINGS.
BUT I WILL GLADLY GIVE WHAT COUNSEL I CAN.
TELL ME *EVERYTHING.*

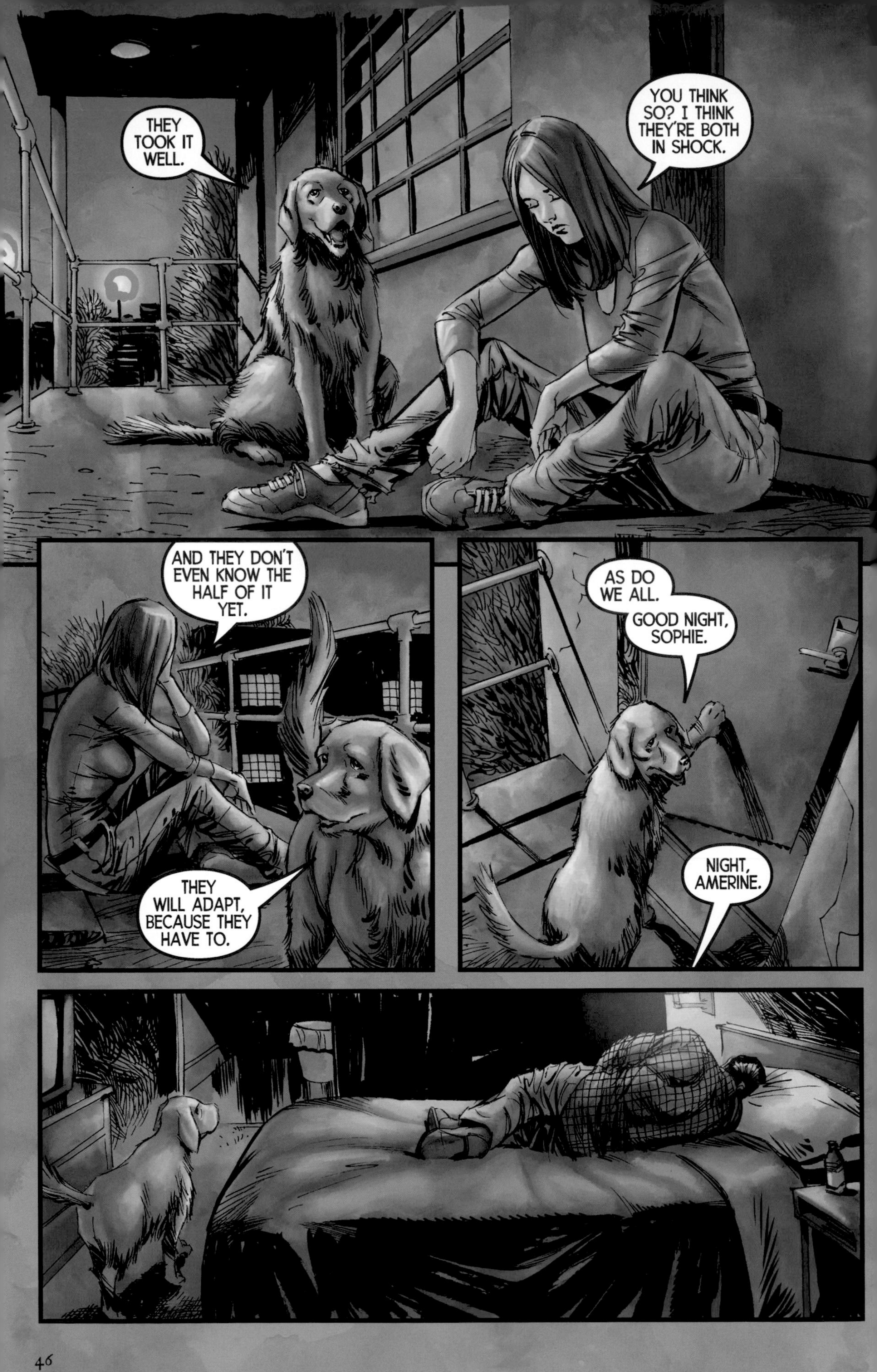
THEY TOOK IT WELL.
YOU THINK SO? I THINK THEY'RE BOTH IN SHOCK.
AND THEY DON'T EVEN KNOW THE HALF OF IT YET.
THEY WILL ADAPT, BECAUSE THEY HAVE TO.
AS DO WE ALL.
GOOD NIGHT, SOPHIE.
NIGHT, AMERINE.

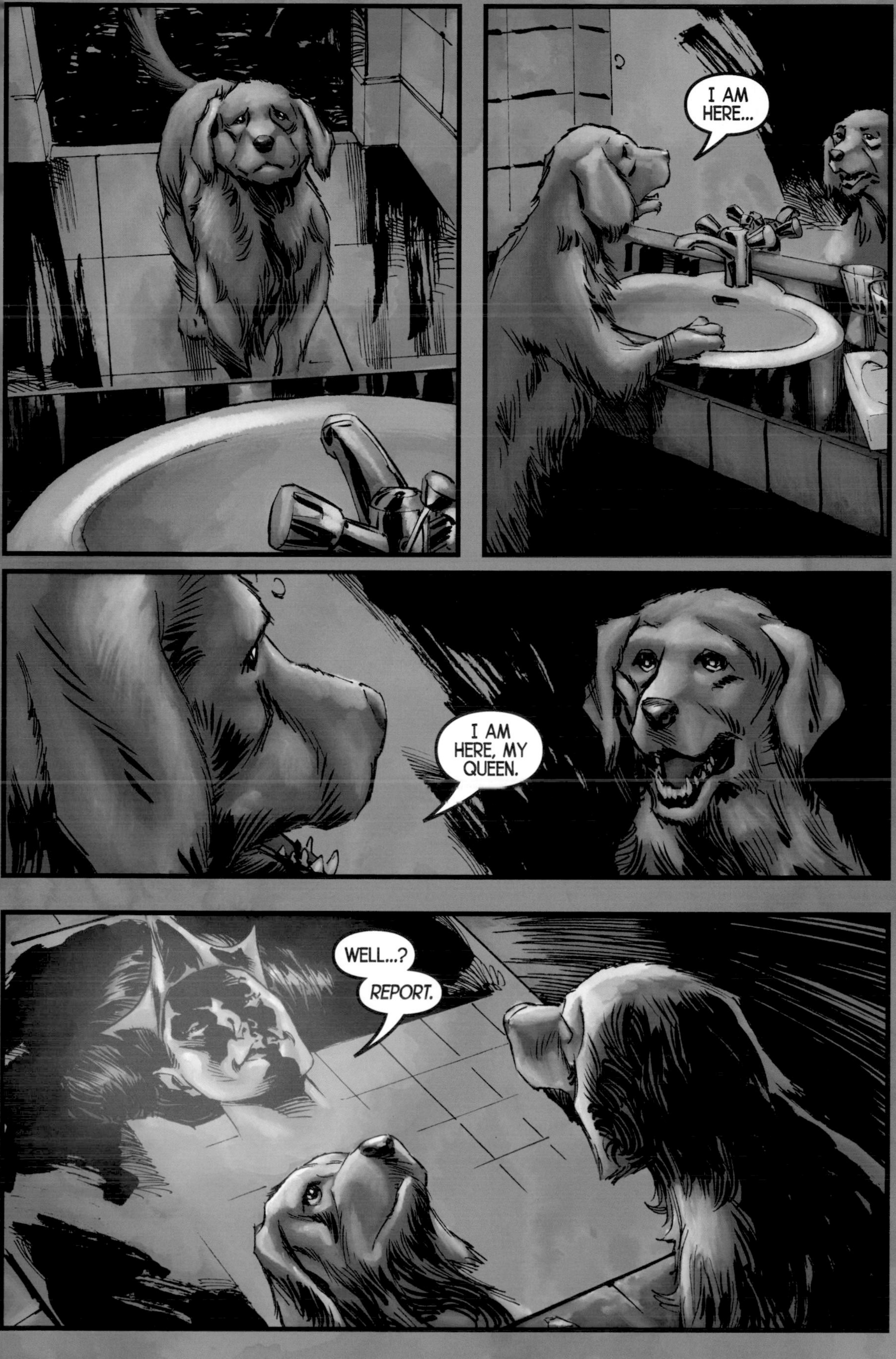
I AM HERE...
I AM HERE, MY QUEEN.
WELL...?
REPORT.

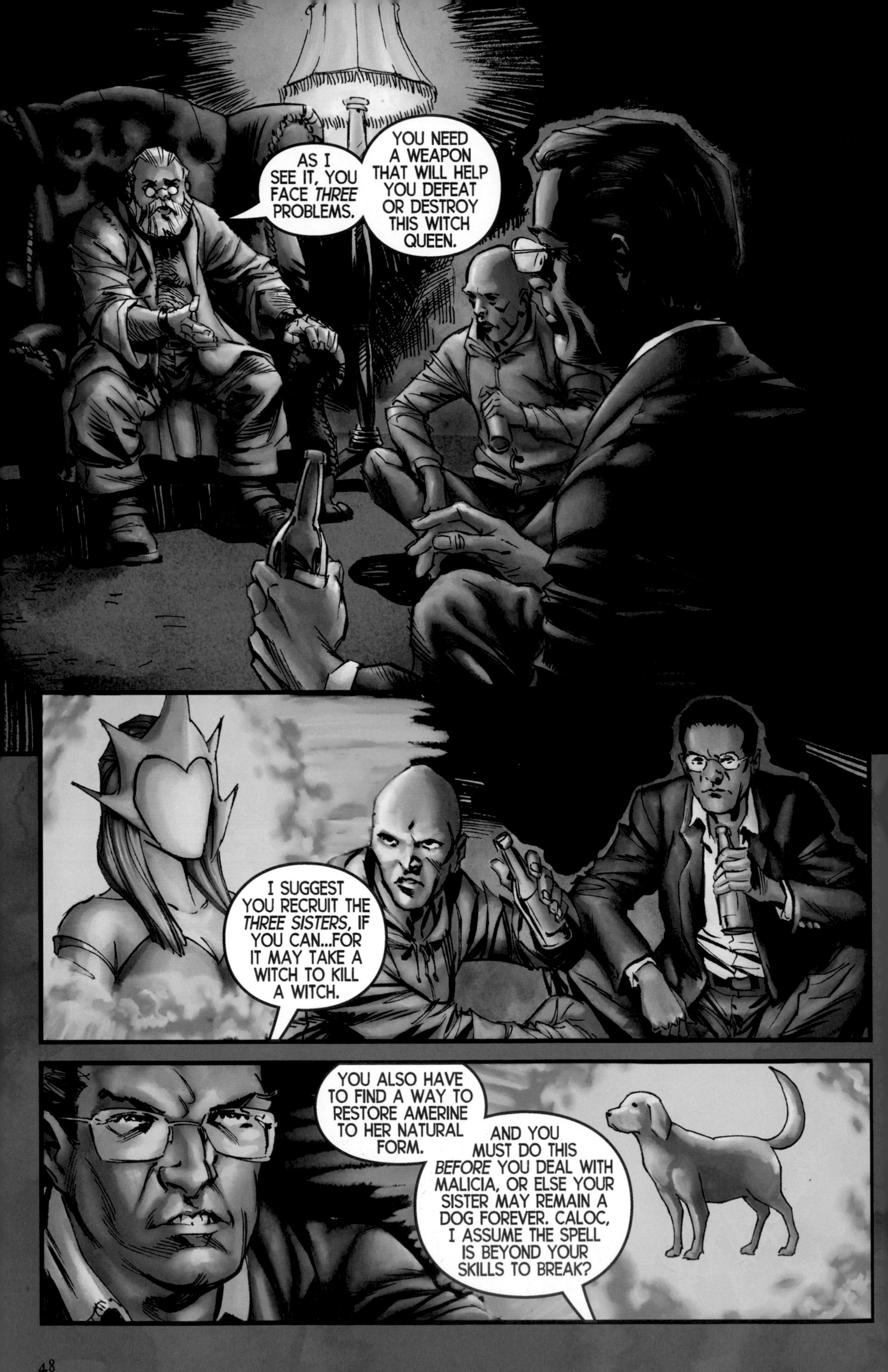
AS I SEE IT, YOU FACE *THREE* PROBLEMS.
YOU NEED A WEAPON THAT WILL HELP YOU DEFEAT OR DESTROY THIS WITCH QUEEN.
I SUGGEST YOU RECRUIT THE *THREE SISTERS*, IF YOU CAN...FOR IT MAY TAKE A WITCH TO KILL A WITCH.
YOU ALSO HAVE TO FIND A WAY TO RESTORE AMERINE TO HER NATURAL FORM.
AND YOU MUST DO THIS *BEFORE* YOU DEAL WITH MALICIA, OR ELSE YOUR SISTER MAY REMAIN A DOG FOREVER. CALOC, I ASSUME THE SPELL IS BEYOND YOUR SKILLS TO BREAK?

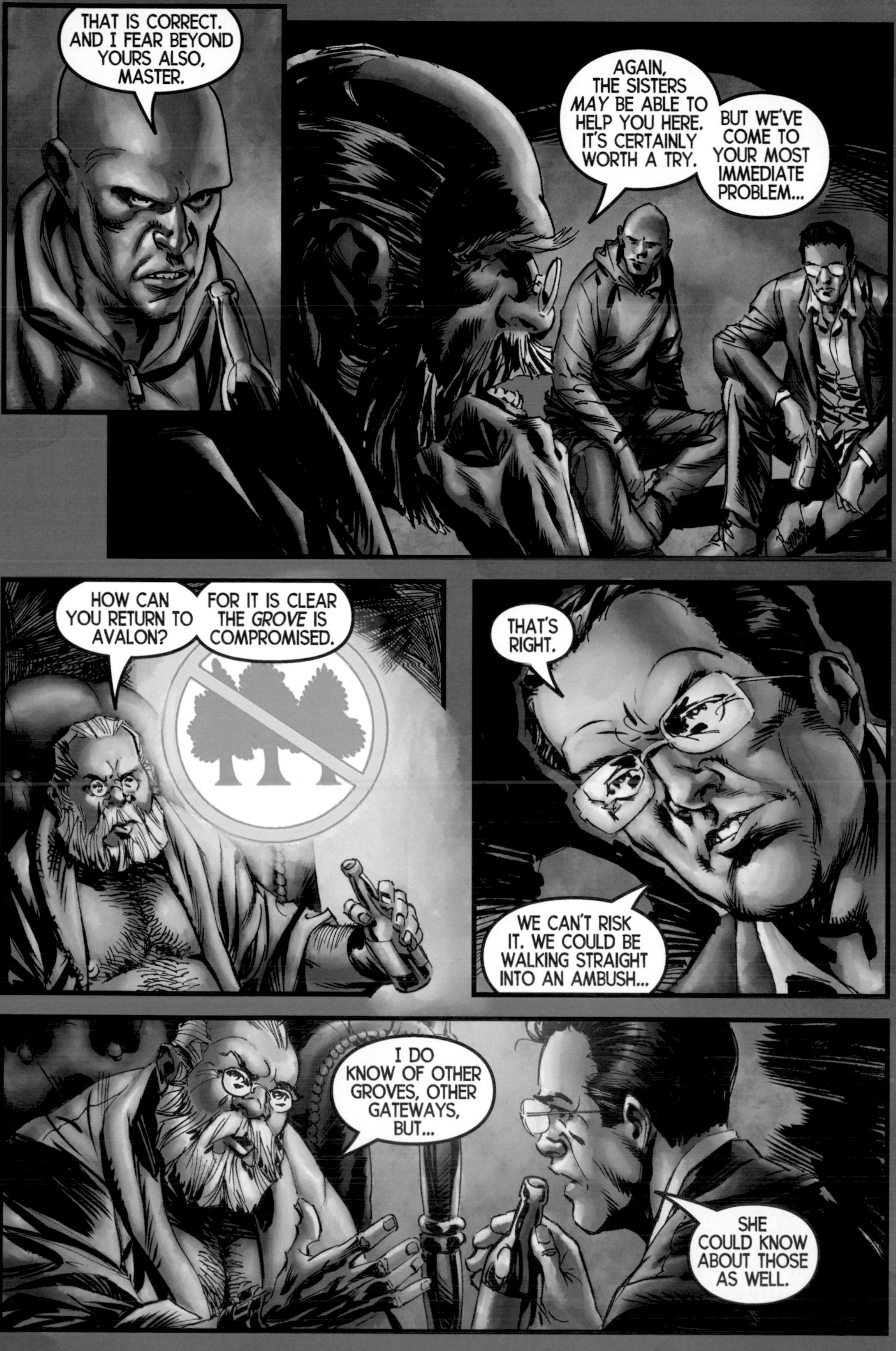
THAT IS CORRECT. AND I FEAR BEYOND YOURS ALSO, MASTER.
AGAIN, THE SISTERS *MAY* BE ABLE TO HELP YOU HERE. IT'S CERTAINLY WORTH A TRY.
BUT WE'VE COME TO YOUR MOST IMMEDIATE PROBLEM...
HOW CAN YOU RETURN TO AVALON?
FOR IT IS CLEAR THE *GROVE* IS COMPROMISED.
THAT'S RIGHT.
WE CAN'T RISK IT. WE COULD BE WALKING STRAIGHT INTO AN AMBUSH...
I DO KNOW OF OTHER GROVES, OTHER GATEWAYS, BUT...
SHE COULD KNOW ABOUT THOSE AS WELL.

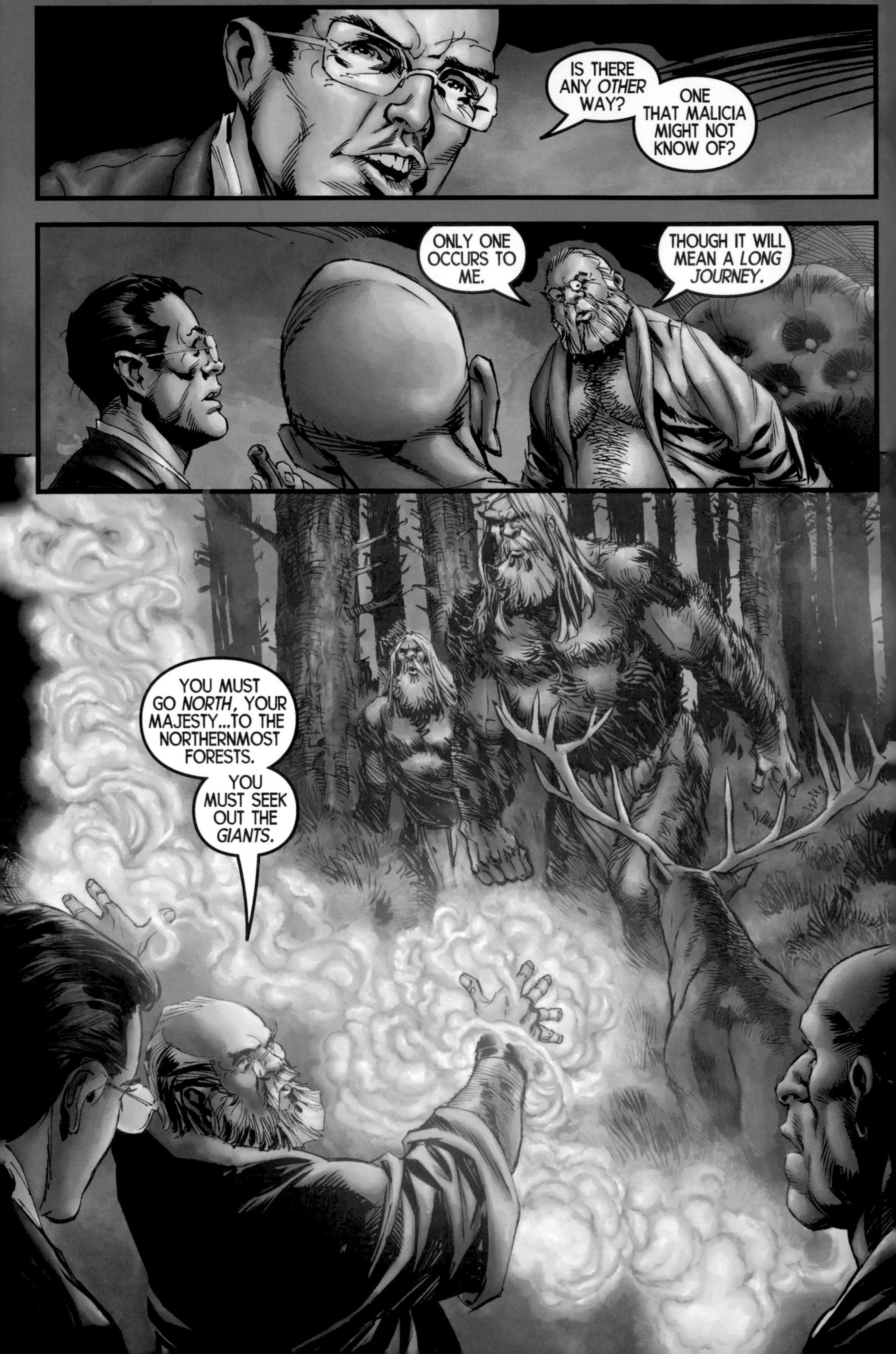
IS THERE ANY OTHER WAY?
ONE THAT MALICIA MIGHT NOT KNOW OF?
ONLY ONE OCCURS TO ME.
THOUGH IT WILL MEAN A LONG JOURNEY.
YOU MUST GO NORTH, YOUR MAJESTY...TO THE NORTHERNMOST FORESTS.
YOU MUST SEEK OUT THE GIANTS.

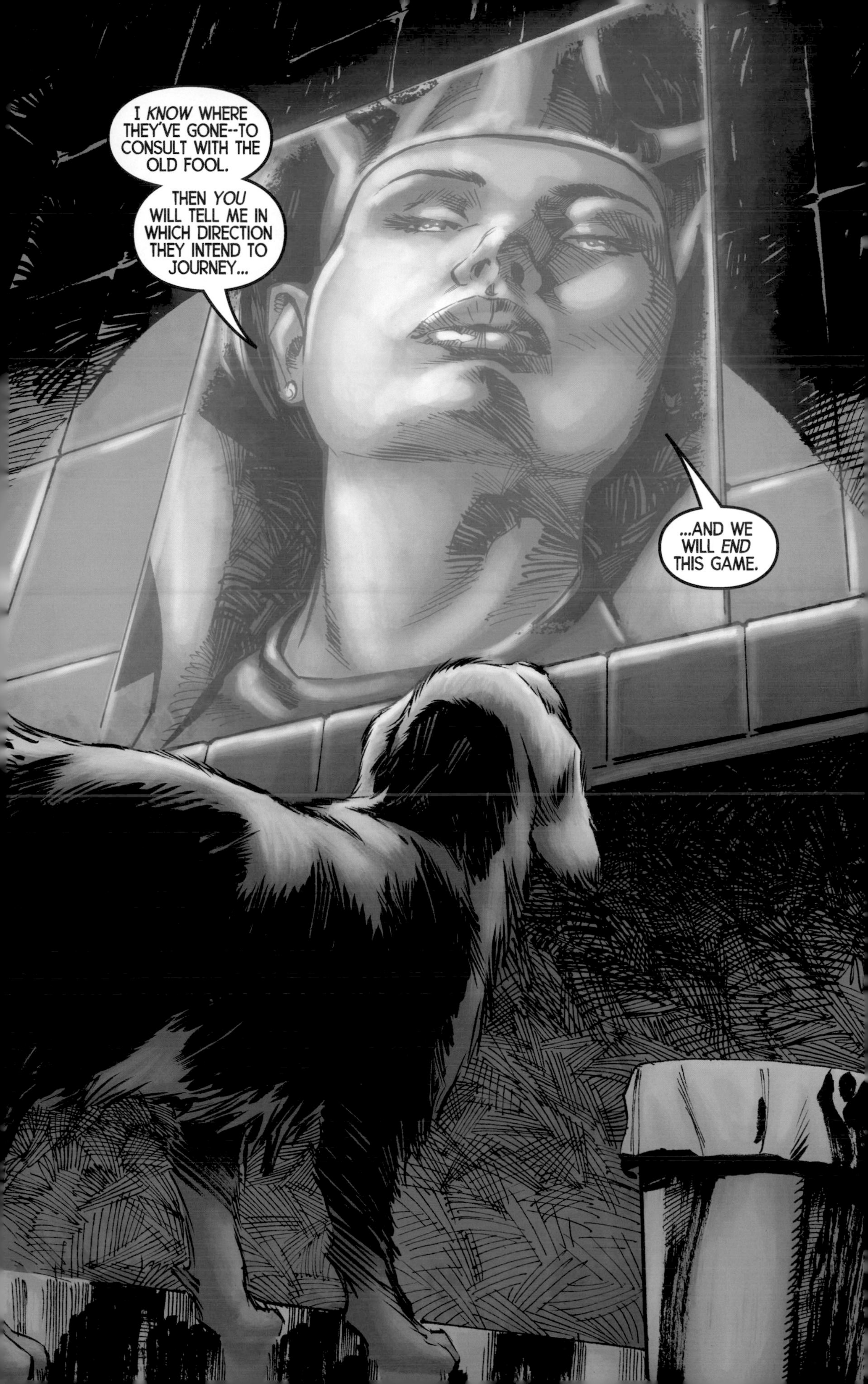
I *KNOW* WHERE THEY'VE GONE--TO CONSULT WITH THE OLD FOOL.
THEN *YOU* WILL TELL ME IN WHICH DIRECTION THEY INTEND TO JOURNEY...
...AND WE WILL *END* THIS GAME.

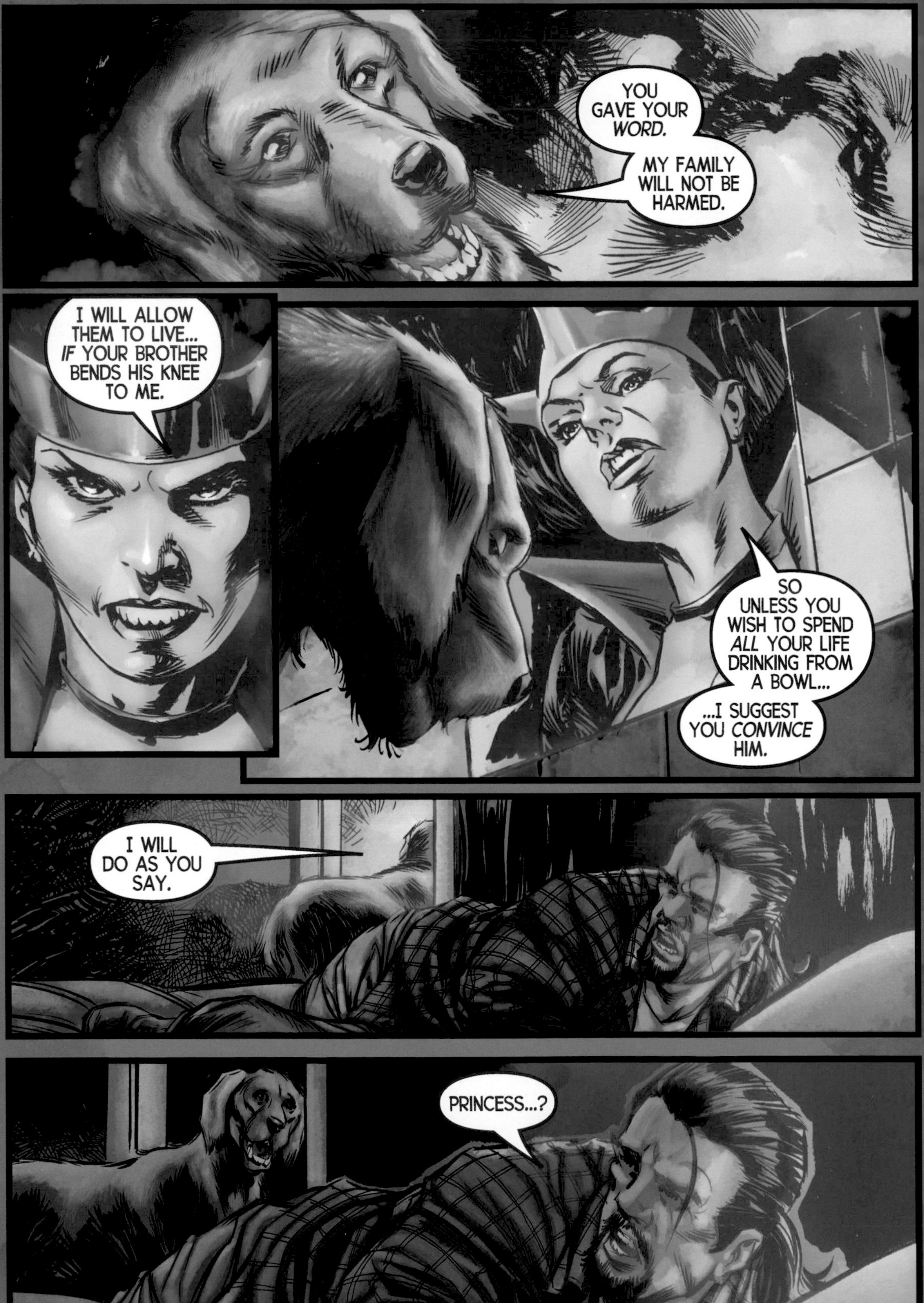
YOU GAVE YOUR *WORD.*
MY FAMILY WILL NOT BE HARMED.
I WILL ALLOW THEM TO LIVE... *IF* YOUR BROTHER BENDS HIS KNEE TO ME.
SO UNLESS YOU WISH TO SPEND *ALL* YOUR LIFE DRINKING FROM A BOWL...
...I SUGGEST YOU *CONVINCE* HIM.
I WILL DO AS YOU SAY.
PRINCESS...?

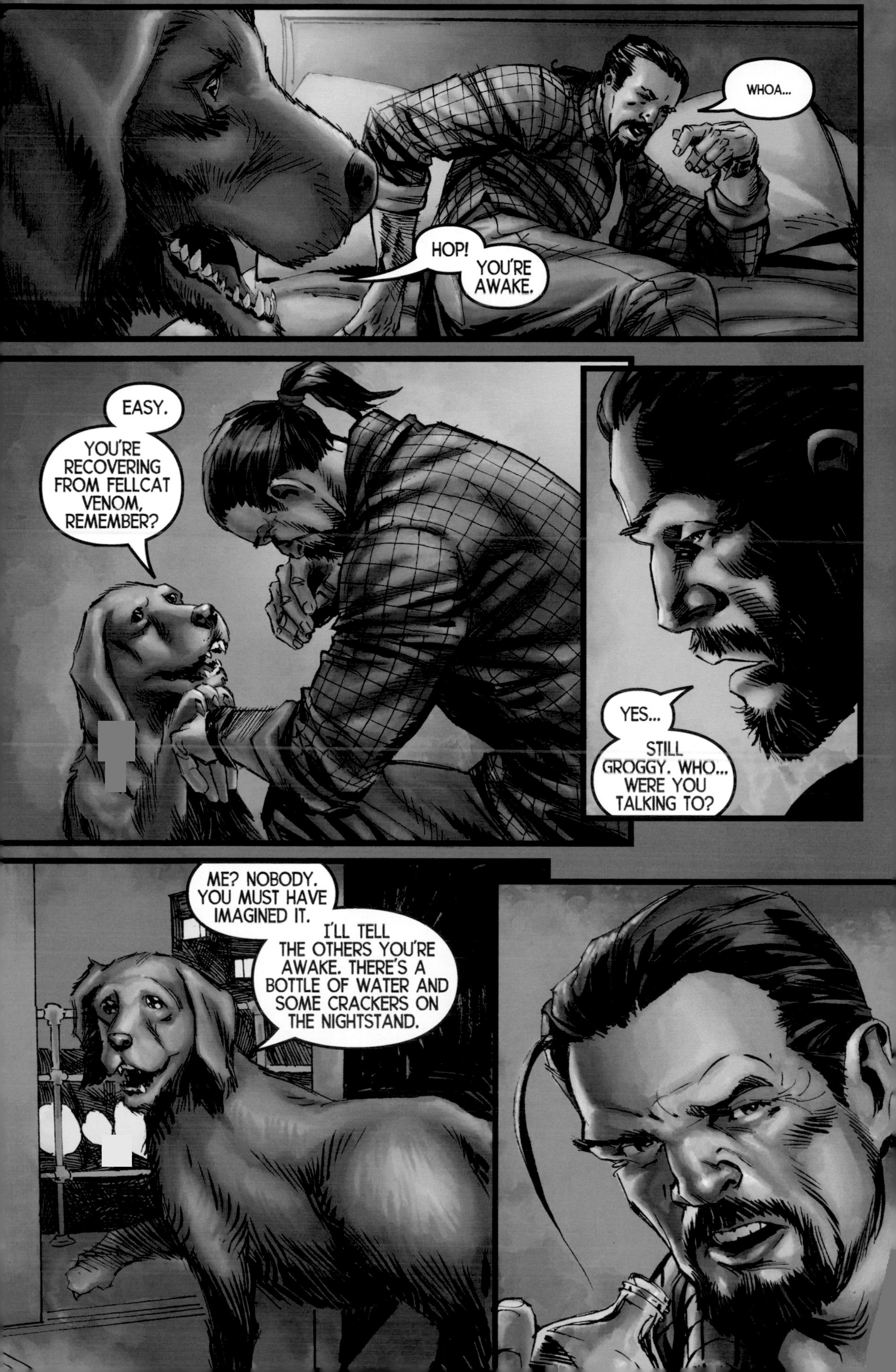
WHOA...
HOP! YOU'RE AWAKE.
EASY.
YOU'RE RECOVERING FROM FELLCAT VENOM, REMEMBER?
YES...
STILL GROGGY. WHO... WERE YOU TALKING TO?
ME? NOBODY. YOU MUST HAVE IMAGINED IT.
I'LL TELL THE OTHERS YOU'RE AWAKE. THERE'S A BOTTLE OF WATER AND SOME CRACKERS ON THE NIGHTSTAND.

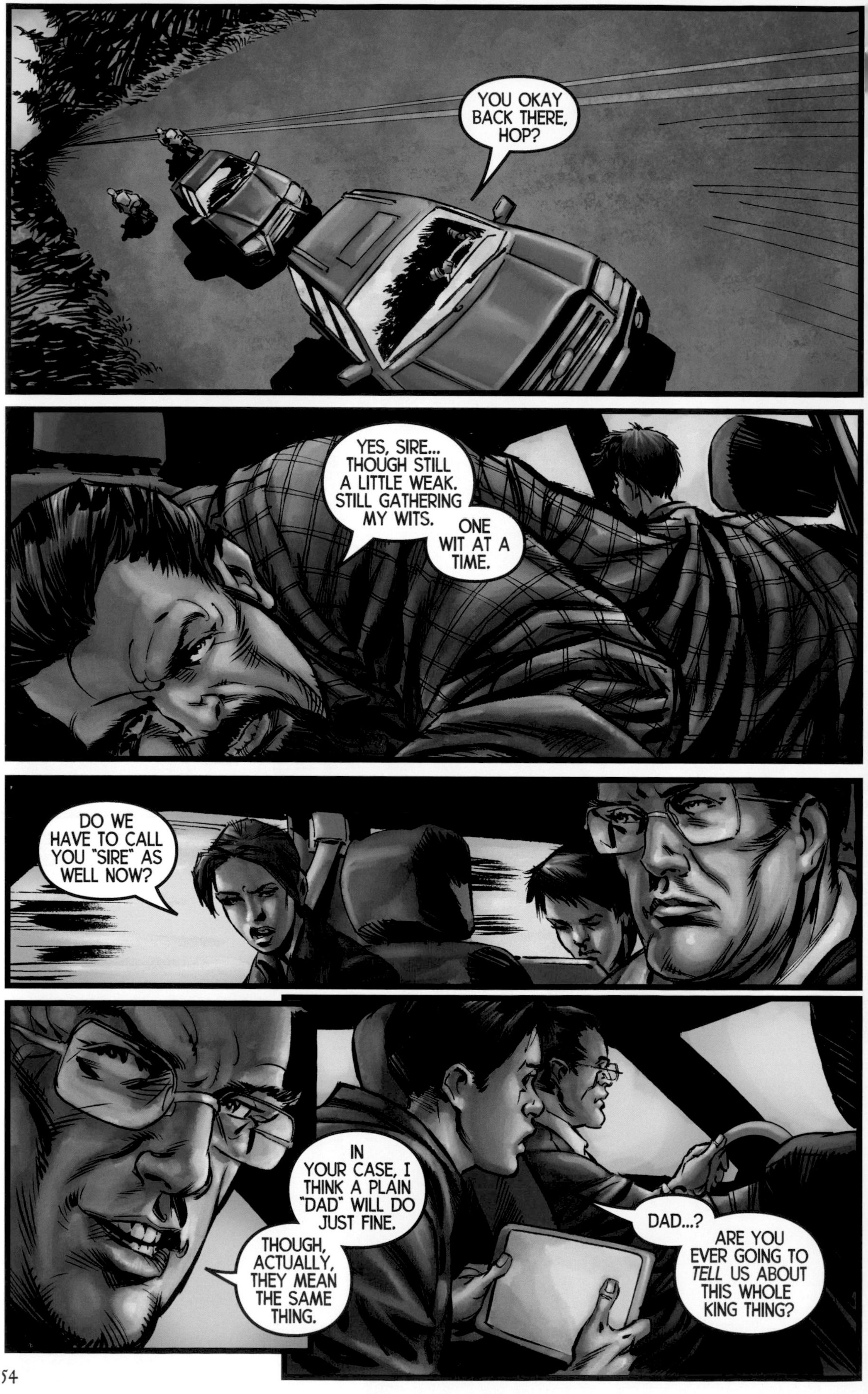
YOU OKAY BACK THERE, HOP?
YES, SIRE... THOUGH STILL A LITTLE WEAK. STILL GATHERING MY WITS.
ONE WIT AT A TIME.
DO WE HAVE TO CALL YOU "SIRE" AS WELL NOW?
IN YOUR CASE, I THINK A PLAIN "DAD" WILL DO JUST FINE.
THOUGH, ACTUALLY, THEY MEAN THE SAME THING.
DAD...?
ARE YOU EVER GOING TO *TELL* US ABOUT THIS WHOLE KING THING?

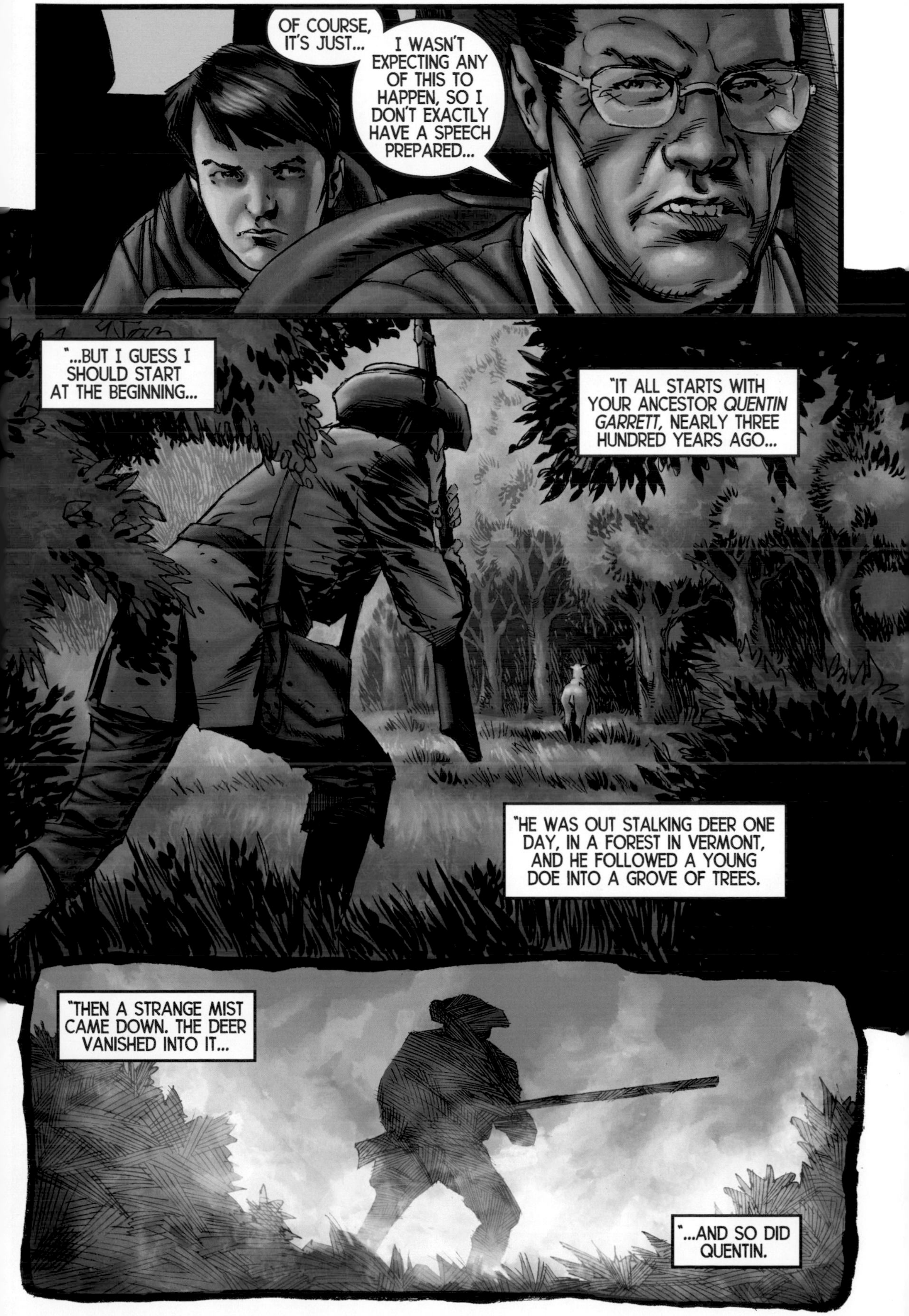
OF COURSE, IT'S JUST...
I WASN'T EXPECTING ANY OF THIS TO HAPPEN, SO I DON'T EXACTLY HAVE A SPEECH PREPARED...
"...BUT I GUESS I SHOULD START AT THE BEGINNING...
"IT ALL STARTS WITH YOUR ANCESTOR *QUENTIN GARRETT,* NEARLY THREE HUNDRED YEARS AGO...
"HE WAS OUT STALKING DEER ONE DAY, IN A FOREST IN VERMONT, AND HE FOLLOWED A YOUNG DOE INTO A GROVE OF TREES.
"THEN A STRANGE MIST CAME DOWN. THE DEER VANISHED INTO IT...
"...AND SO DID QUENTIN.

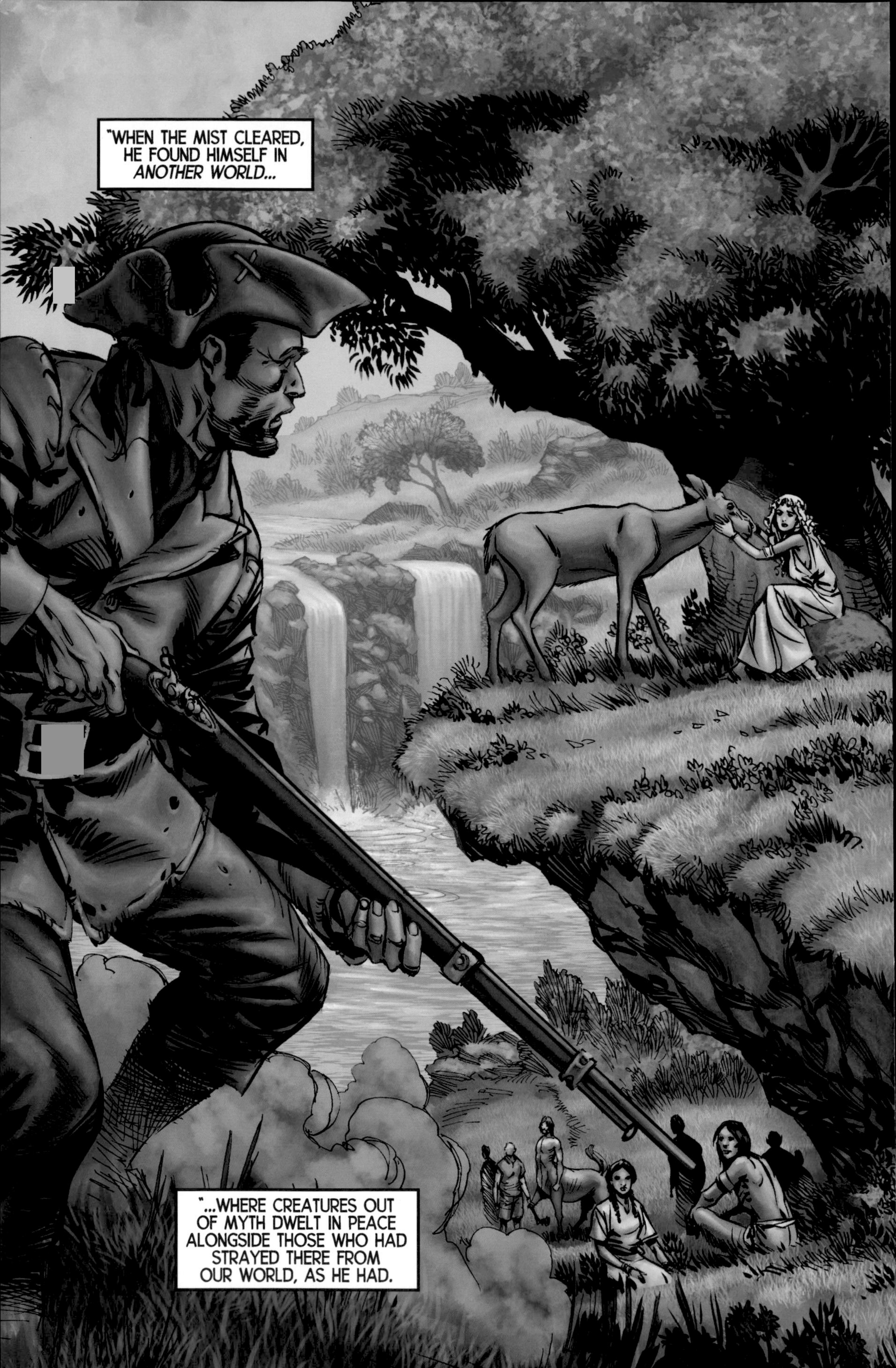
"WHEN THE MIST CLEARED, HE FOUND HIMSELF IN *ANOTHER WORLD*...
"...WHERE CREATURES OUT OF MYTH DWELT IN PEACE ALONGSIDE THOSE WHO HAD STRAYED THERE FROM OUR WORLD, AS HE HAD.

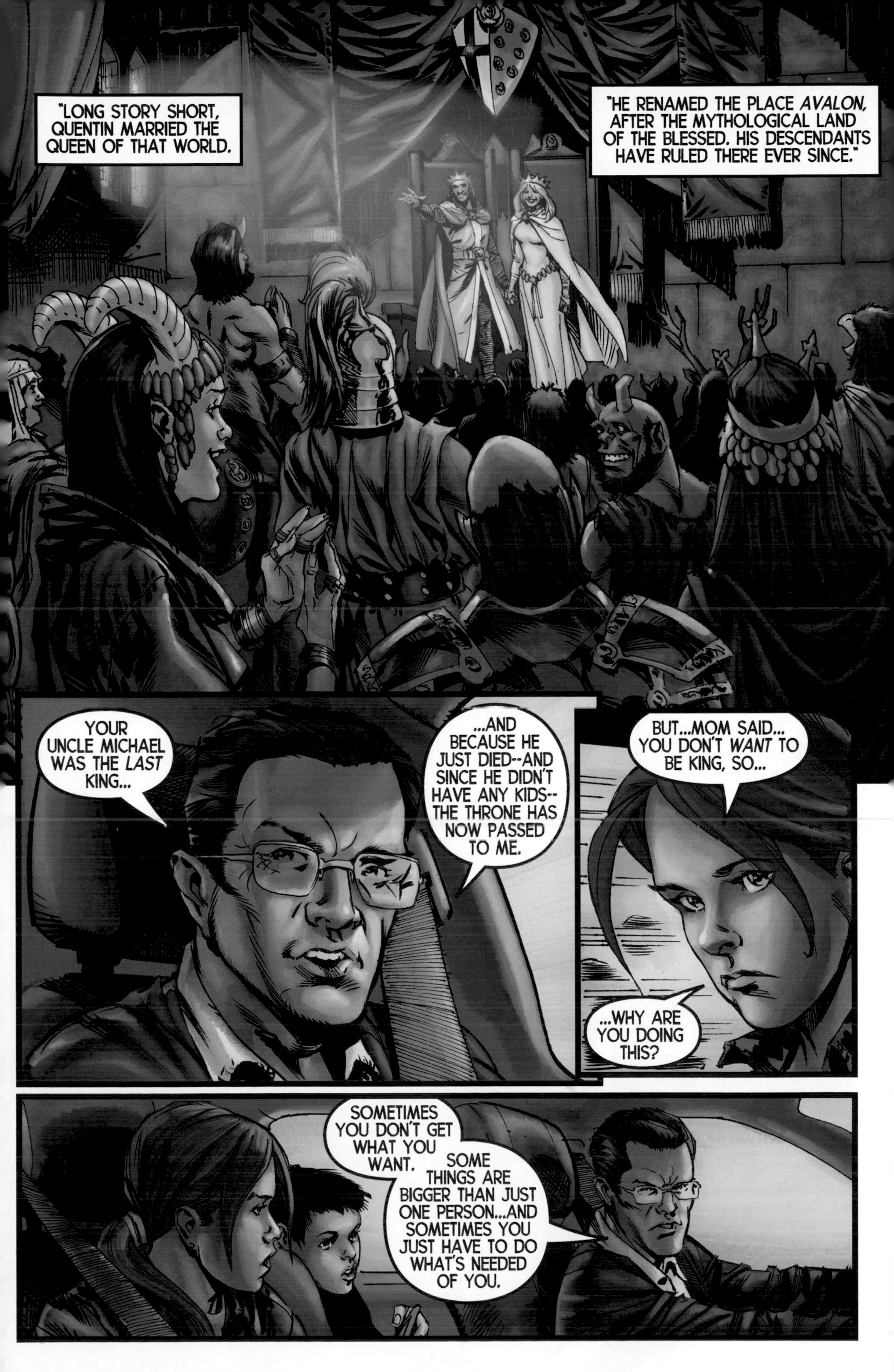
"LONG STORY SHORT, QUENTIN MARRIED THE QUEEN OF THAT WORLD.
"HE RENAMED THE PLACE *AVALON*, AFTER THE MYTHOLOGICAL LAND OF THE BLESSED. HIS DESCENDANTS HAVE RULED THERE EVER SINCE."
YOUR UNCLE MICHAEL WAS THE *LAST* KING...
...AND BECAUSE HE JUST DIED--AND SINCE HE DIDN'T HAVE ANY KIDS--THE THRONE HAS NOW PASSED TO ME.
BUT...MOM SAID... YOU DON'T *WANT* TO BE KING, SO...
...WHY ARE YOU DOING THIS?
SOMETIMES YOU DON'T GET WHAT YOU WANT.
SOME THINGS ARE BIGGER THAN JUST ONE PERSON...AND SOMETIMES YOU JUST HAVE TO DO WHAT'S NEEDED OF YOU.

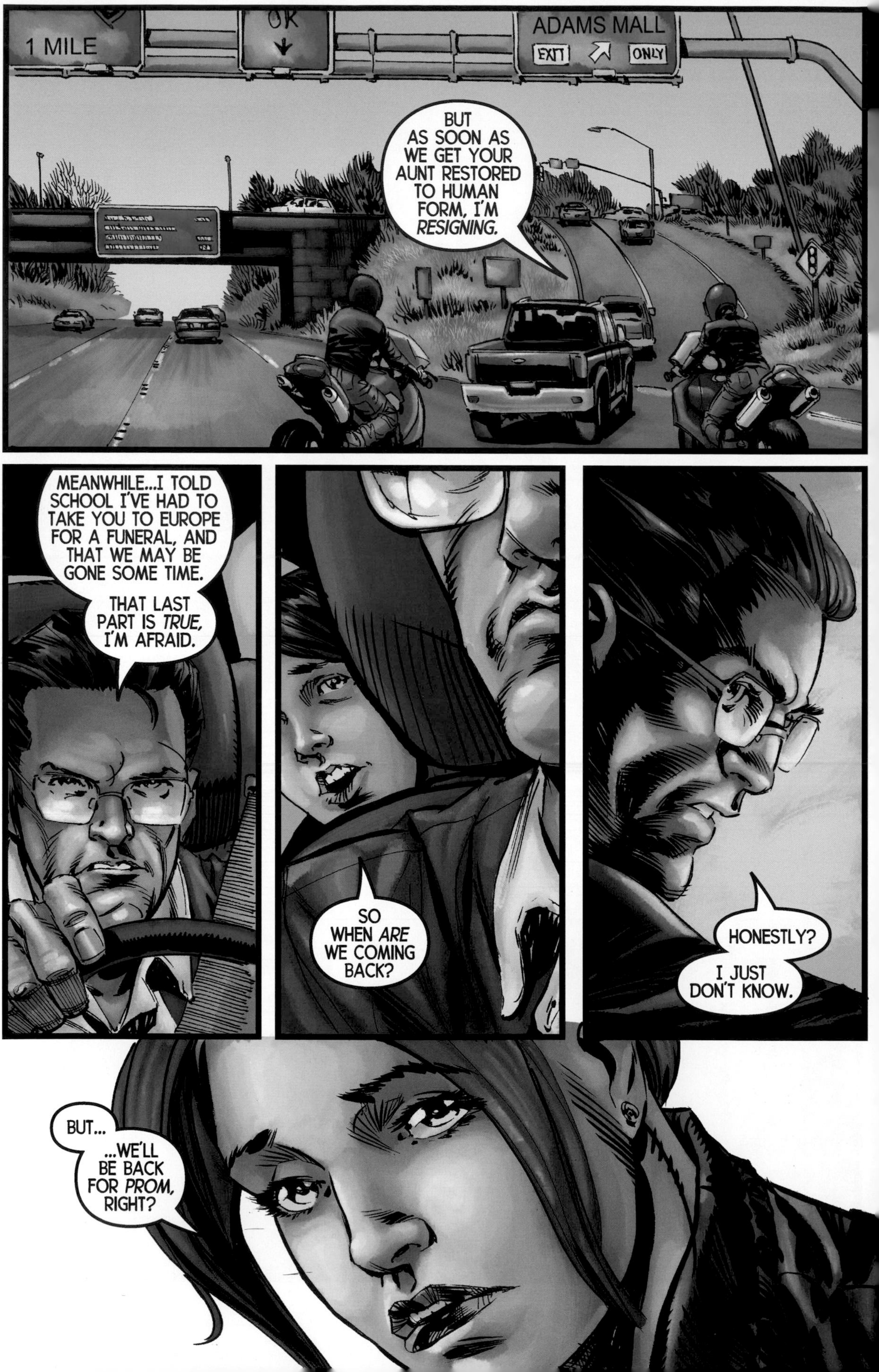
1 MILE
OK
ADAMS MALL
EXIT ONLY
BUT AS SOON AS WE GET YOUR AUNT RESTORED TO HUMAN FORM, I'M *RESIGNING.*
MEANWHILE...I TOLD SCHOOL I'VE HAD TO TAKE YOU TO EUROPE FOR A FUNERAL, AND THAT WE MAY BE GONE SOME TIME.
THAT LAST PART IS *TRUE,* I'M AFRAID.
SO WHEN *ARE* WE COMING BACK?
HONESTLY?
I JUST DON'T KNOW.
BUT...
...WE'LL BE BACK FOR *PROM,* RIGHT?

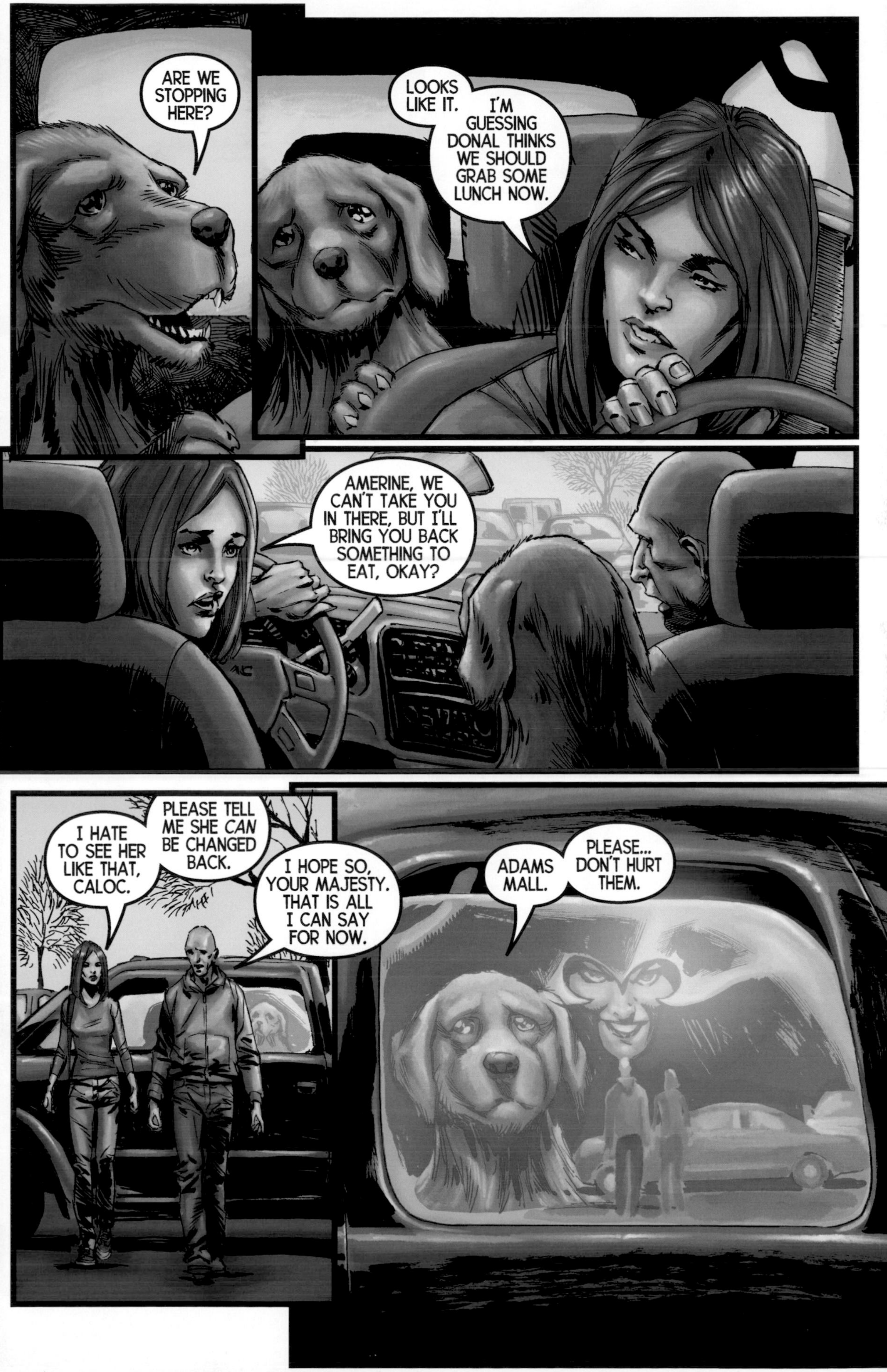
ARE WE STOPPING HERE?
LOOKS LIKE IT.
I'M GUESSING DONAL THINKS WE SHOULD GRAB SOME LUNCH NOW.
AMERINE, WE CAN'T TAKE YOU IN THERE, BUT I'LL BRING YOU BACK SOMETHING TO EAT, OKAY?
I HATE TO SEE HER LIKE THAT, CALOC.
PLEASE TELL ME SHE *CAN* BE CHANGED BACK.
I HOPE SO, YOUR MAJESTY. THAT IS ALL I CAN SAY FOR NOW.
ADAMS MALL.
PLEASE... DON'T HURT THEM.

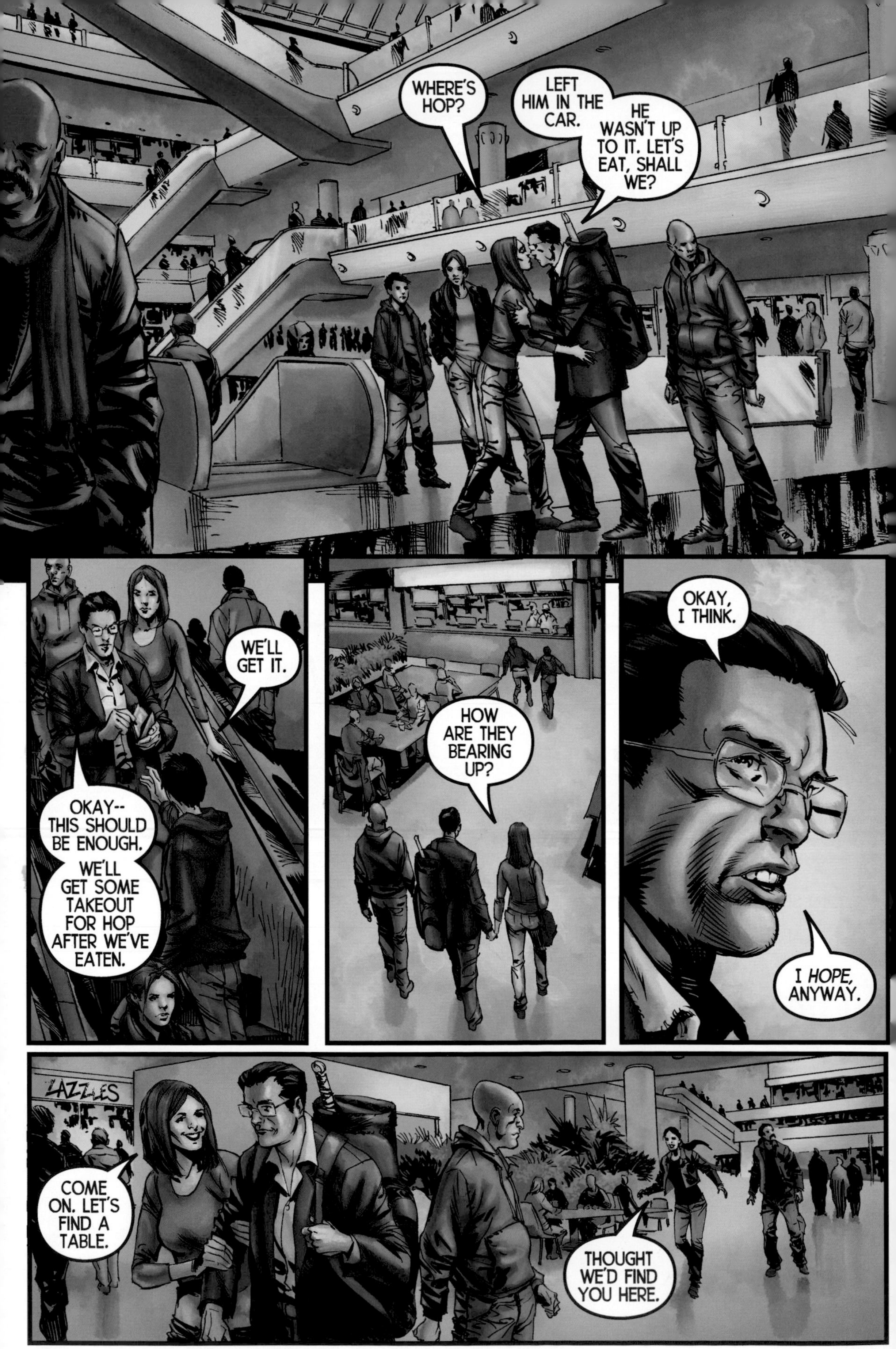
WHERE'S HOP?
LEFT HIM IN THE CAR.
HE WASN'T UP TO IT. LET'S EAT, SHALL WE?
WE'LL GET IT.
OKAY-- THIS SHOULD BE ENOUGH.
WE'LL GET SOME TAKEOUT FOR HOP AFTER WE'VE EATEN.
HOW ARE THEY BEARING UP?
OKAY, I THINK.
I *HOPE*, ANYWAY.
LAZZLES
COME ON. LET'S FIND A TABLE.
THOUGHT WE'D FIND YOU HERE.

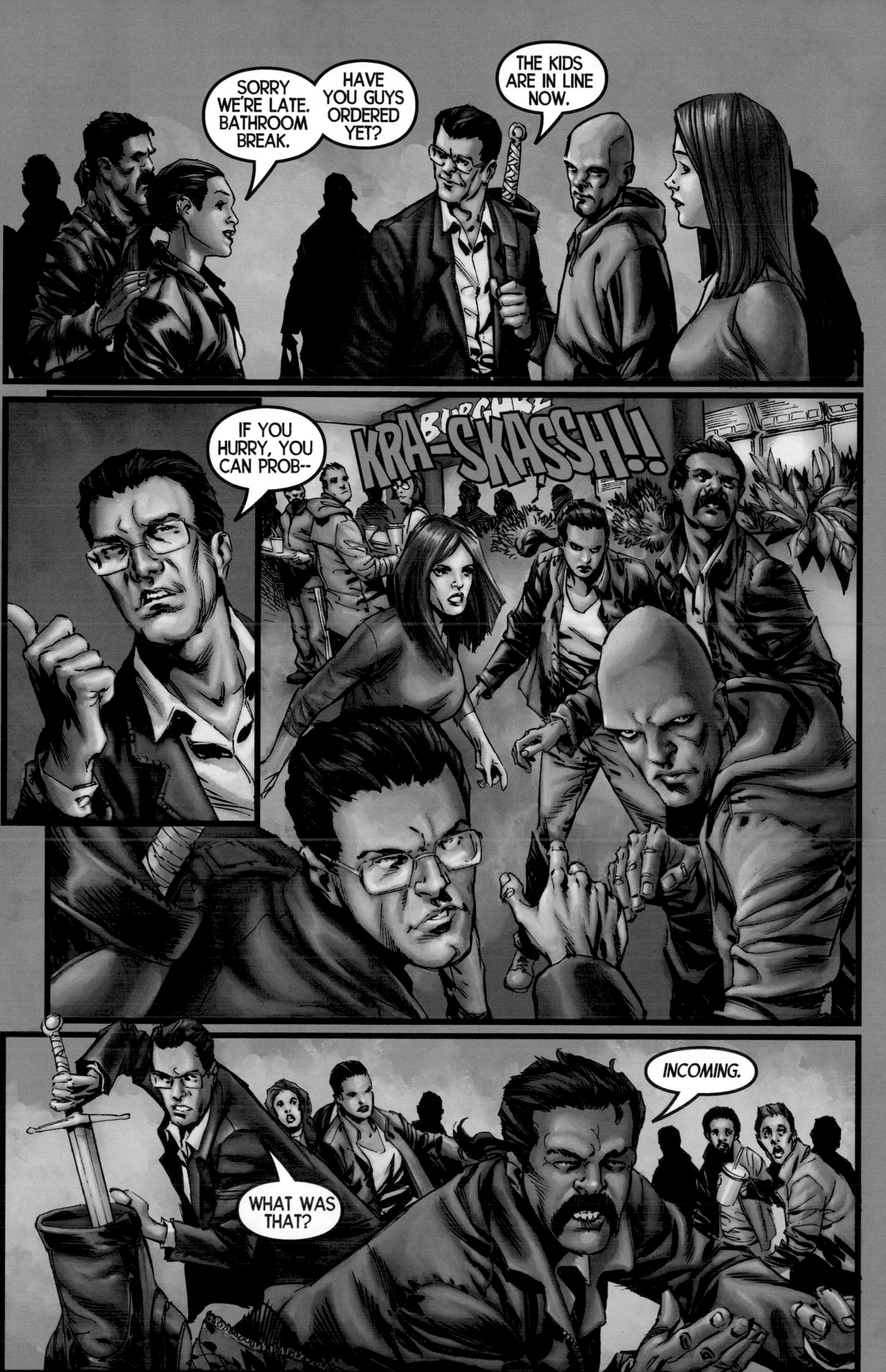
SORRY WE'RE LATE. BATHROOM BREAK.
HAVE YOU GUYS ORDERED YET?
THE KIDS ARE IN LINE NOW.
IF YOU HURRY, YOU CAN PROB--
KRA-SKASSH!!
WHAT WAS THAT?
INCOMING.

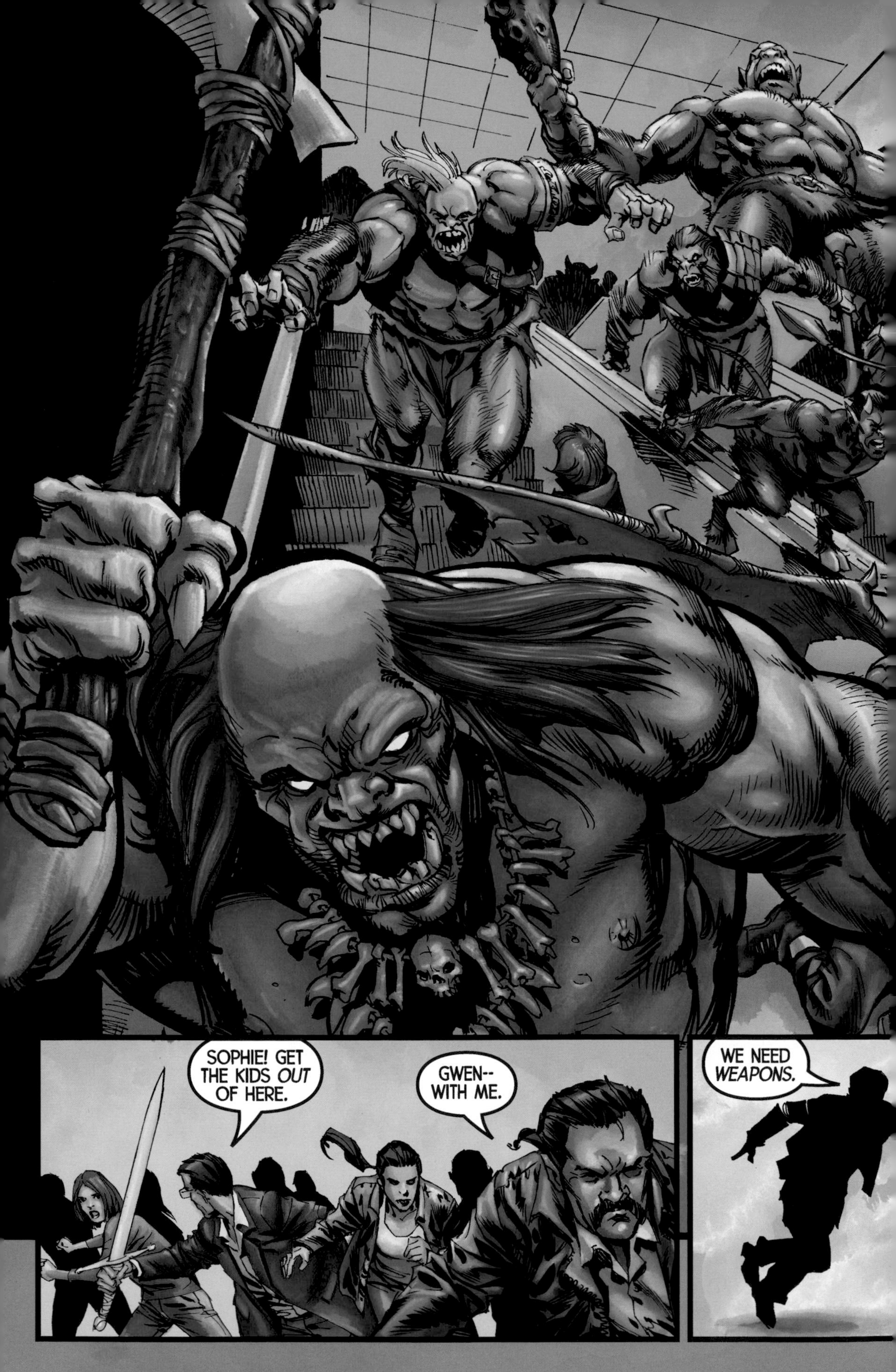
SOPHIE! GET THE KIDS *OUT* OF HERE.
GWEN-- WITH ME.
WE NEED *WEAPONS.*

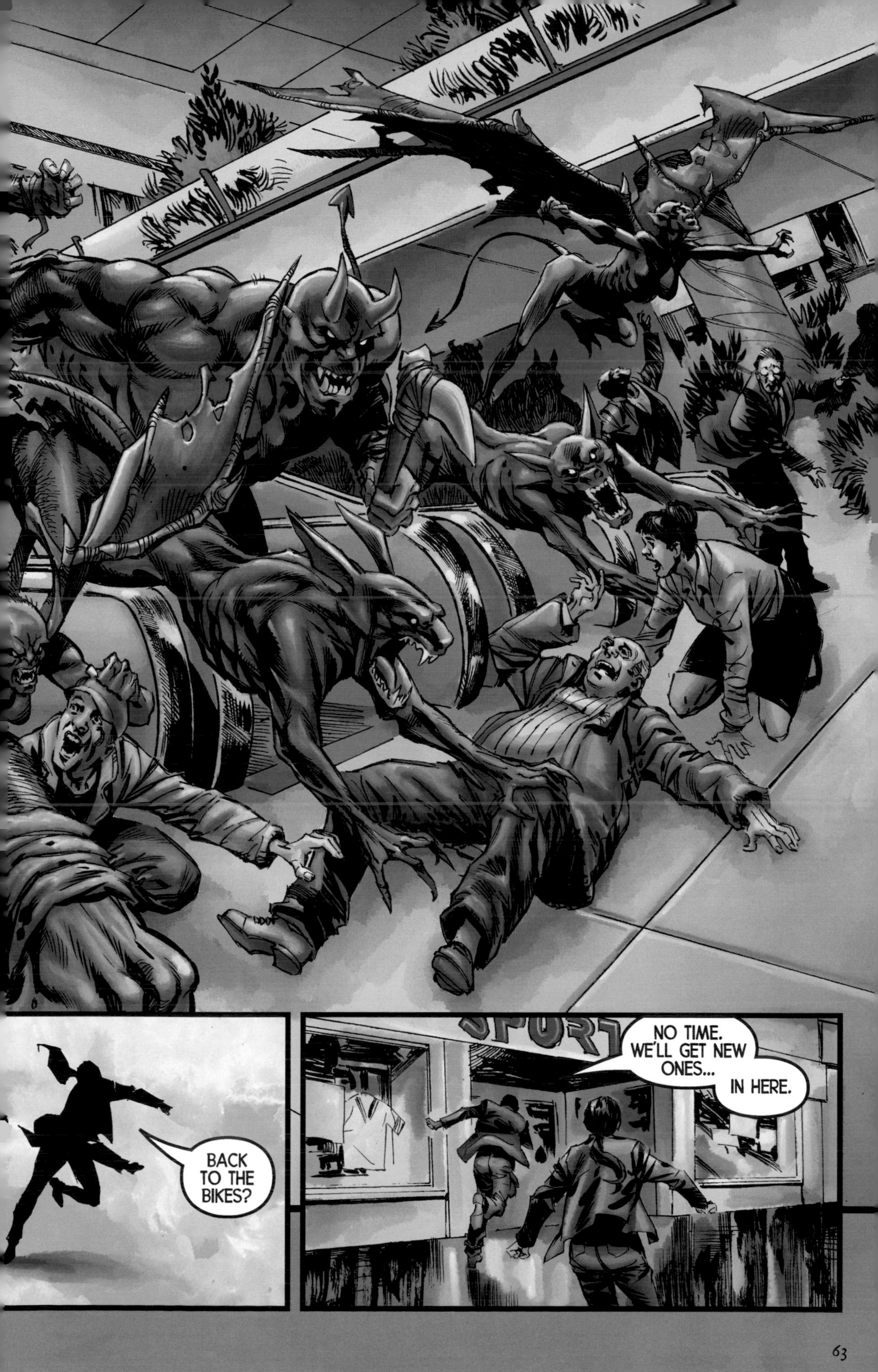
BACK TO THE BIKES?
NO TIME. WE'LL GET NEW ONES...
IN HERE.

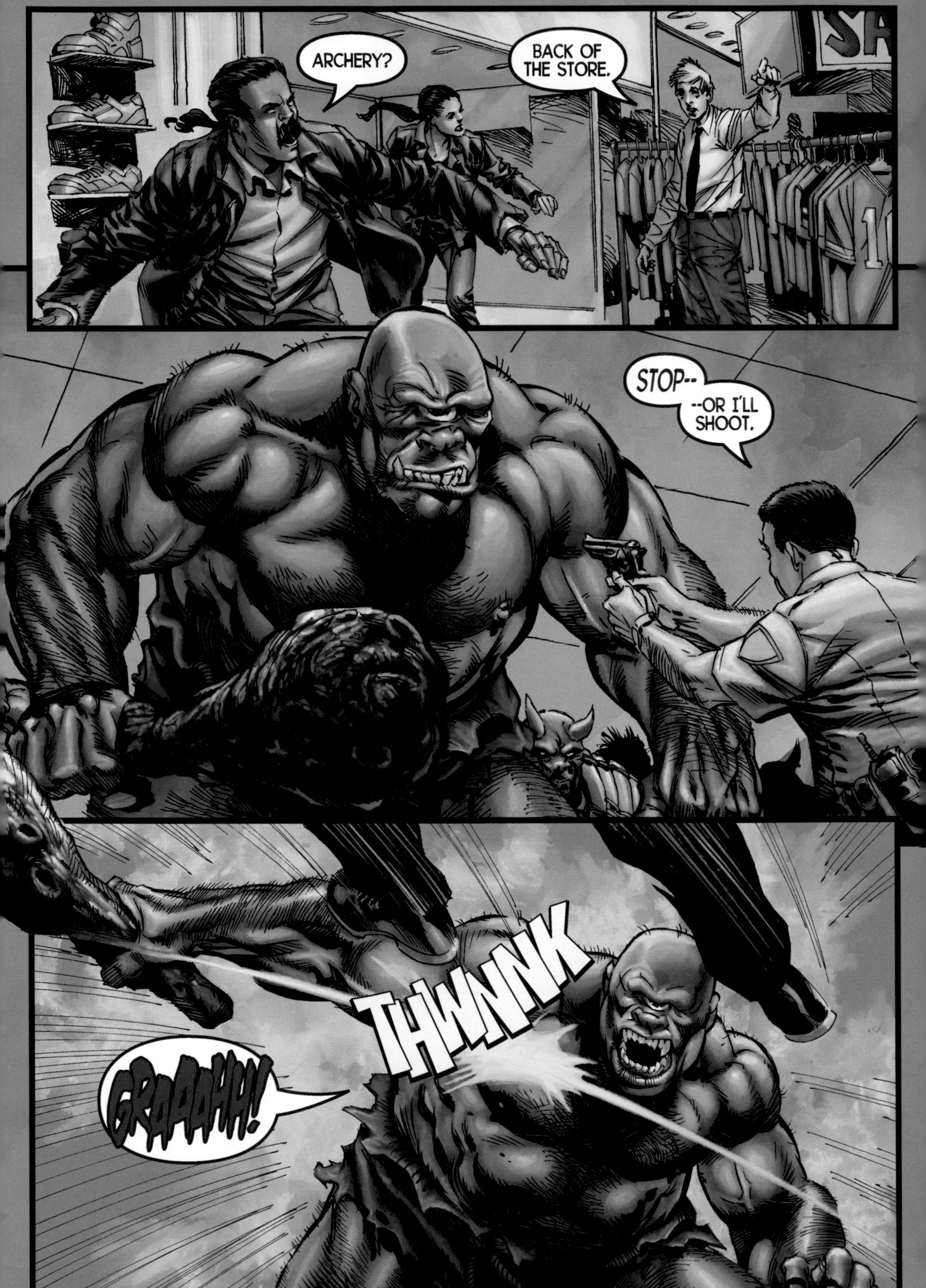
ARCHERY?
BACK OF THE STORE.
STOP--
--OR I'LL SHOOT.
THWNNK
GRAAAHH!

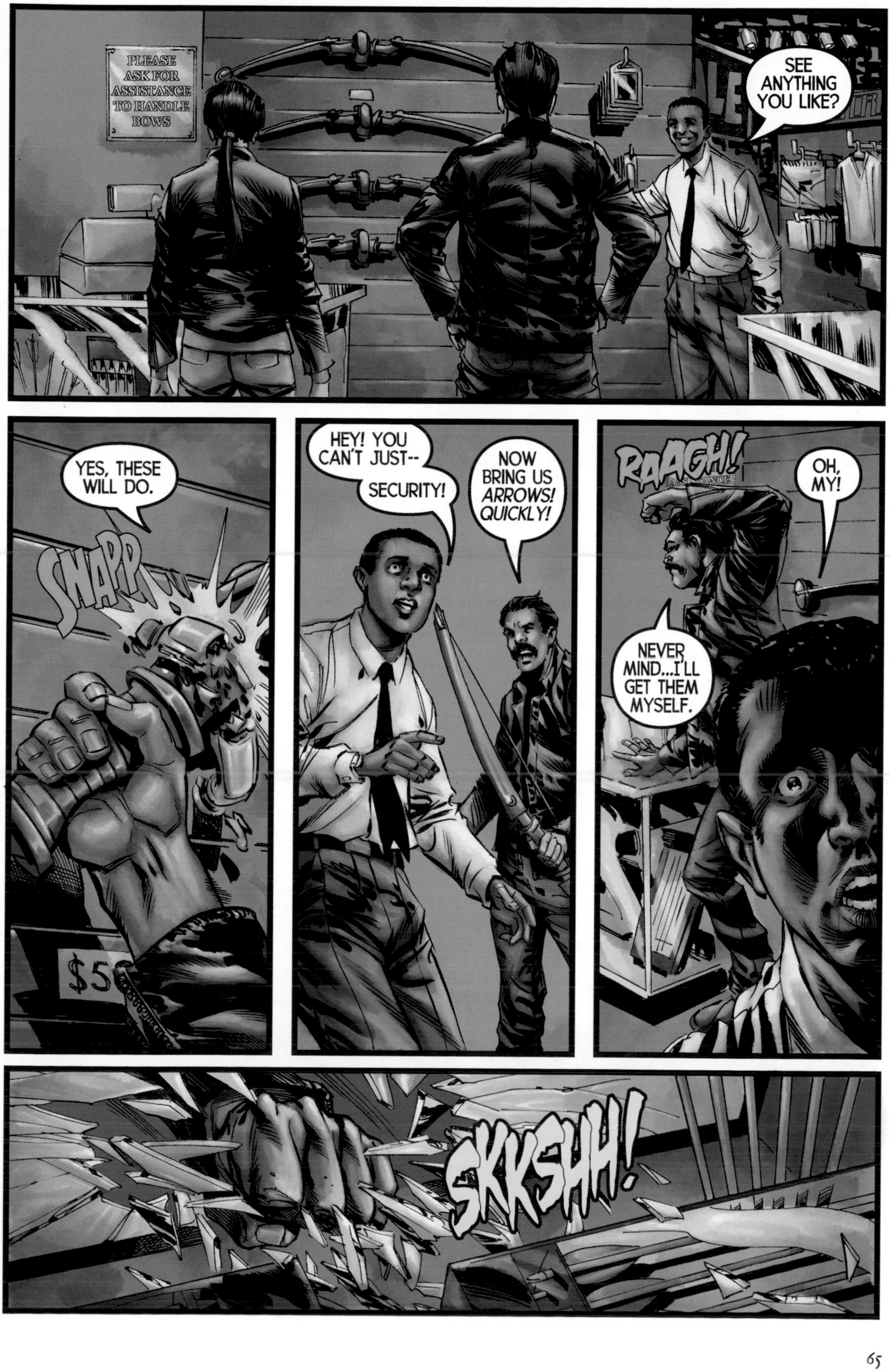
PLEASE ASK FOR ASSISTANCE TO HANDLE BOWS
SEE ANYTHING YOU LIKE?
YES, THESE WILL DO.
SNAPP
$5
HEY! YOU CAN'T JUST--
SECURITY!
NOW BRING US *ARROWS! QUICKLY!*
RAAGH!
OH, MY!
NEVER MIND...I'LL GET THEM MYSELF.
SKKSHH!

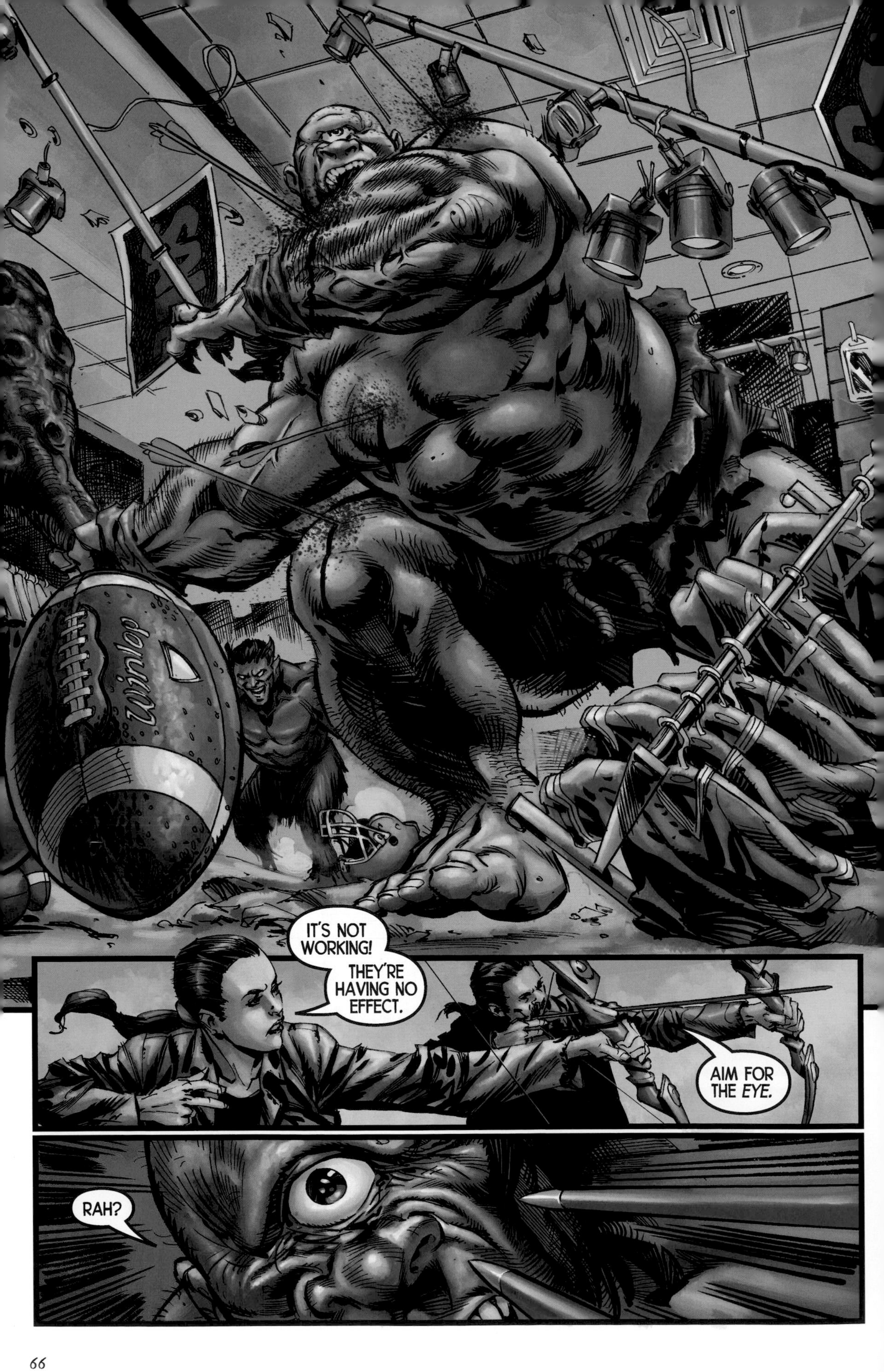

Winlop
IT'S NOT WORKING!
THEY'RE HAVING NO EFFECT.
AIM FOR THE *EYE.*
RAH?

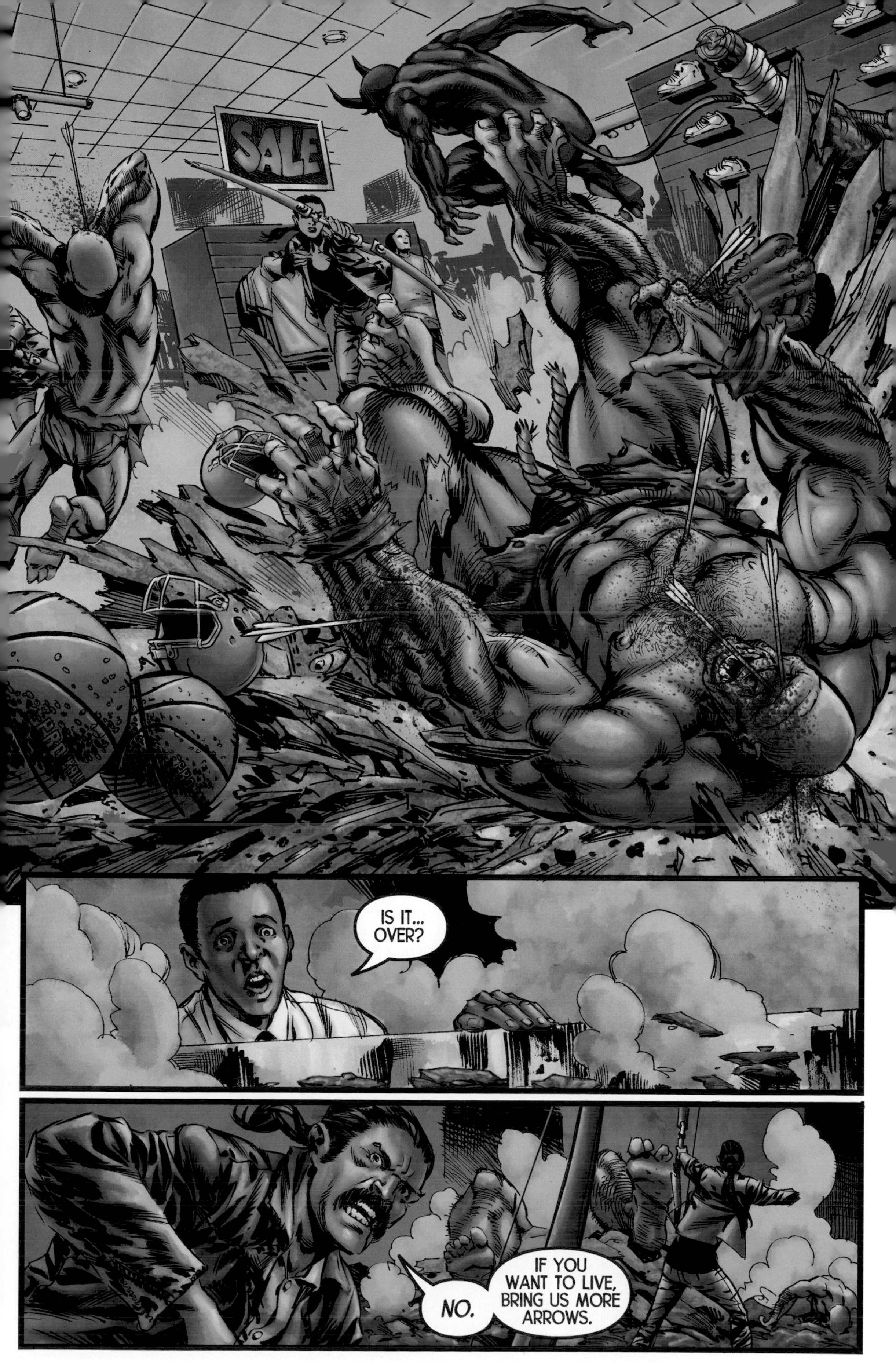
SALE
IS IT... OVER?
NO.
IF YOU WANT TO LIVE, BRING US MORE ARROWS.

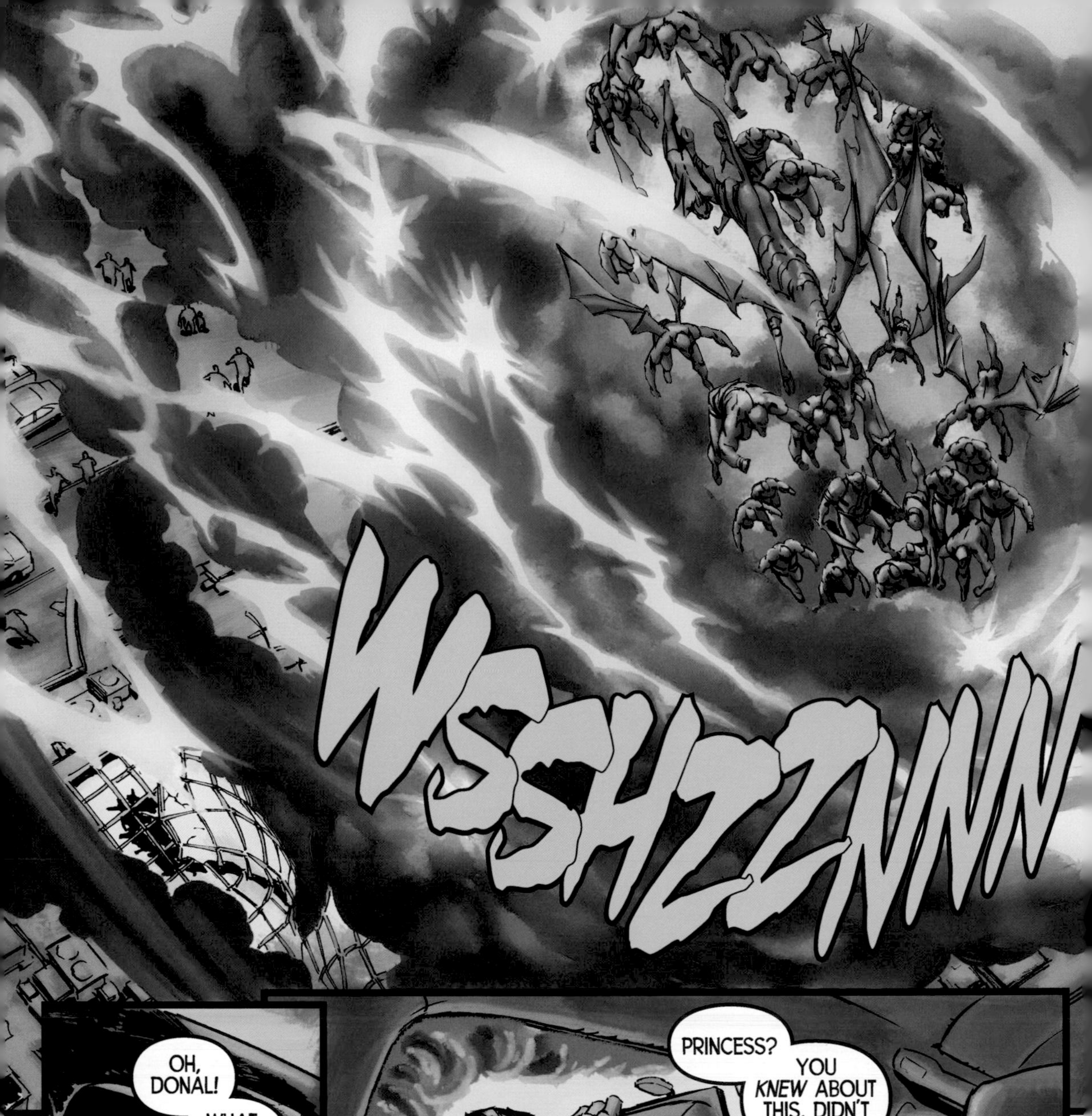
WSSHZZNNN

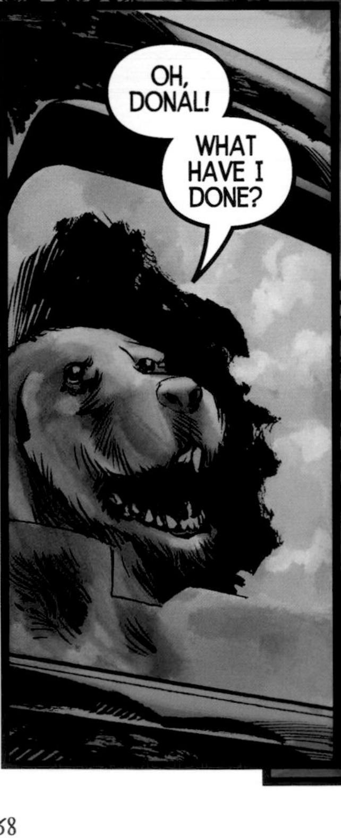
OH, DONAL!
WHAT HAVE I DONE?

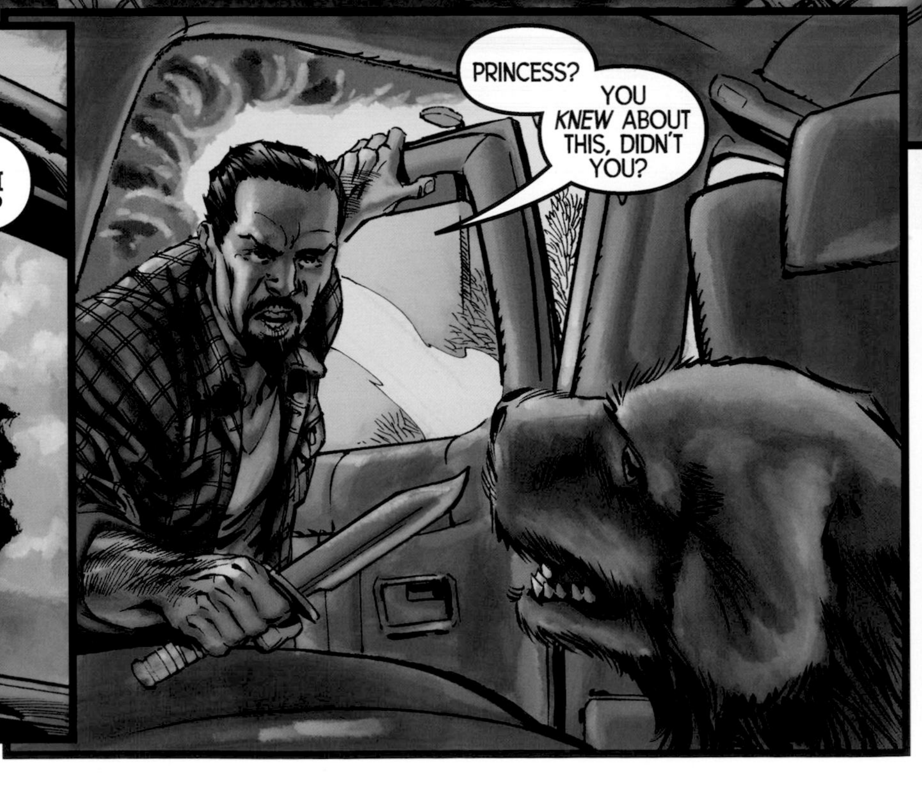
PRINCESS?
YOU *KNEW* ABOUT THIS, DIDN'T YOU?

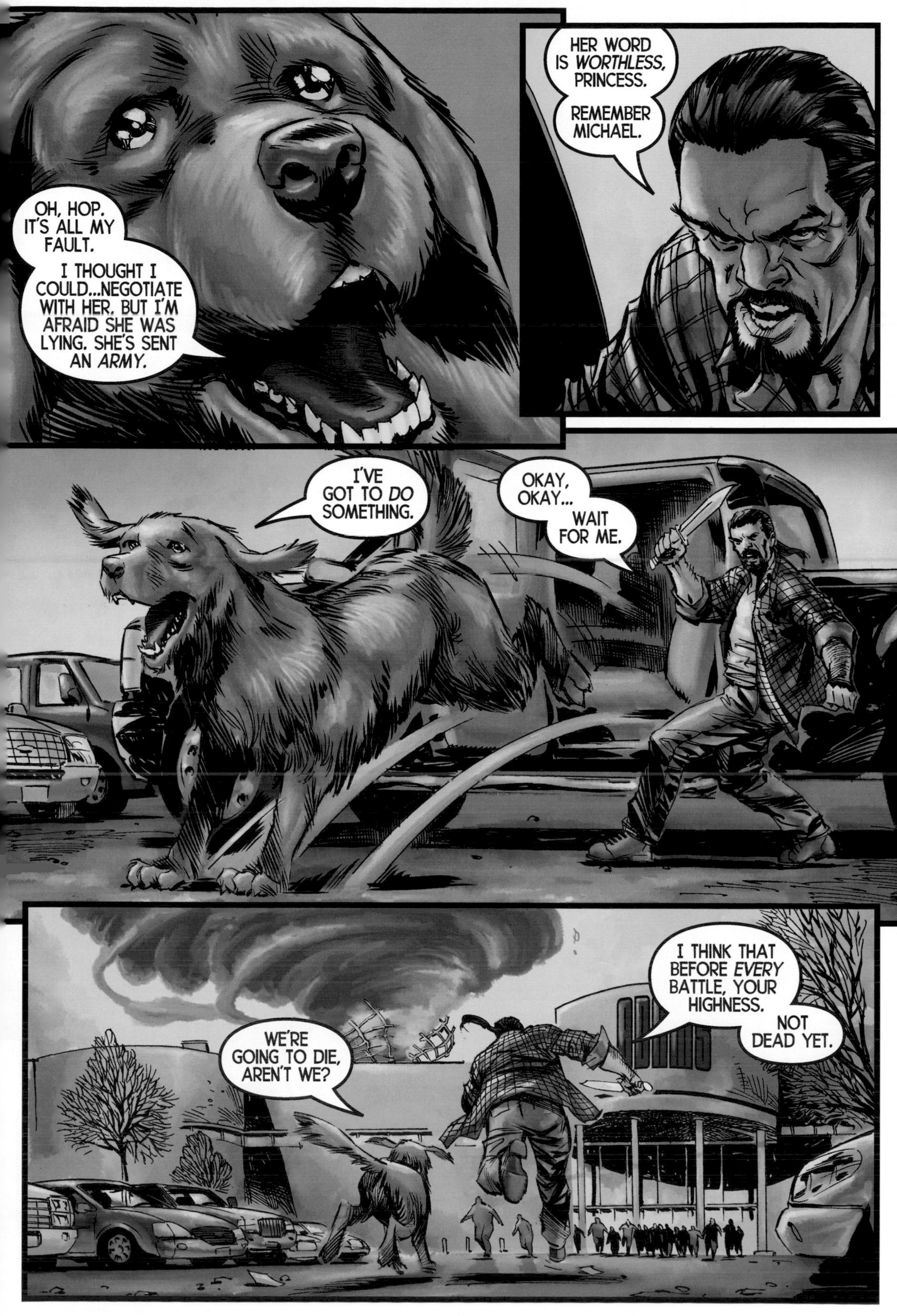
OH, HOP. IT'S ALL MY FAULT.
I THOUGHT I COULD...NEGOTIATE WITH HER. BUT I'M AFRAID SHE WAS LYING. SHE'S SENT AN *ARMY.*
HER WORD IS *WORTHLESS,* PRINCESS.
REMEMBER MICHAEL.
I'VE GOT TO *DO* SOMETHING.
OKAY, OKAY...
WAIT FOR ME.
WE'RE GOING TO DIE, AREN'T WE?
I THINK THAT BEFORE *EVERY* BATTLE, YOUR HIGHNESS.
NOT DEAD YET.

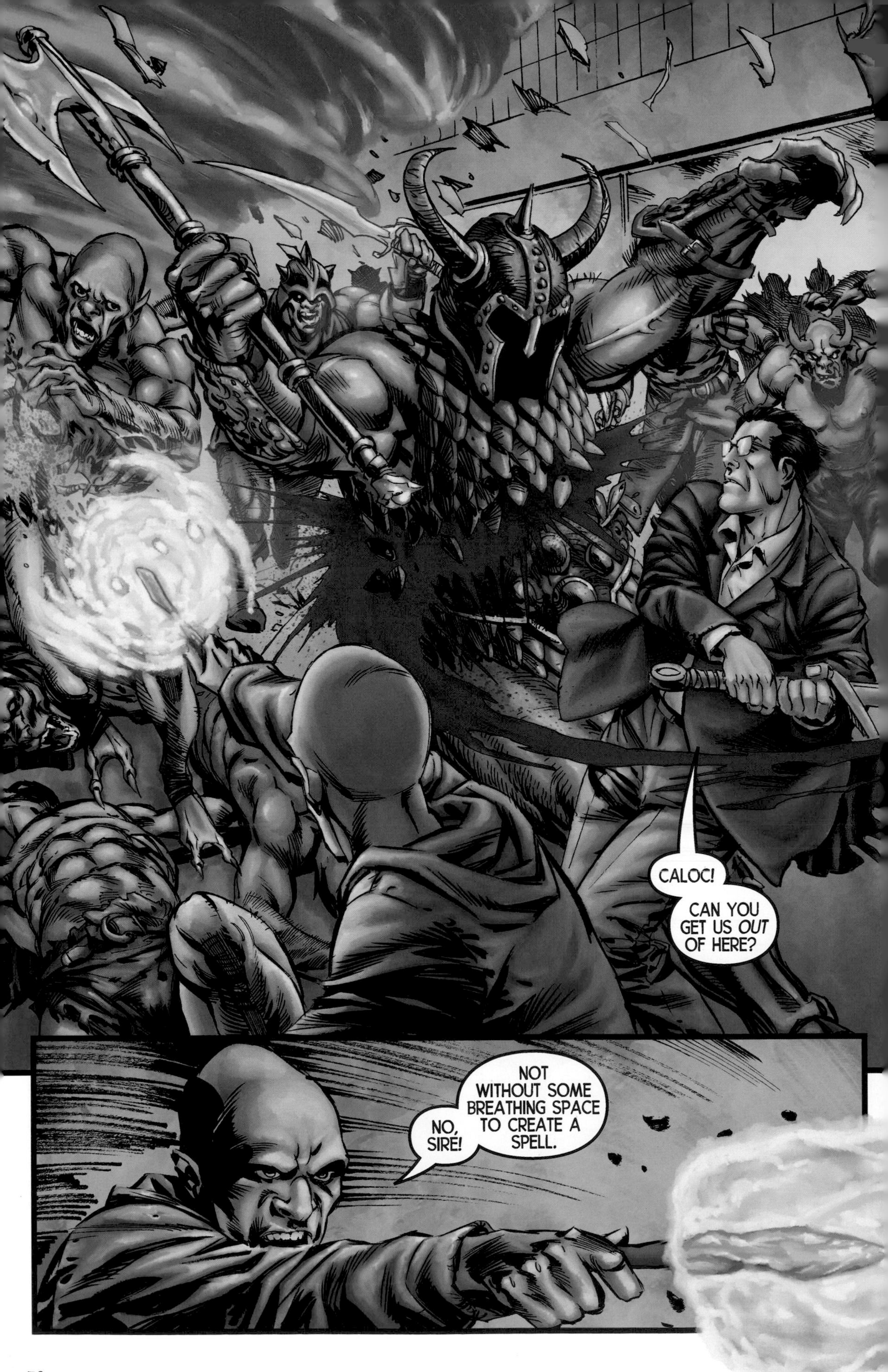
CALOC!
CAN YOU GET US *OUT* OF HERE?
NO, SIRE!
NOT WITHOUT SOME BREATHING SPACE TO CREATE A SPELL.

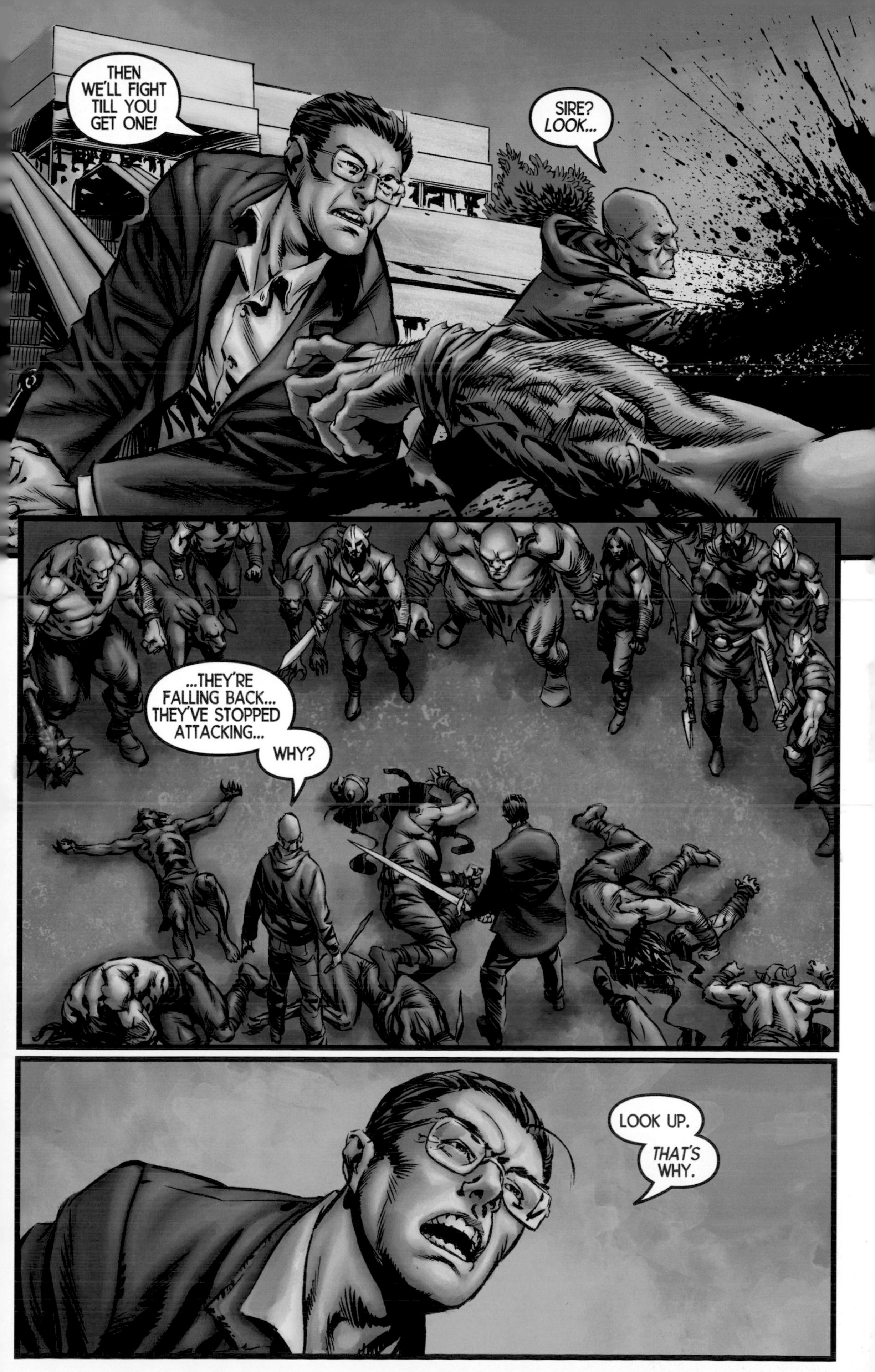
THEN WE'LL FIGHT TILL YOU GET ONE!
SIRE? *LOOK...*
...THEY'RE FALLING BACK... THEY'VE STOPPED ATTACKING...
WHY?
LOOK UP.
THAT'S WHY.

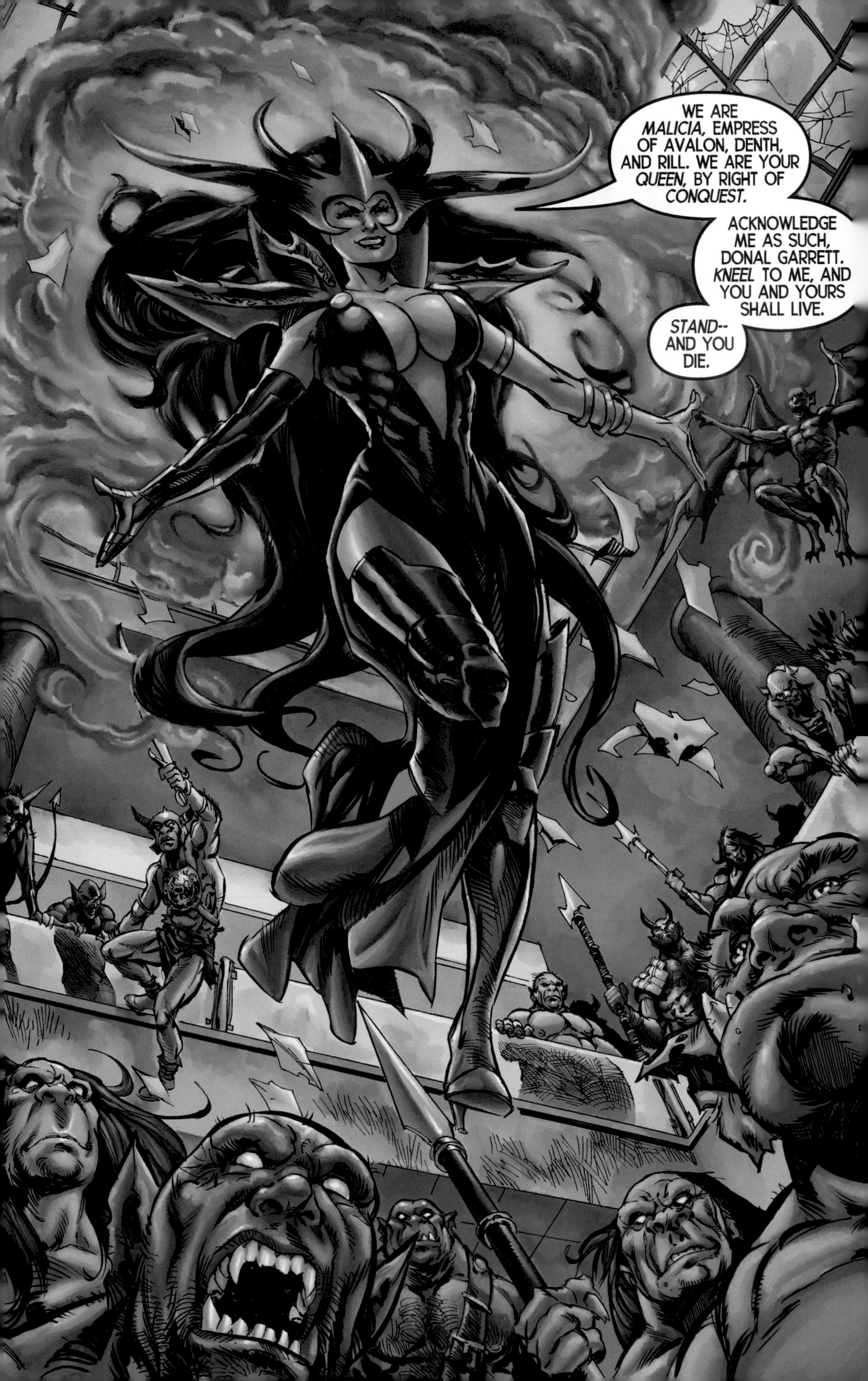
WE ARE *MALICIA,* EMPRESS OF AVALON, DENTH, AND RILL. WE ARE YOUR *QUEEN,* BY RIGHT OF *CONQUEST.*
ACKNOWLEDGE ME AS SUCH, DONAL GARRETT. *KNEEL* TO ME, AND YOU AND YOURS SHALL LIVE.
STAND-- AND YOU DIE.

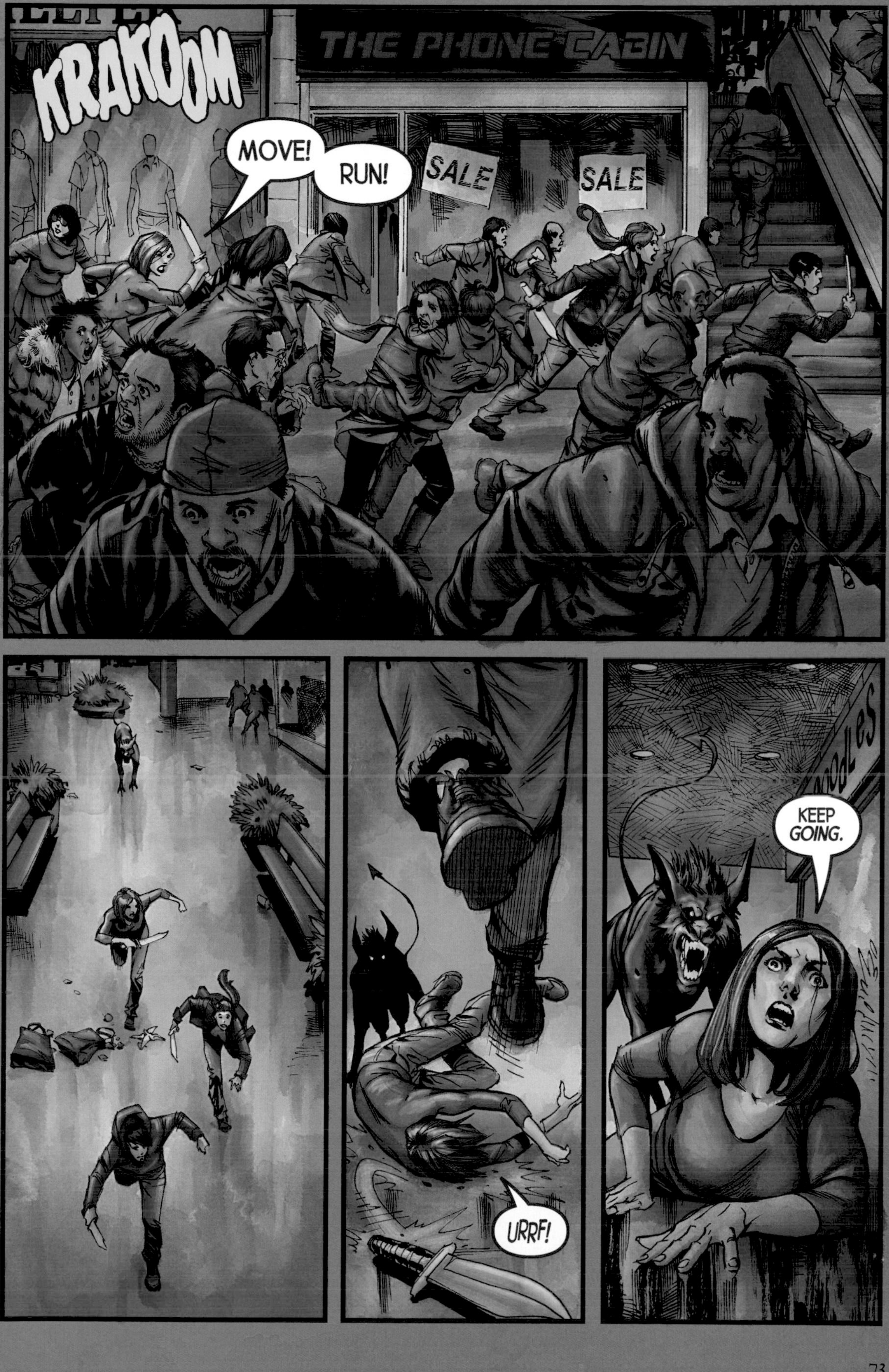
KRAKOOM
THE PHONE CABIN
MOVE!
RUN!
SALE
SALE
URRF!
KEEP GOING.

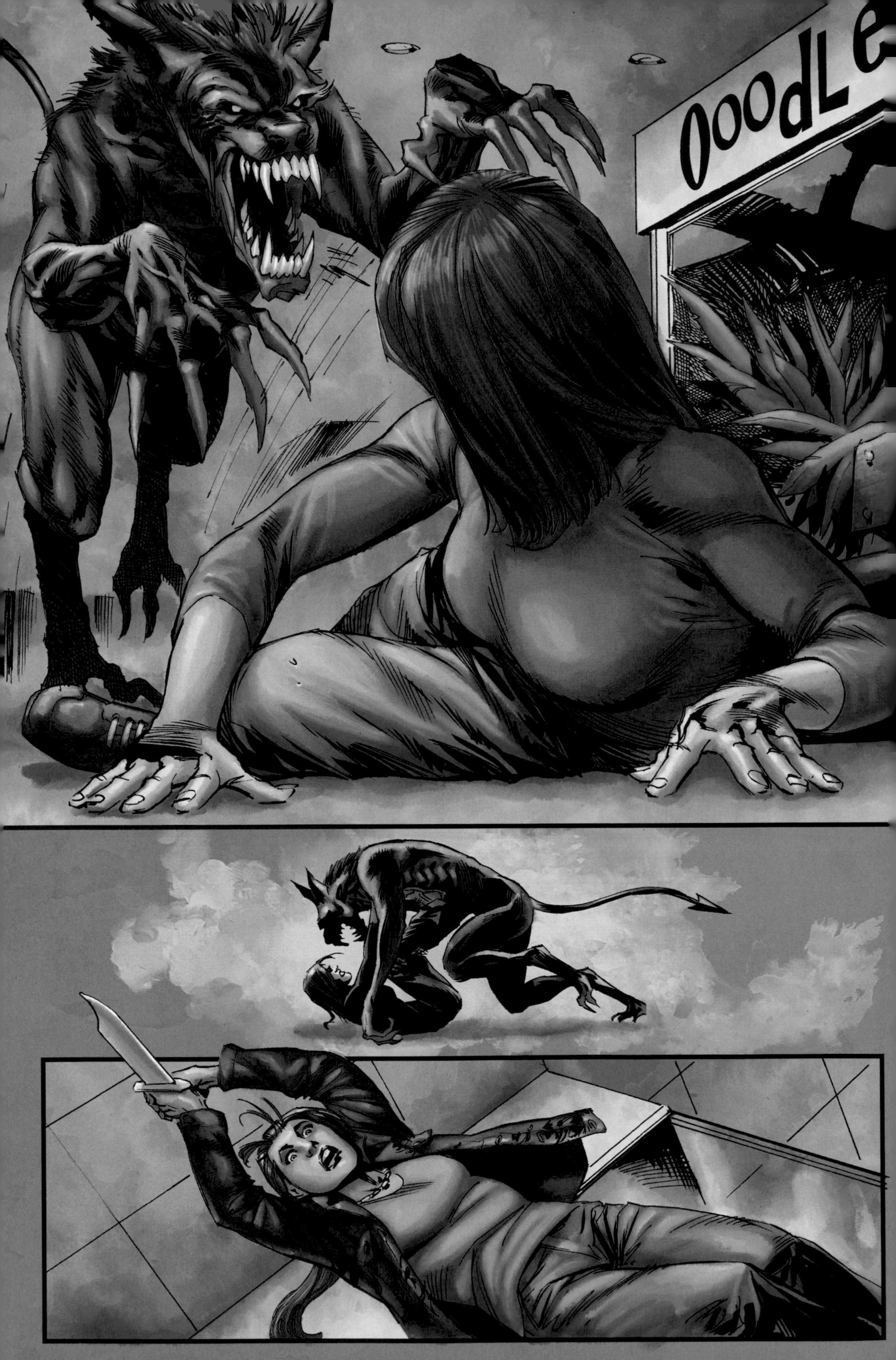
OOODLE

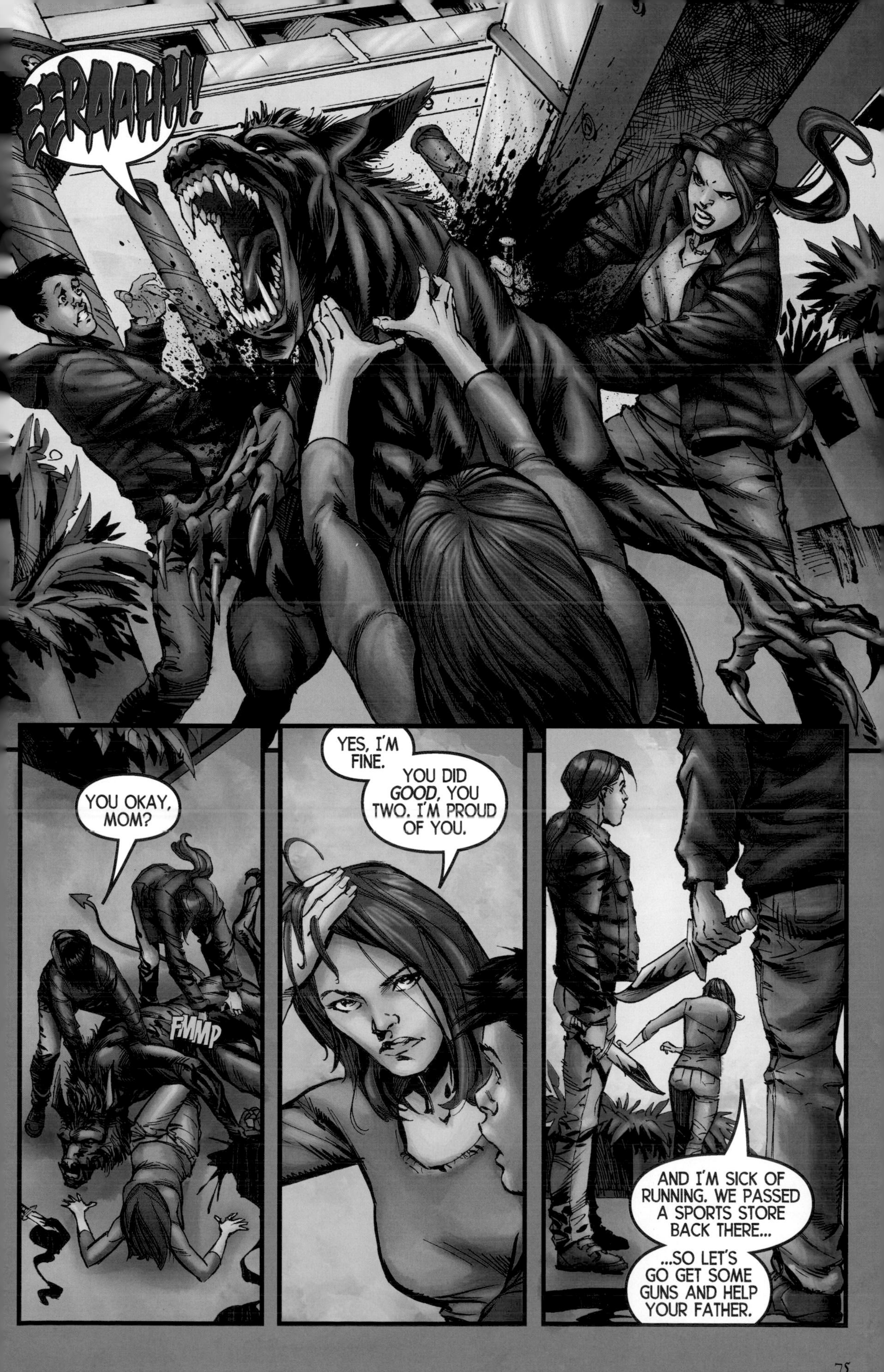
EERAAHH!
YOU OKAY, MOM?
FMMP
YES, I'M FINE.
YOU DID *GOOD*, YOU TWO. I'M PROUD OF YOU.
AND I'M SICK OF RUNNING. WE PASSED A SPORTS STORE BACK THERE...
...SO LET'S GO GET SOME GUNS AND HELP YOUR FATHER.

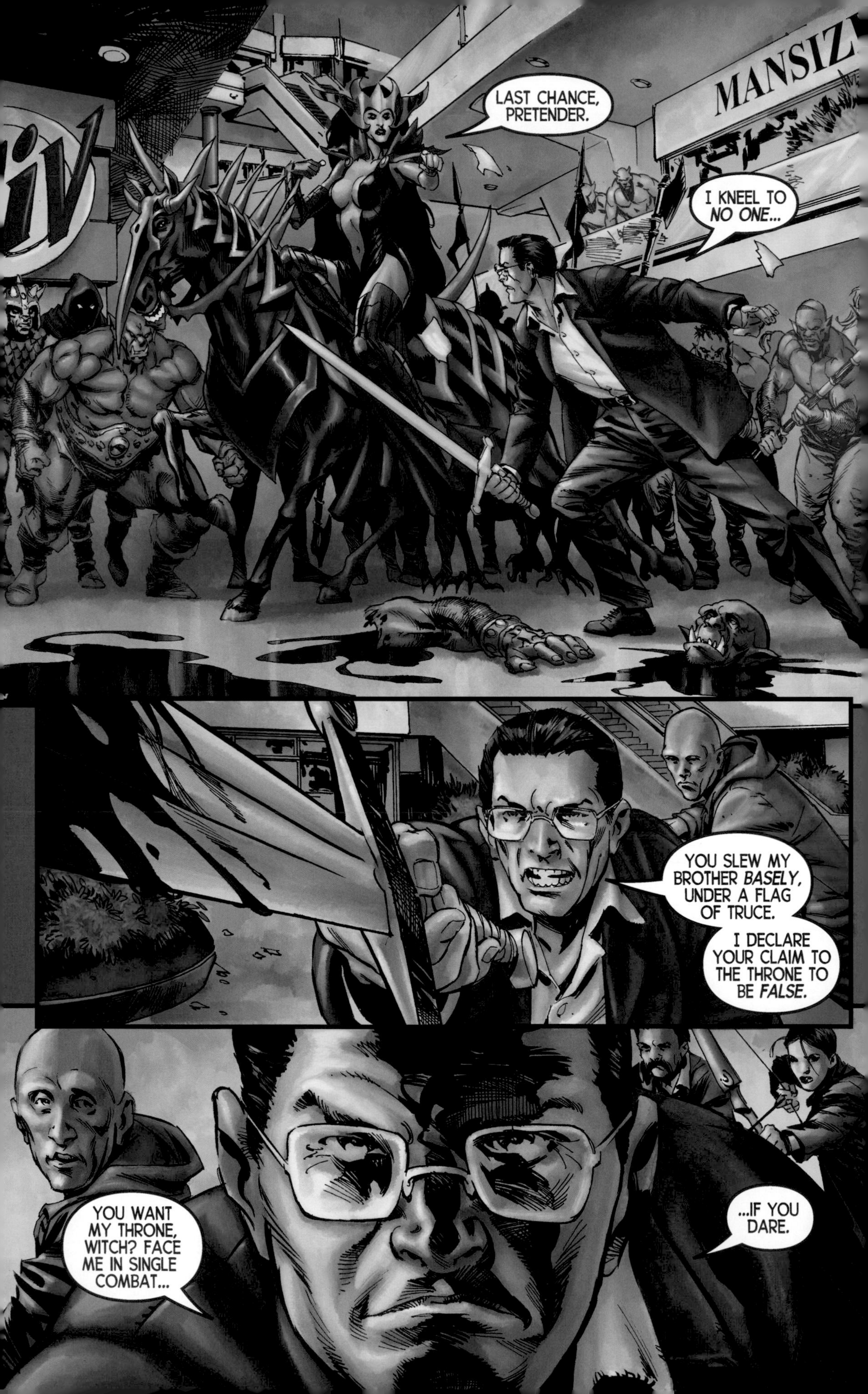
MANSIZ
LAST CHANCE, PRETENDER.
I KNEEL TO *NO ONE*...
YOU SLEW MY BROTHER *BASELY*, UNDER A FLAG OF TRUCE.
I DECLARE YOUR CLAIM TO THE THRONE TO BE *FALSE*.
YOU WANT MY THRONE, WITCH? FACE ME IN SINGLE COMBAT...
...IF YOU DARE.

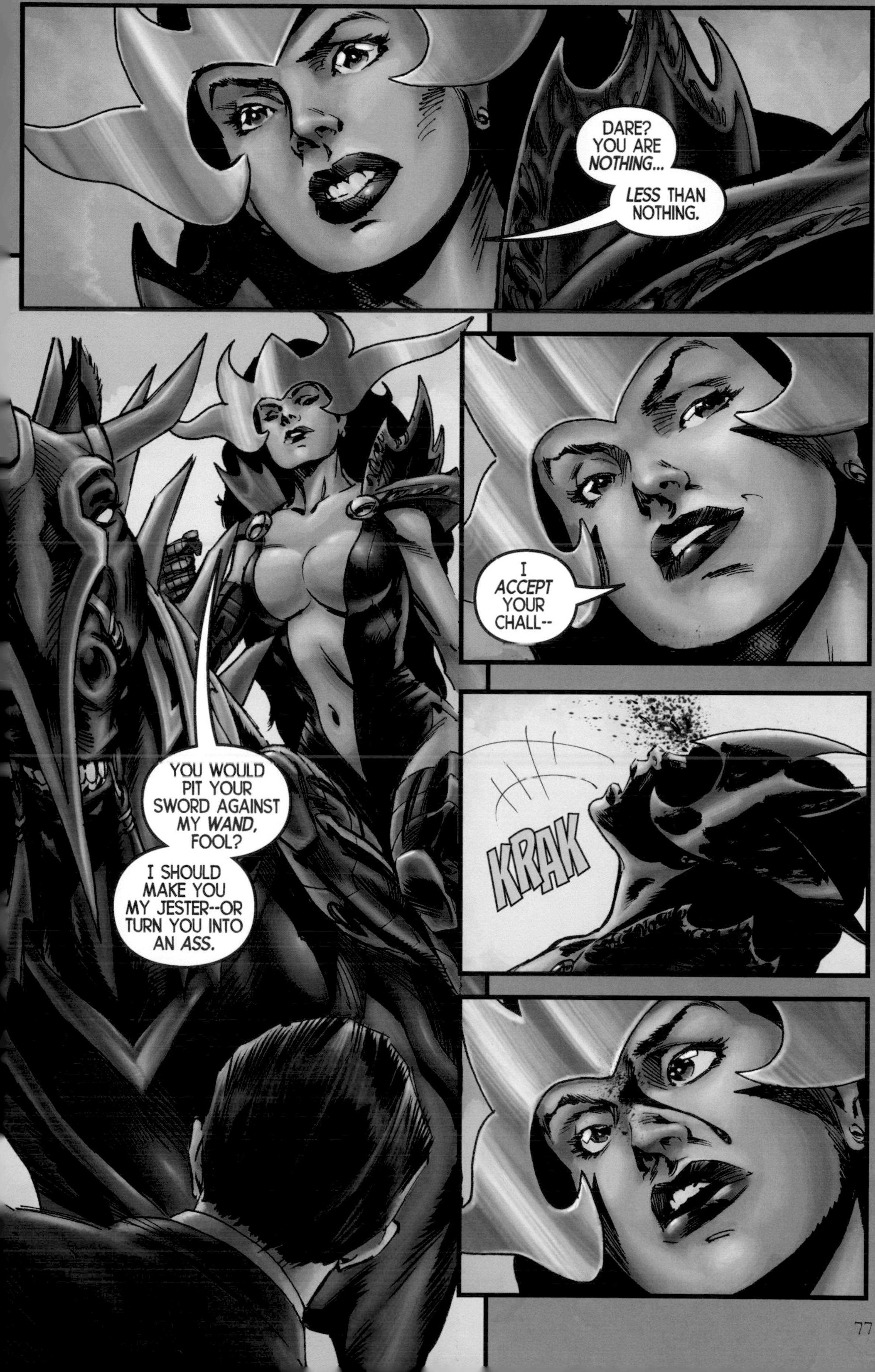
DARE? YOU ARE NOTHING...
LESS THAN NOTHING.
YOU WOULD PIT YOUR SWORD AGAINST MY WAND, FOOL?
I SHOULD MAKE YOU MY JESTER--OR TURN YOU INTO AN ASS.
I ACCEPT YOUR CHALL--
KRAK

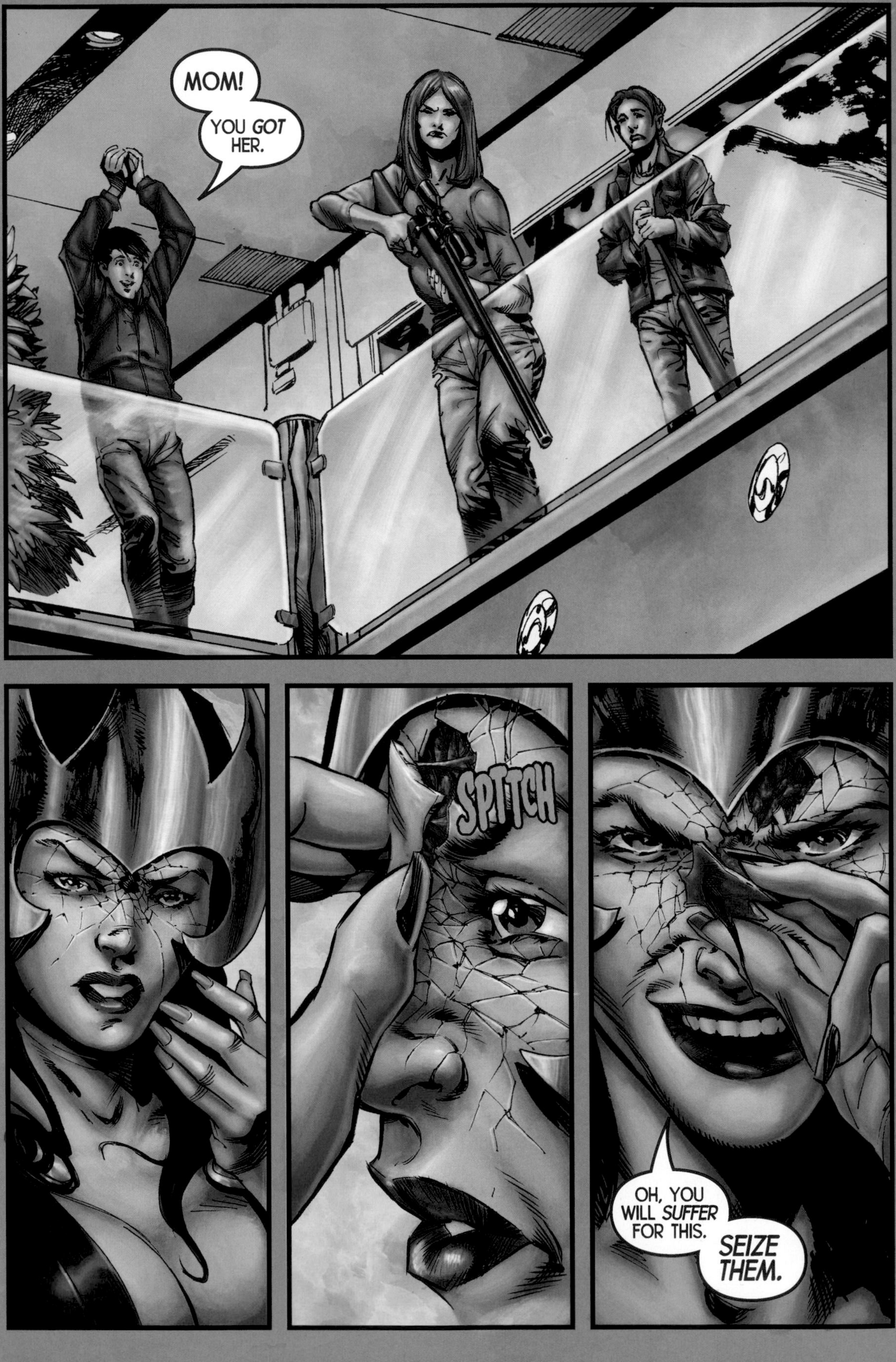
MOM!
YOU GOT HER.
SPTTCH
OH, YOU WILL SUFFER FOR THIS.
SEIZE THEM.

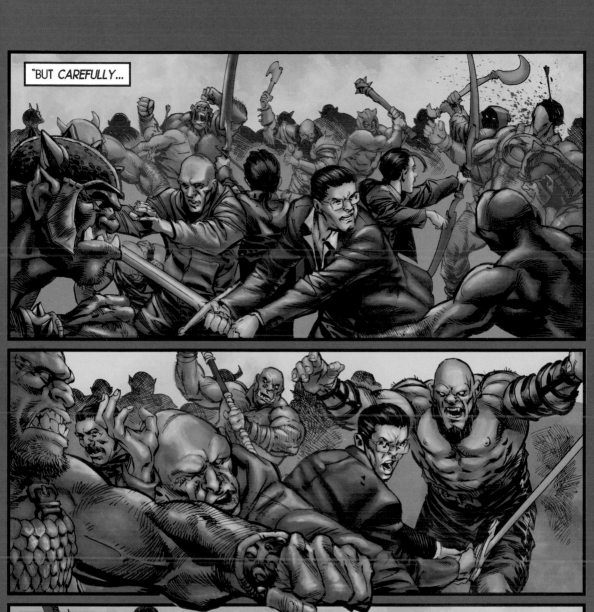

"BUT *CAREFULLY*...

"...I WANT THEM UNHARMED."

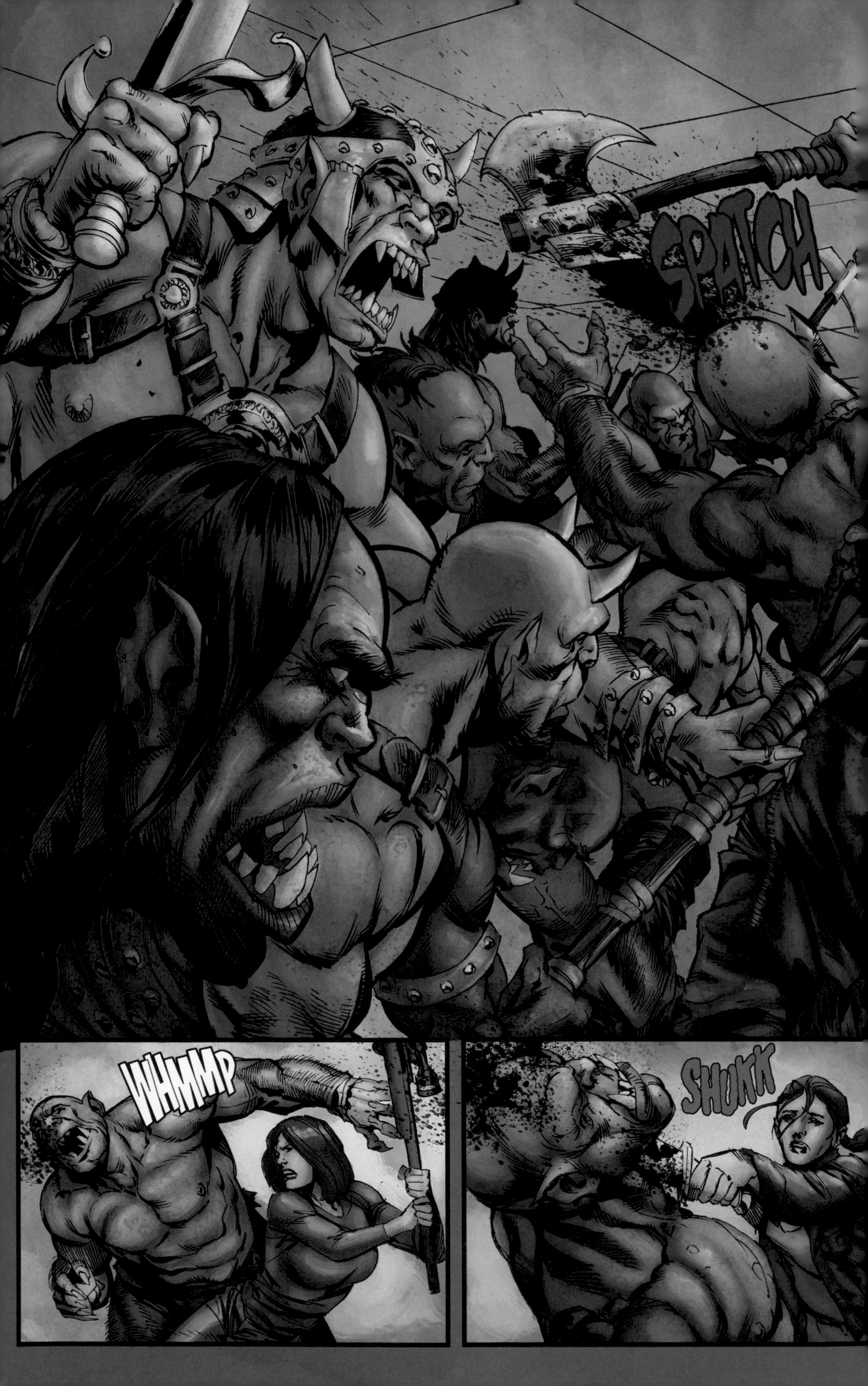
SPATCH
WHMMP
SHUKK

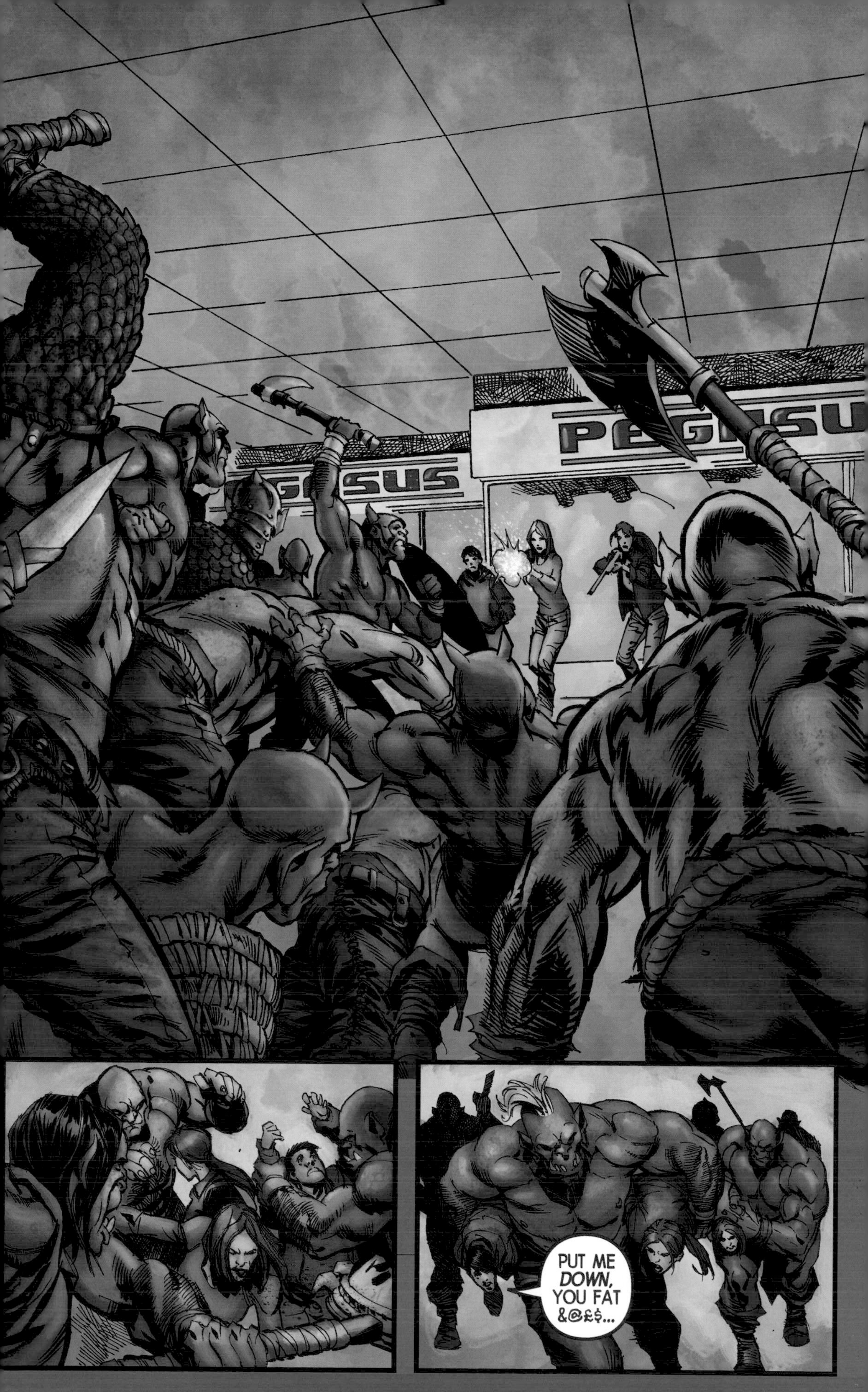
PUT ME *DOWN,* YOU FAT &@£$...

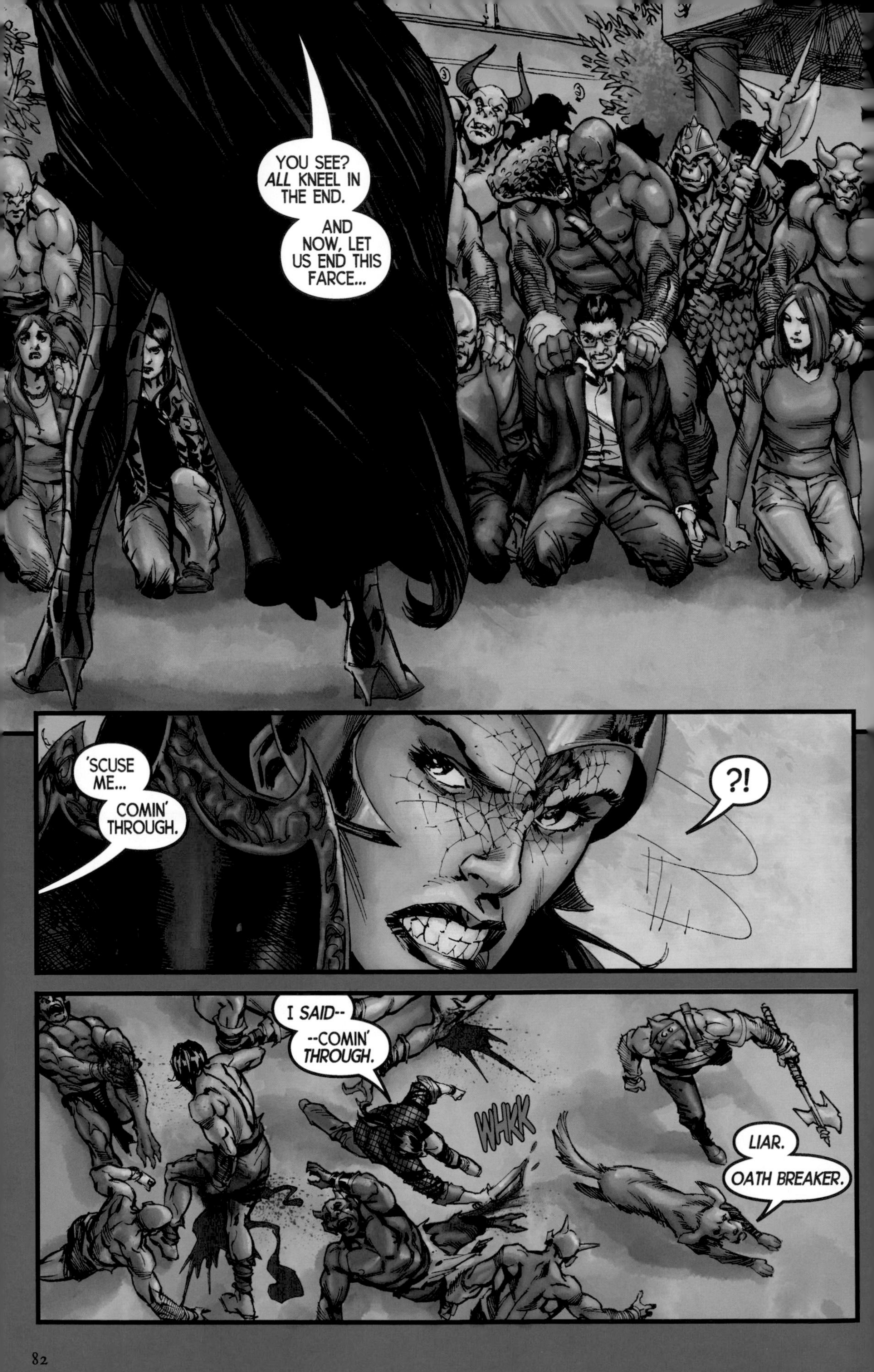
YOU SEE? *ALL* KNEEL IN THE END.
AND NOW, LET US END THIS FARCE...
'SCUSE ME...
COMIN' THROUGH.
?!
I *SAID*--
--COMIN' *THROUGH.*
WHKK
LIAR.
OATH BREAKER.

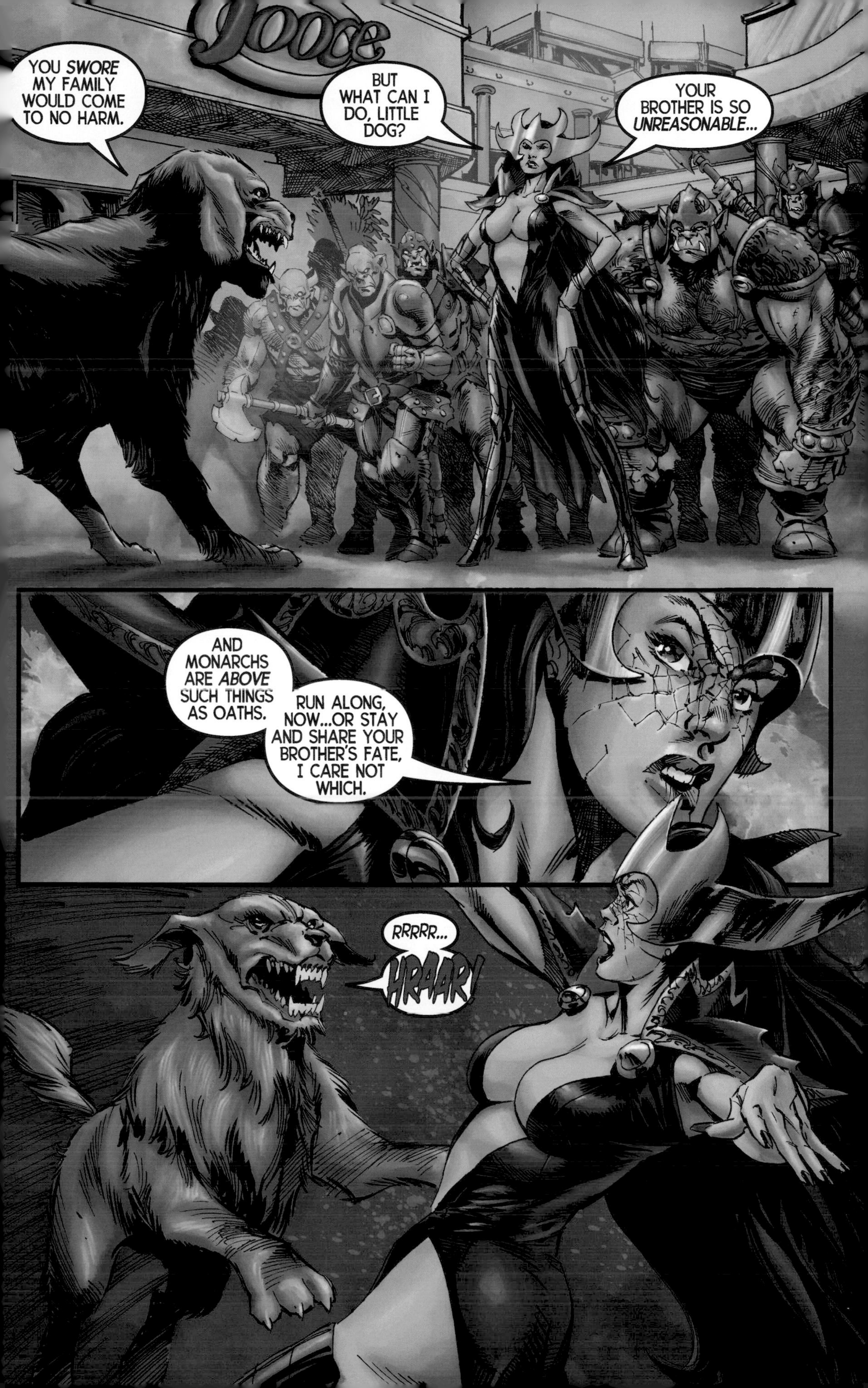
JOOCE
YOU *SWORE* MY FAMILY WOULD COME TO NO HARM.
BUT WHAT CAN I DO, LITTLE DOG?
YOUR BROTHER IS SO *UNREASONABLE*...
AND MONARCHS ARE *ABOVE* SUCH THINGS AS OATHS.
RUN ALONG, NOW...OR STAY AND SHARE YOUR BROTHER'S FATE, I CARE NOT WHICH.
RRRRR...
HRAAR!

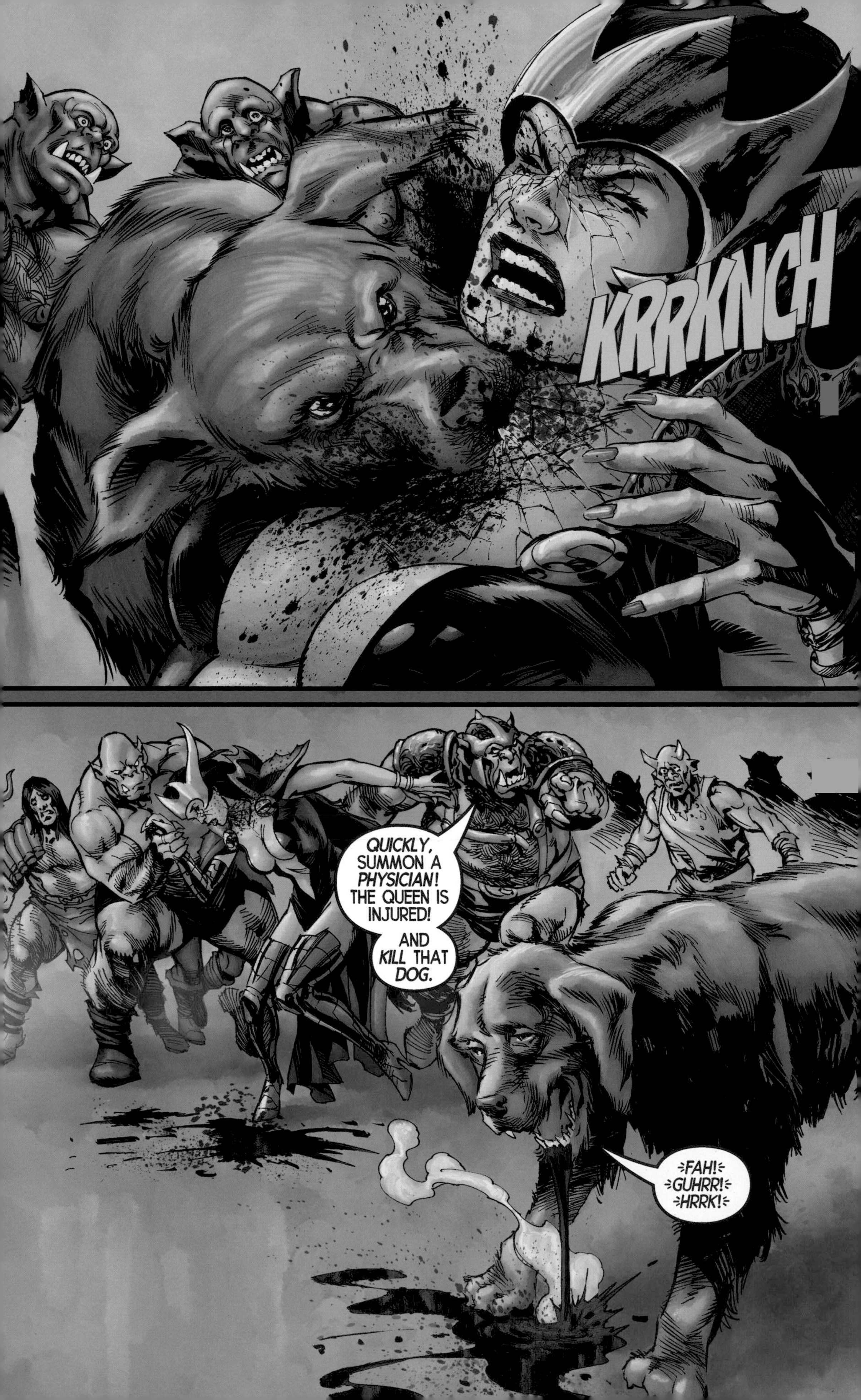
KRRKNCH
QUICKLY, SUMMON A PHYSICIAN! THE QUEEN IS INJURED!
AND KILL THAT DOG.
FAH! GUHRR! HRRK!

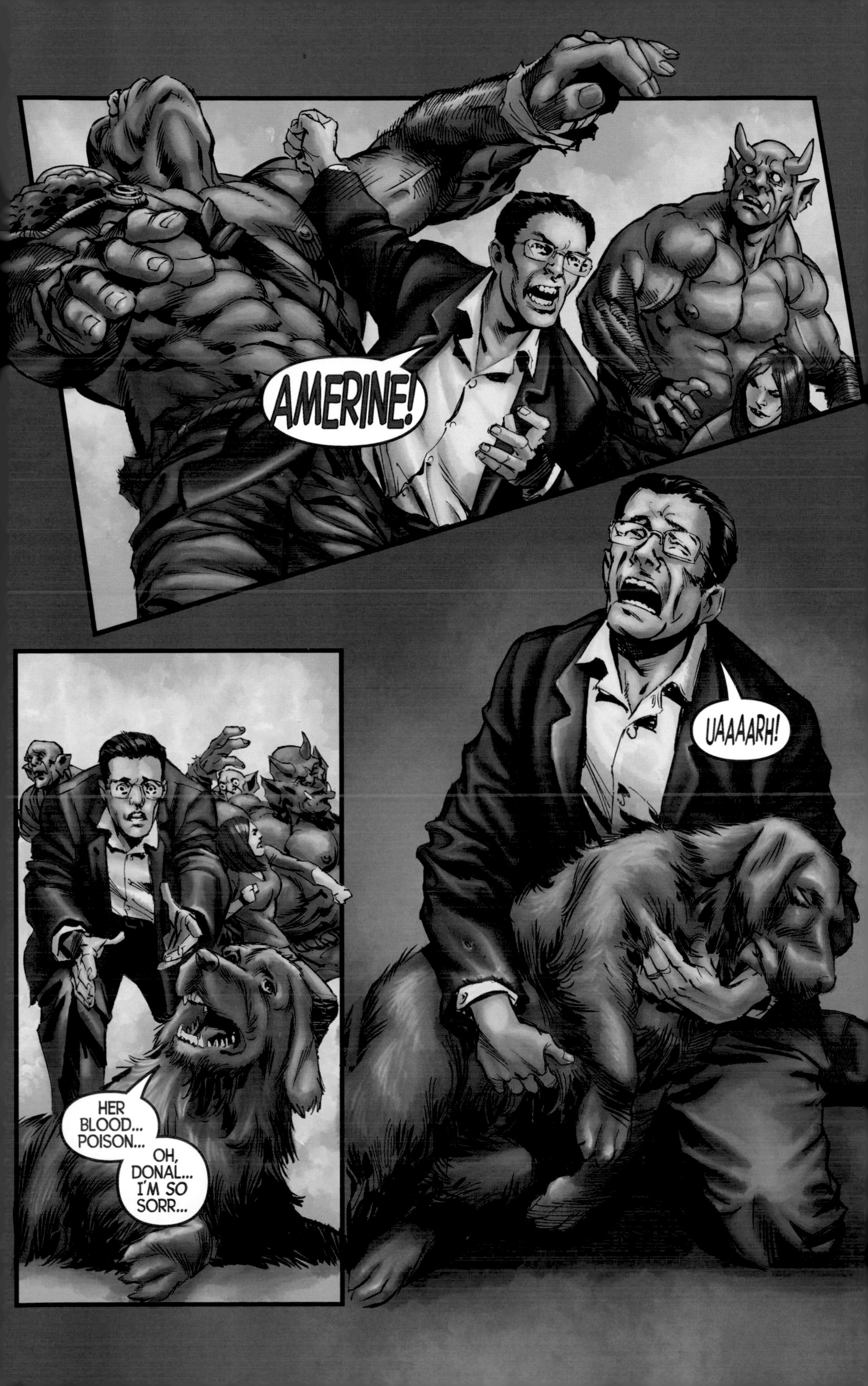
AMERINE!
HER BLOOD... POISON...
OH, DONAL... I'M SO SORR...
UAAAARH!

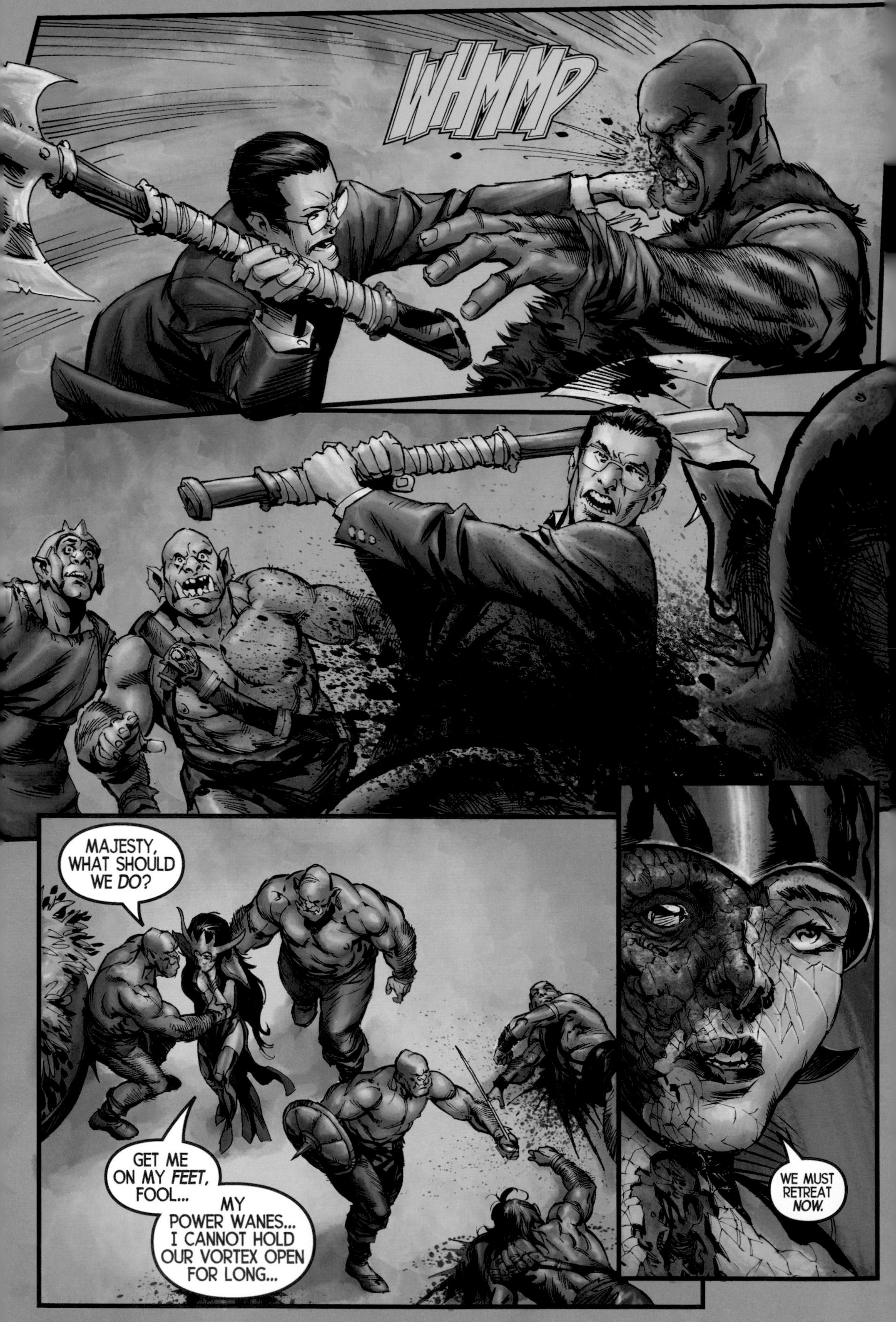
WHMMP
MAJESTY, WHAT SHOULD WE *DO*?
GET ME ON MY *FEET*, FOOL...
MY POWER WANES... I CANNOT HOLD OUR VORTEX OPEN FOR LONG...
WE MUST RETREAT *NOW*.

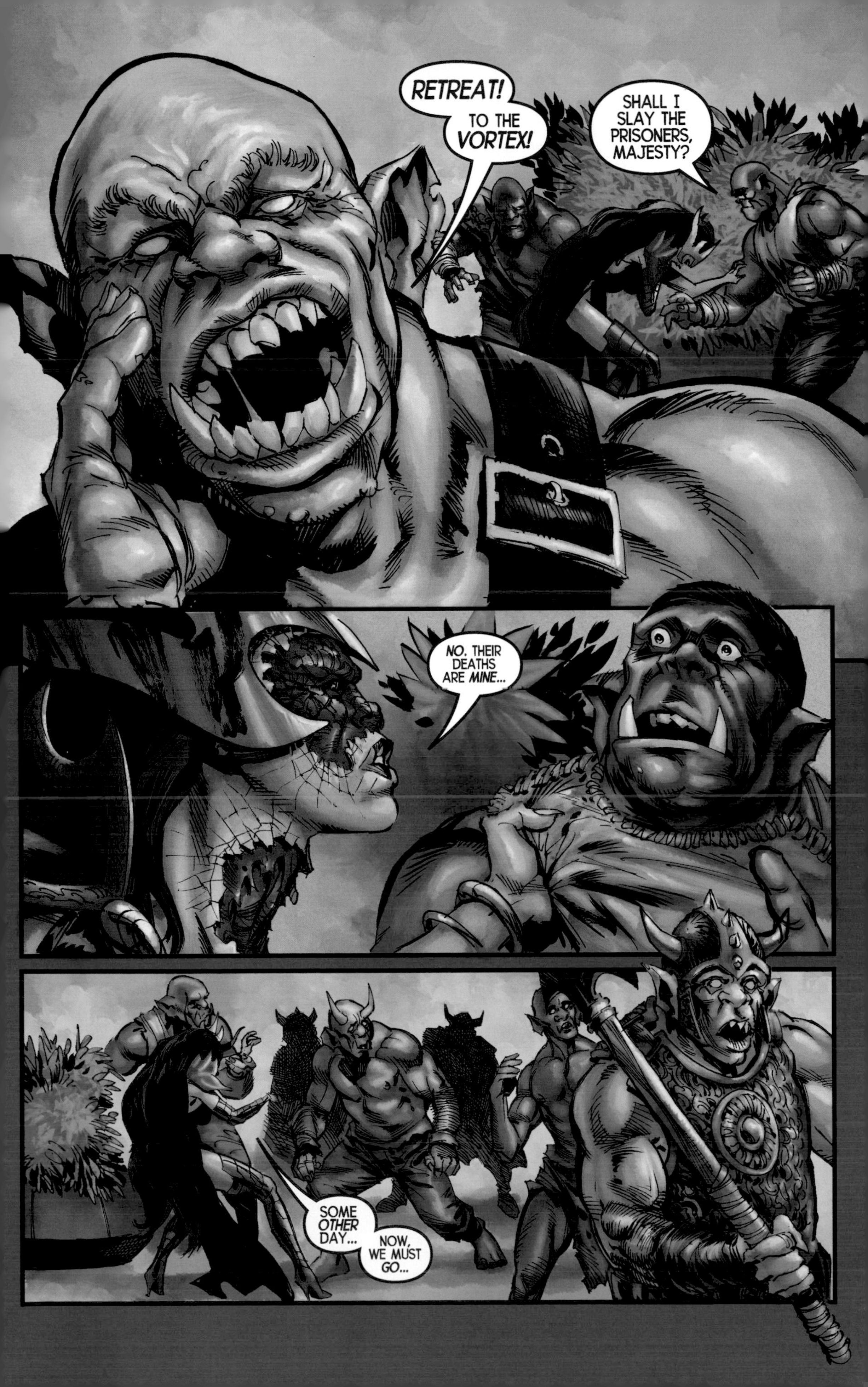
RETREAT! TO THE VORTEX!
SHALL I SLAY THE PRISONERS, MAJESTY?
NO. THEIR DEATHS ARE MINE...
SOME OTHER DAY...
NOW, WE MUST GO...

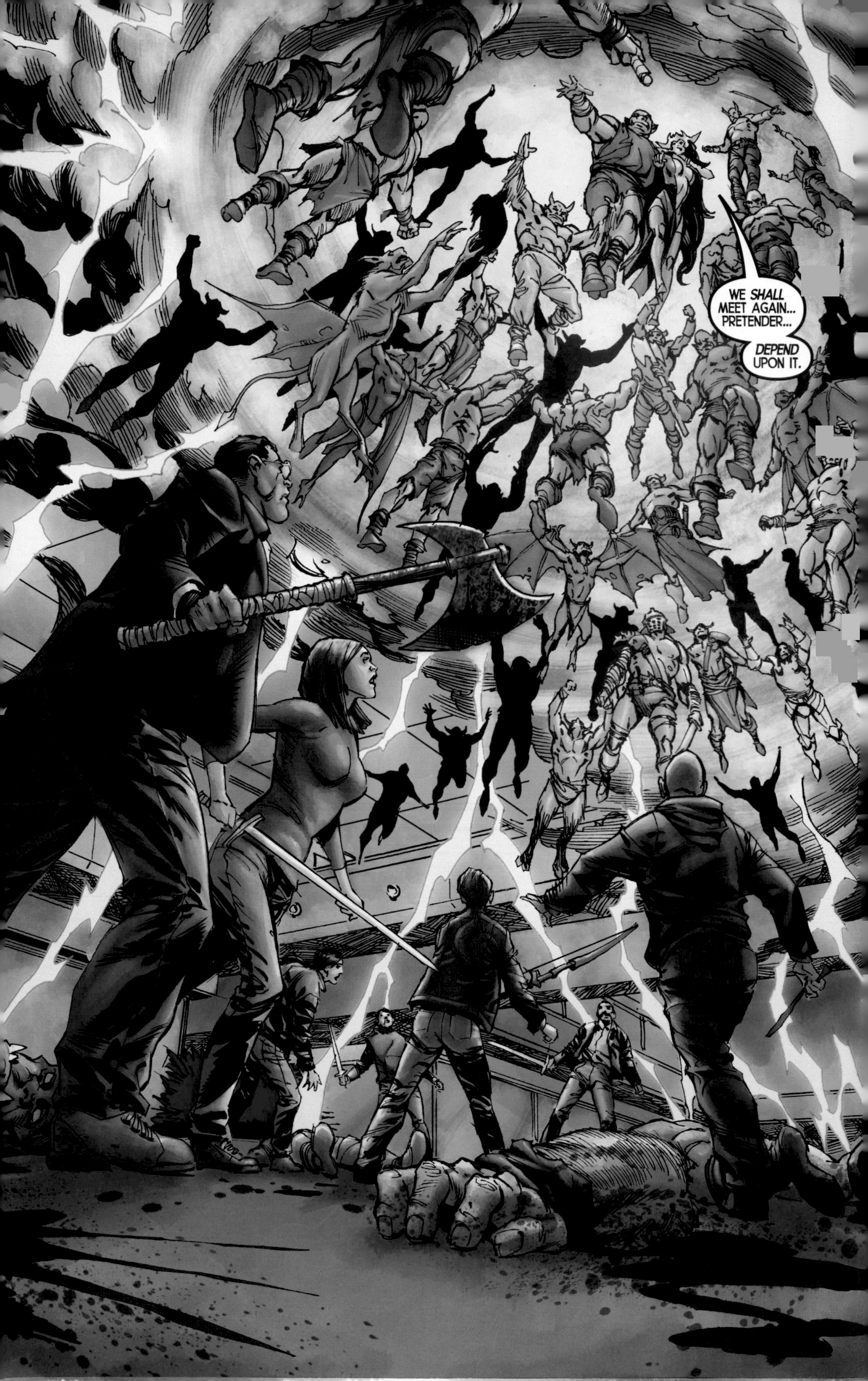
WE SHALL MEET AGAIN... PRETENDER...
DEPEND UPON IT.

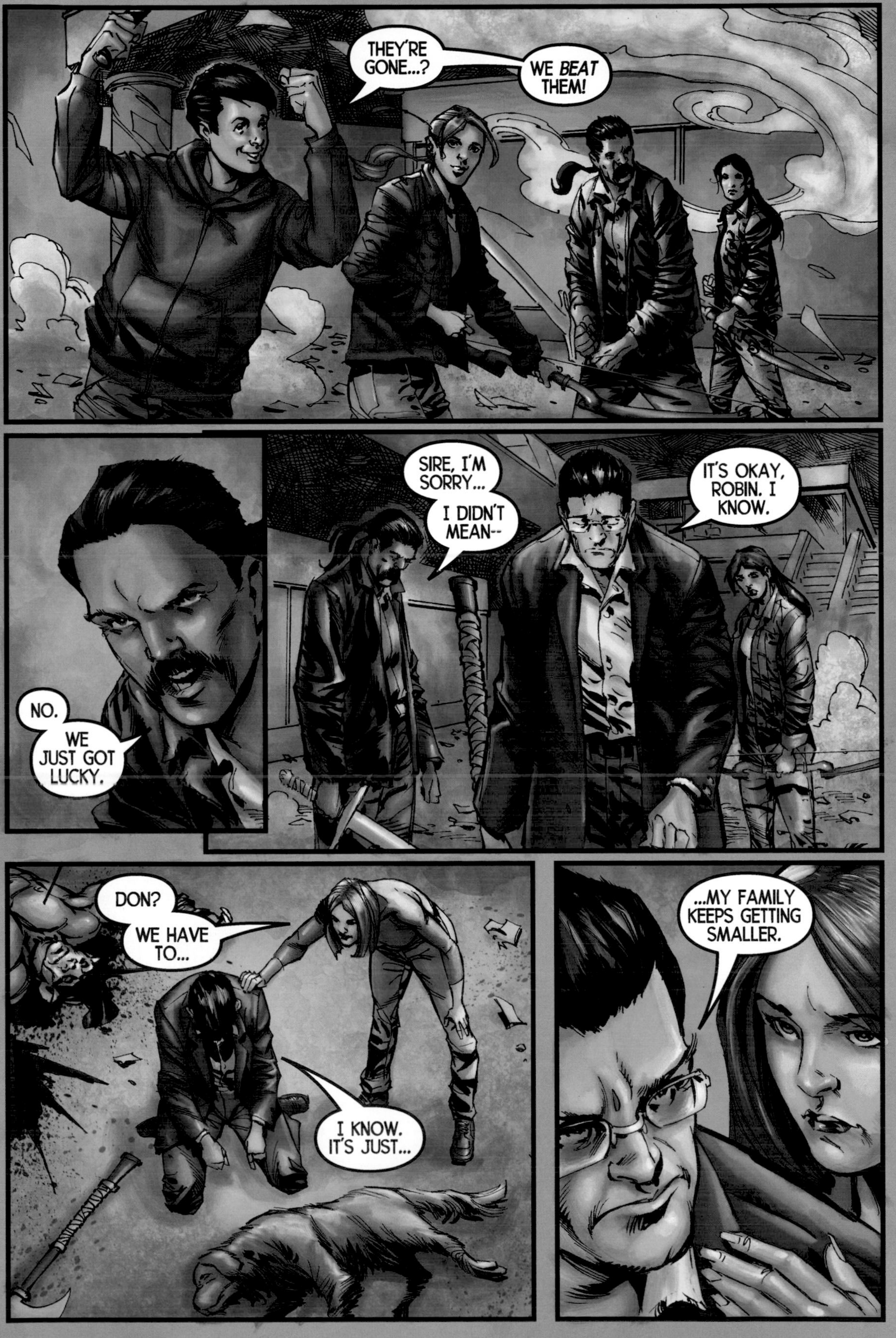
THEY'RE GONE...?
WE BEAT THEM!
NO.
WE JUST GOT LUCKY.
SIRE, I'M SORRY...
I DIDN'T MEAN--
IT'S OKAY, ROBIN. I KNOW.
DON?
WE HAVE TO...
I KNOW. IT'S JUST...
...MY FAMILY KEEPS GETTING SMALLER.

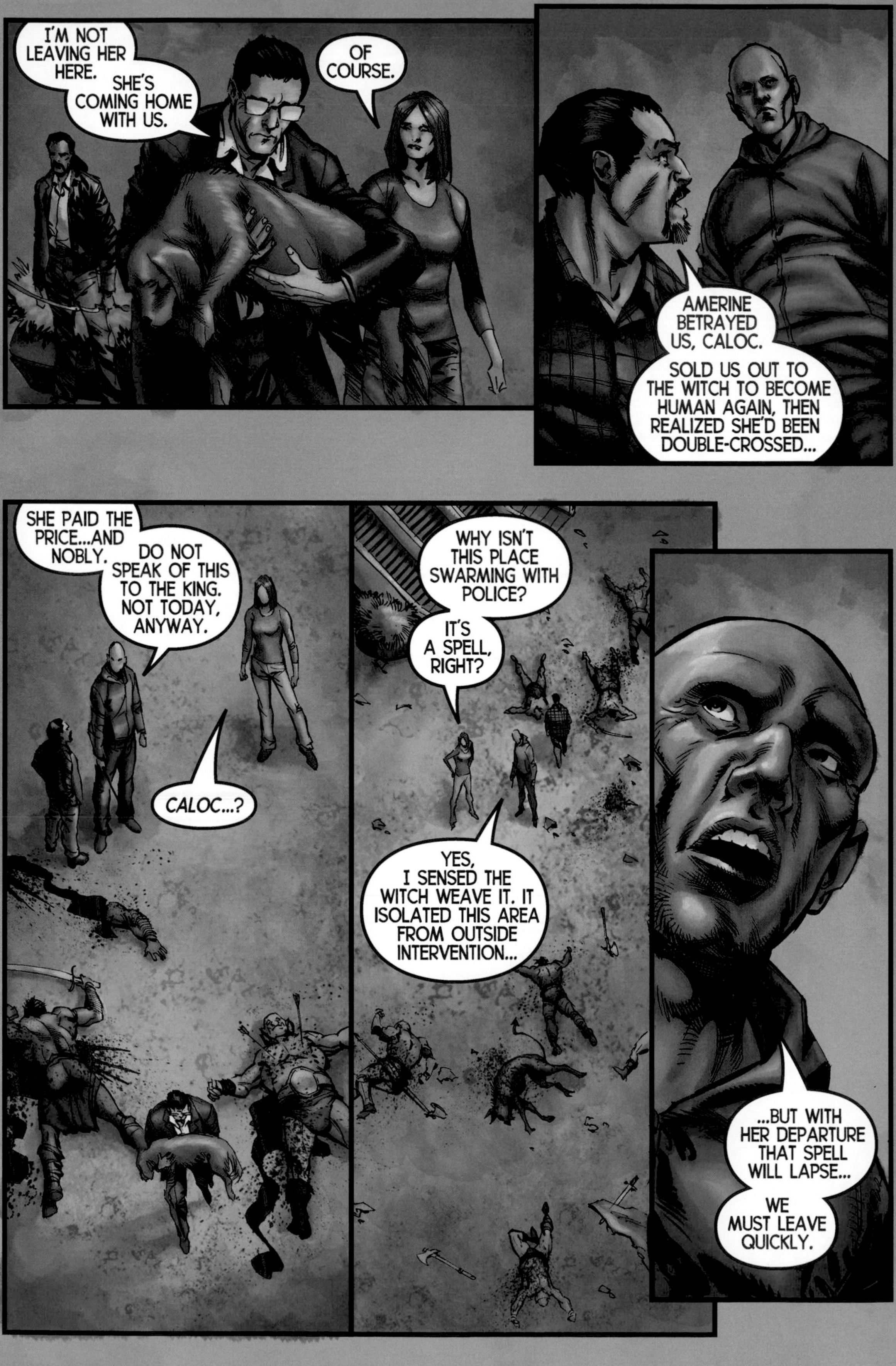
I'M NOT LEAVING HER HERE.
SHE'S COMING HOME WITH US.
OF COURSE.
AMERINE BETRAYED US, CALOC.
SOLD US OUT TO THE WITCH TO BECOME HUMAN AGAIN, THEN REALIZED SHE'D BEEN DOUBLE-CROSSED...
SHE PAID THE PRICE...AND NOBLY.
DO NOT SPEAK OF THIS TO THE KING. NOT TODAY, ANYWAY.
CALOC...?
WHY ISN'T THIS PLACE SWARMING WITH POLICE?
IT'S A SPELL, RIGHT?
YES, I SENSED THE WITCH WEAVE IT. IT ISOLATED THIS AREA FROM OUTSIDE INTERVENTION...
...BUT WITH HER DEPARTURE THAT SPELL WILL LAPSE...
WE MUST LEAVE QUICKLY.

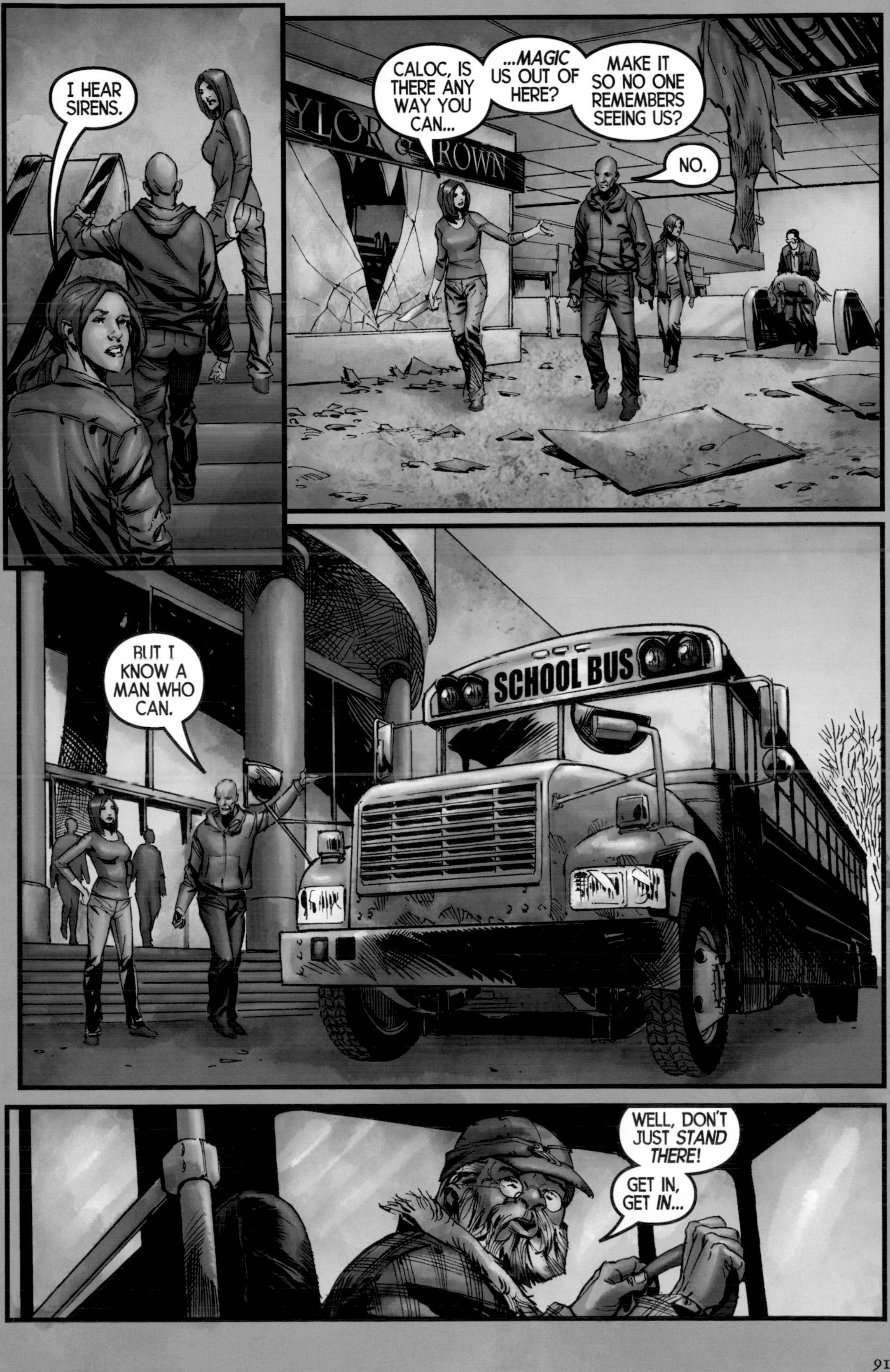
I HEAR SIRENS.
CALOC, IS THERE ANY WAY YOU CAN...
...MAGIC US OUT OF HERE?
MAKE IT SO NO ONE REMEMBERS SEEING US?
NO.
BUT I KNOW A MAN WHO CAN.
SCHOOL BUS
WELL, DON'T JUST *STAND THERE*!
GET IN, GET *IN*...

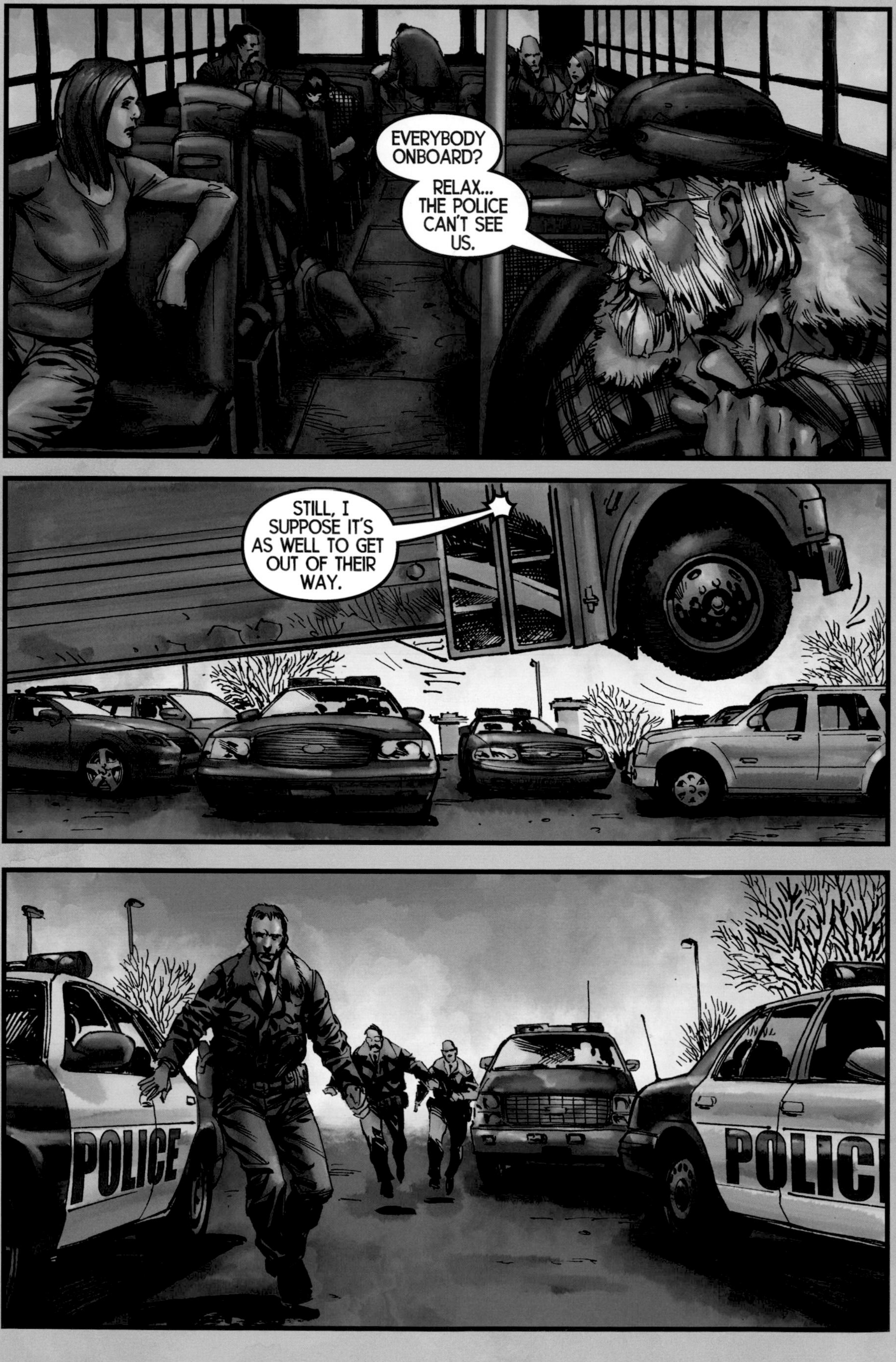
EVERYBODY ONBOARD?
RELAX... THE POLICE CAN'T SEE US.
STILL, I SUPPOSE IT'S AS WELL TO GET OUT OF THEIR WAY.
POLICE
POLICE

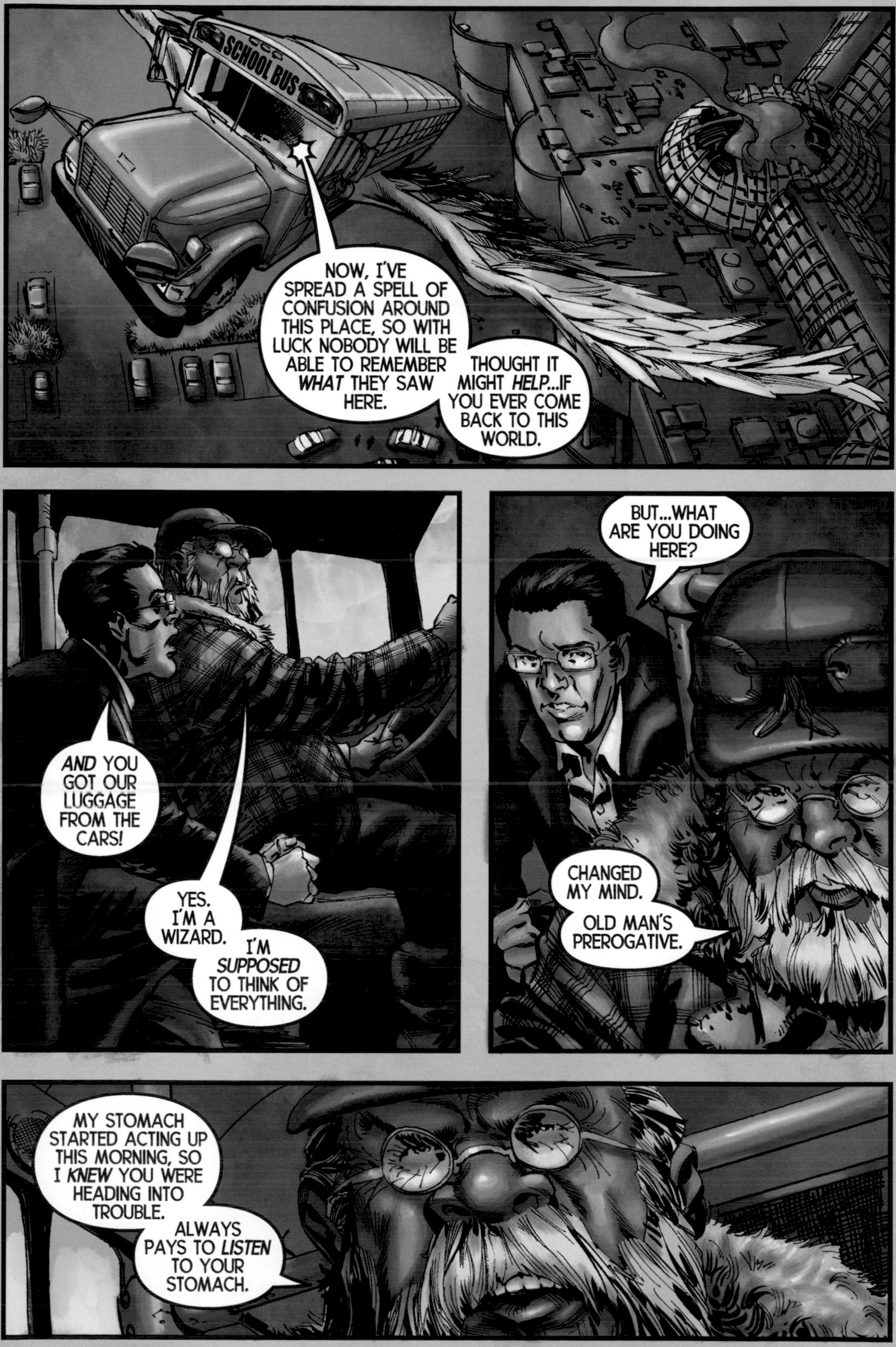
SCHOOL BUS
NOW, I'VE SPREAD A SPELL OF CONFUSION AROUND THIS PLACE, SO WITH LUCK NOBODY WILL BE ABLE TO REMEMBER WHAT THEY SAW HERE.
THOUGHT IT MIGHT HELP...IF YOU EVER COME BACK TO THIS WORLD.
AND YOU GOT OUR LUGGAGE FROM THE CARS!
YES. I'M A WIZARD.
I'M SUPPOSED TO THINK OF EVERYTHING.
BUT...WHAT ARE YOU DOING HERE?
CHANGED MY MIND.
OLD MAN'S PREROGATIVE.
MY STOMACH STARTED ACTING UP THIS MORNING, SO I KNEW YOU WERE HEADING INTO TROUBLE.
ALWAYS PAYS TO LISTEN TO YOUR STOMACH.

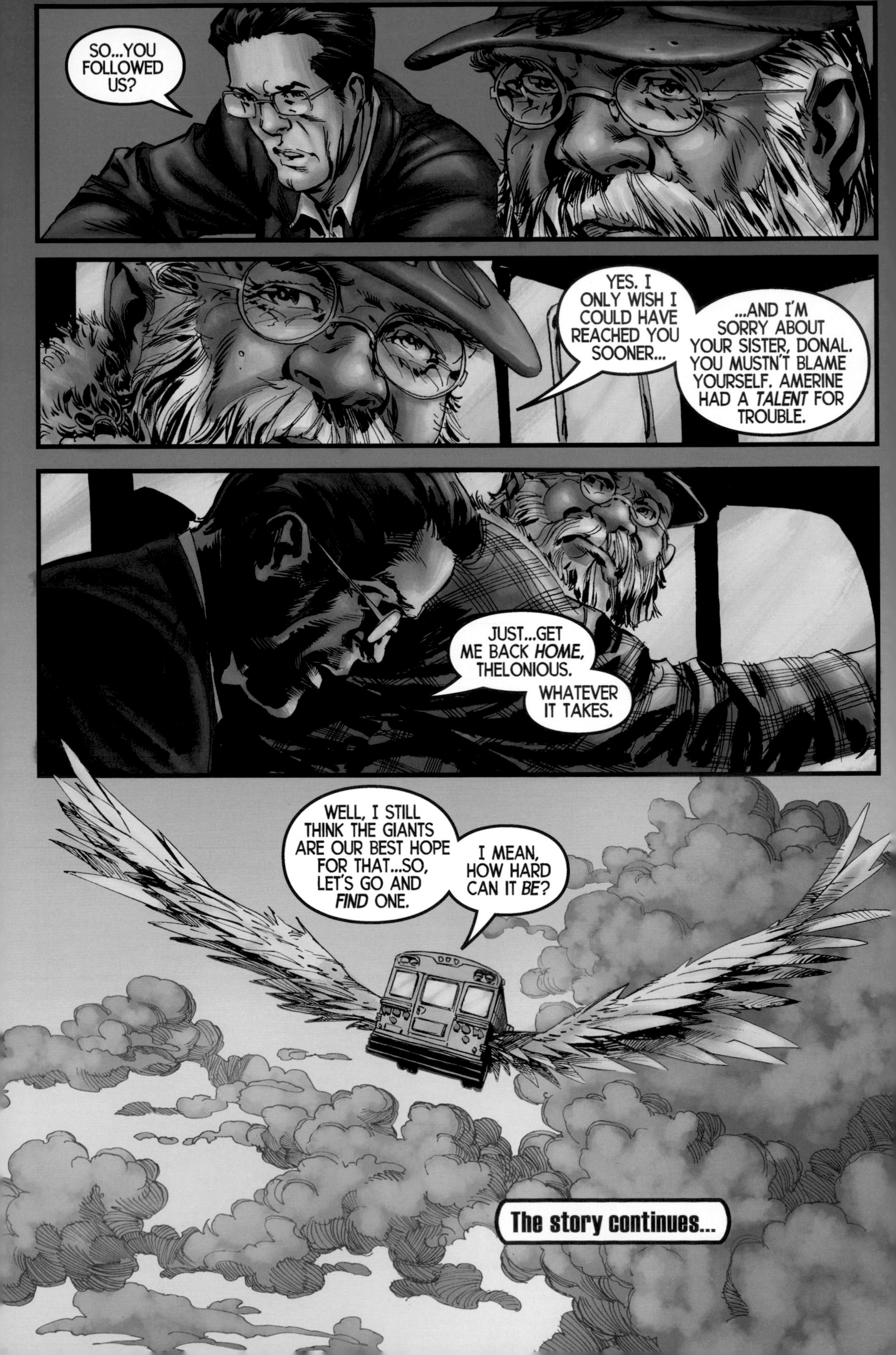
SO...YOU FOLLOWED US?
YES. I ONLY WISH I COULD HAVE REACHED YOU SOONER...
...AND I'M SORRY ABOUT YOUR SISTER, DONAL. YOU MUSTN'T BLAME YOURSELF. AMERINE HAD A *TALENT* FOR TROUBLE.
JUST...GET ME BACK *HOME,* THELONIOUS.
WHATEVER IT TAKES.
WELL, I STILL THINK THE GIANTS ARE OUR BEST HOPE FOR THAT...SO, LET'S GO AND *FIND* ONE.
I MEAN, HOW HARD CAN IT *BE*?
The story continues...

AFTERWORD

The first twenty-four pages of this story initially appeared in eight-page chunks in *Dark Horse Presents*, and the art is by Phil Winslade, who co-created *King's Road* with me. When Phil's commitments took him off elsewhere, I was worried that we'd have a hard time finding a worthy replacement for him. Fortunately, we ended up with Staz Johnson on art (splendidly colored by Douglas Sirois), who came up with the sterling work in the rest of this volume, and I couldn't be happier.

As for the story . . . It begins, like most story ideas, with one simple question: What if . . . ? What if Earth was at war with Mars? What if a magician captured Morpheus, the King of Dreams? What if someone got bitten by a radioactive spider?

I probably first started thinking about *King's Road* as a result of seeing the movie *The King's Speech*. I was really moved by King George's plight—not the fact that the poor guy had a speech impediment, but the fact that because his brother King Edward had abdicated, George got dumped into a job he never thought he'd get and certainly didn't want, just as an impending war was popping up on the horizon. Of course, being British, I was already very familiar with this period of history, but seeing it acted out onscreen carried real emotional power.

I also found myself wondering: What if this happened in a fantasy setting?

And so I came up with Prince Donal, the younger son of the royal house of Avalon, who knew he was never going to be a king and decided to up stakes and try his luck on Earth instead, where half of his family came from. He finds a career, gets married, has a couple of kids, buys a house in the suburbs, and everything works out just fine for a couple of decades . . .

And then the monsters turn up to kill him and all those he loves. His brother the king is dead, and Donal now has no choice but to step up and do his duty to save his family and his homeland.

Back in the 1990s, I wrote half a dozen *Sandman* spinoff stories, and one of the things I learned in the process is that magic suddenly becomes a lot more real when you rub it up against the modern world we all know. A unicorn in an enchanted glade is merely "Meh, so what?"—but a unicorn in Times Square will make you sit up and pay attention. With *King's Road* I figured that the sight of fairy-tale ogres and trolls trashing a shopping mall might be something that readers would enjoy, for sheer novelty value alone.

But now we're about to reverse the flow and take this suburban family back to face the perils of a medieval fantasy world. Our modern teenagers are going to have to cope without electricity, without TV or Wi-Fi, without tablet computers or smartphones or social media. How will they manage? You'll have to wait and see . . .

—Peter Hogan, giant killer and scribe
February 2016

King's Road #1 front cover
inks by Staz Johnson

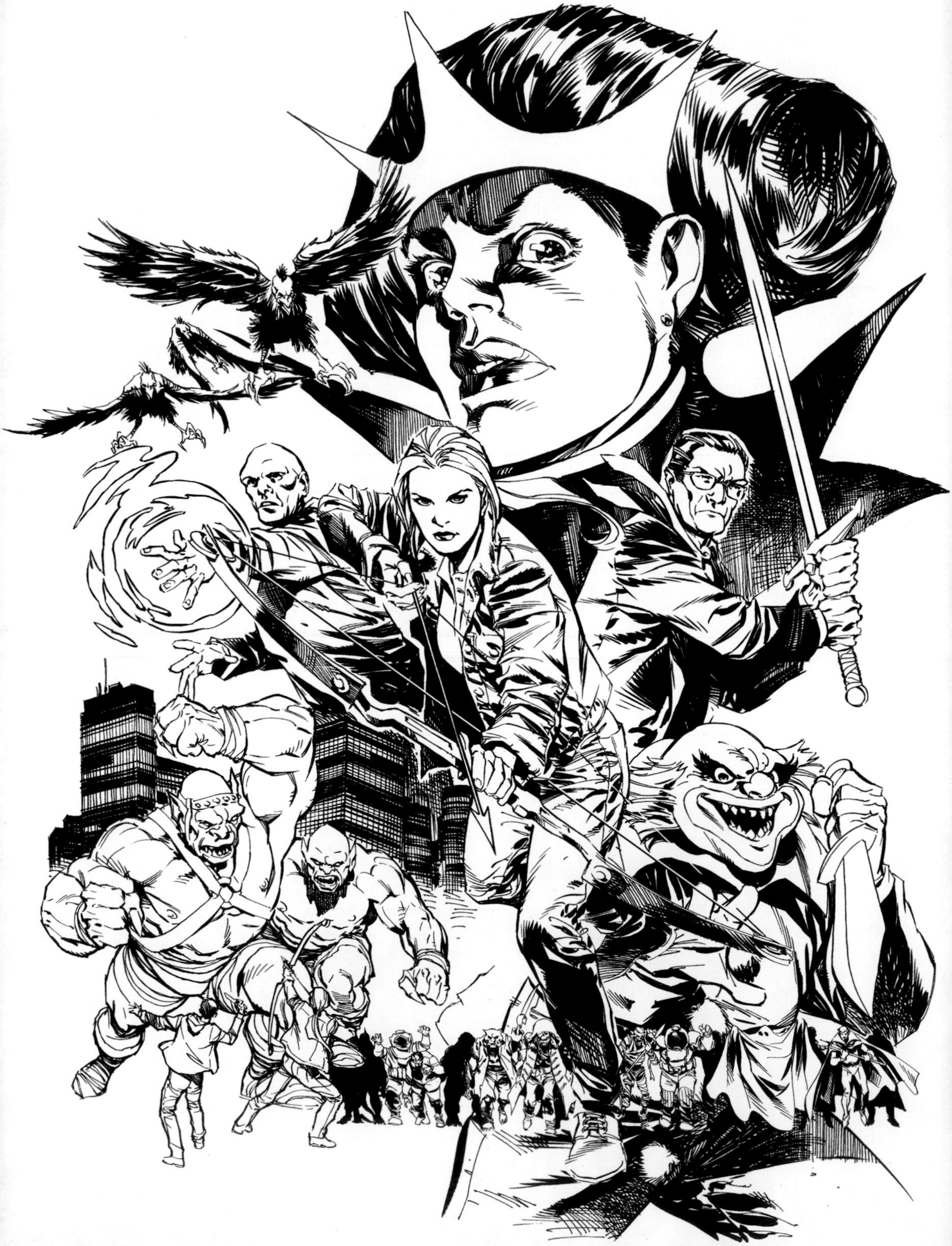

King's Road #1 front cover
colors by Douglas Sirois

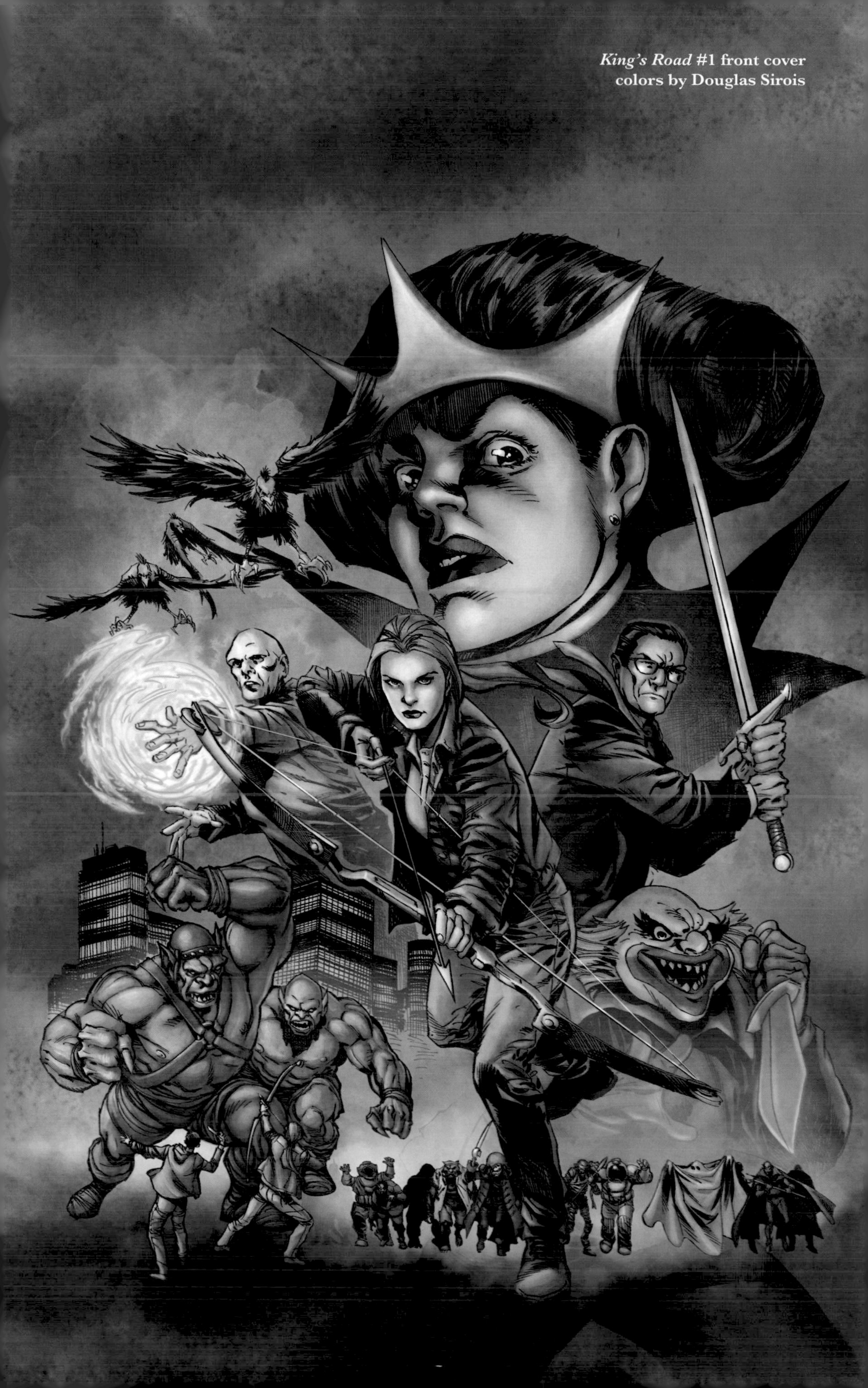

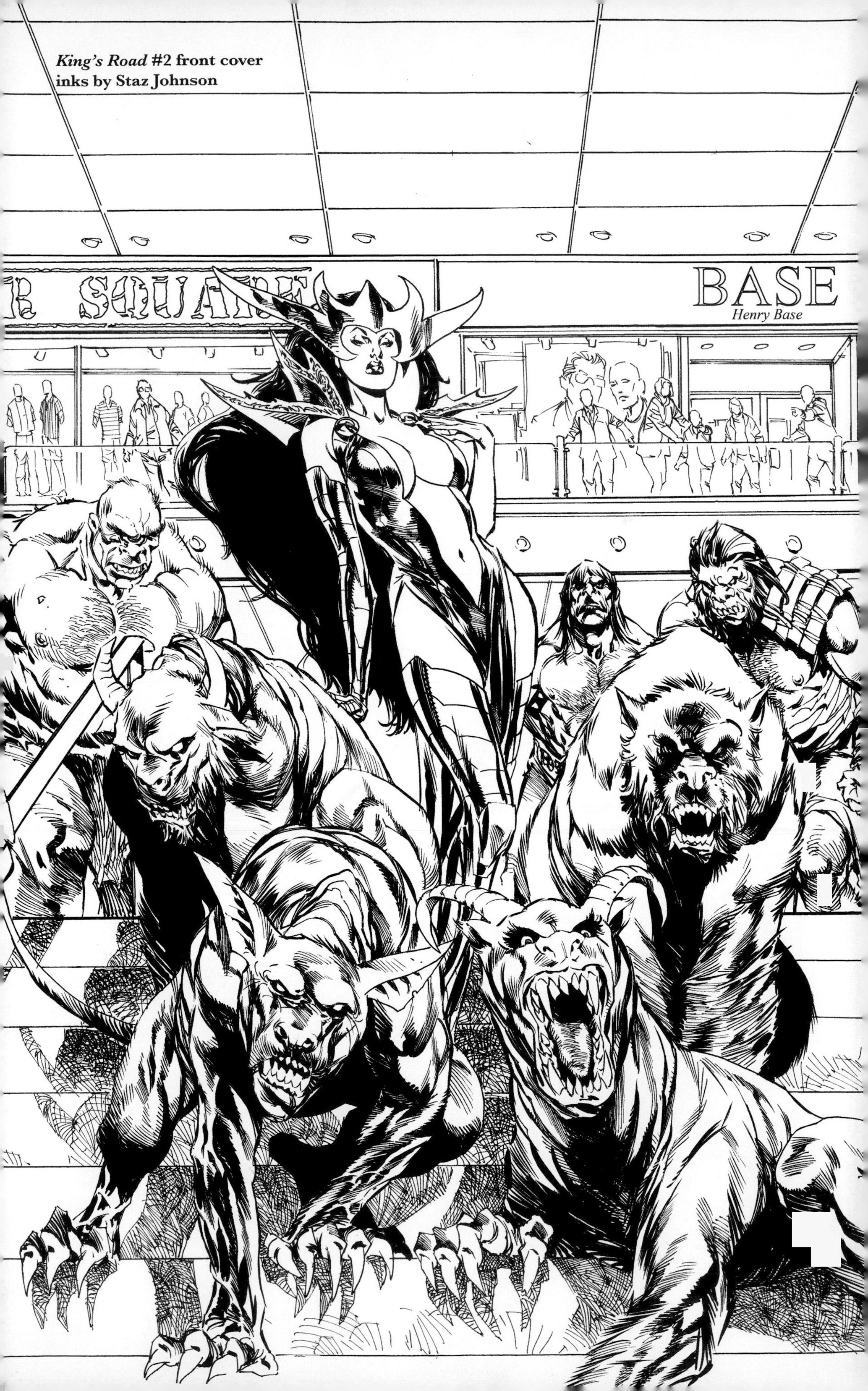
BASE
Henry Base

King's Road #2 front cover
inks by Staz Johnson

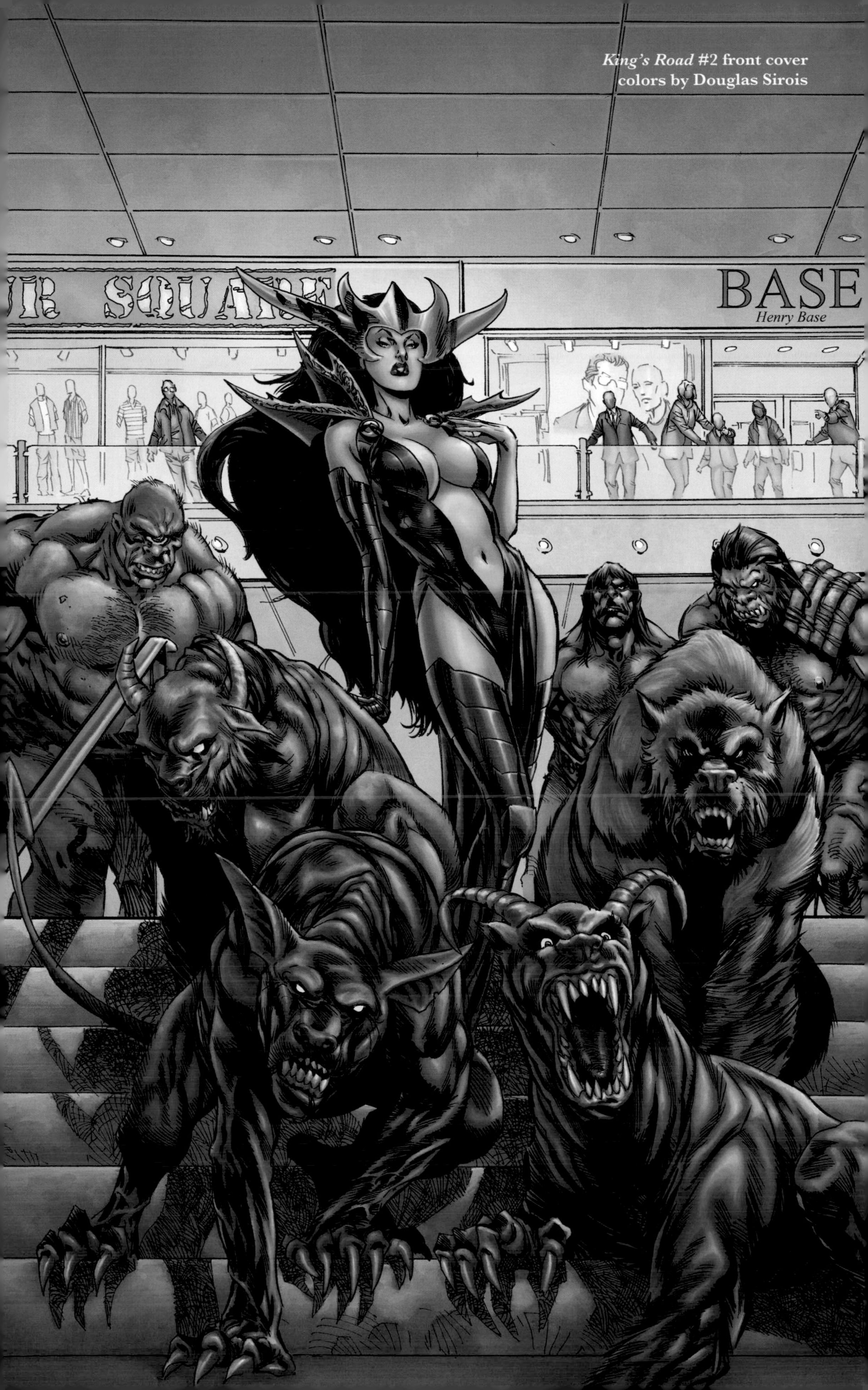
BASE
Henry Base

King's Road #2 front cover
colors by Douglas Sirois

King's Road #3 front cover
inks by Staz Johnson

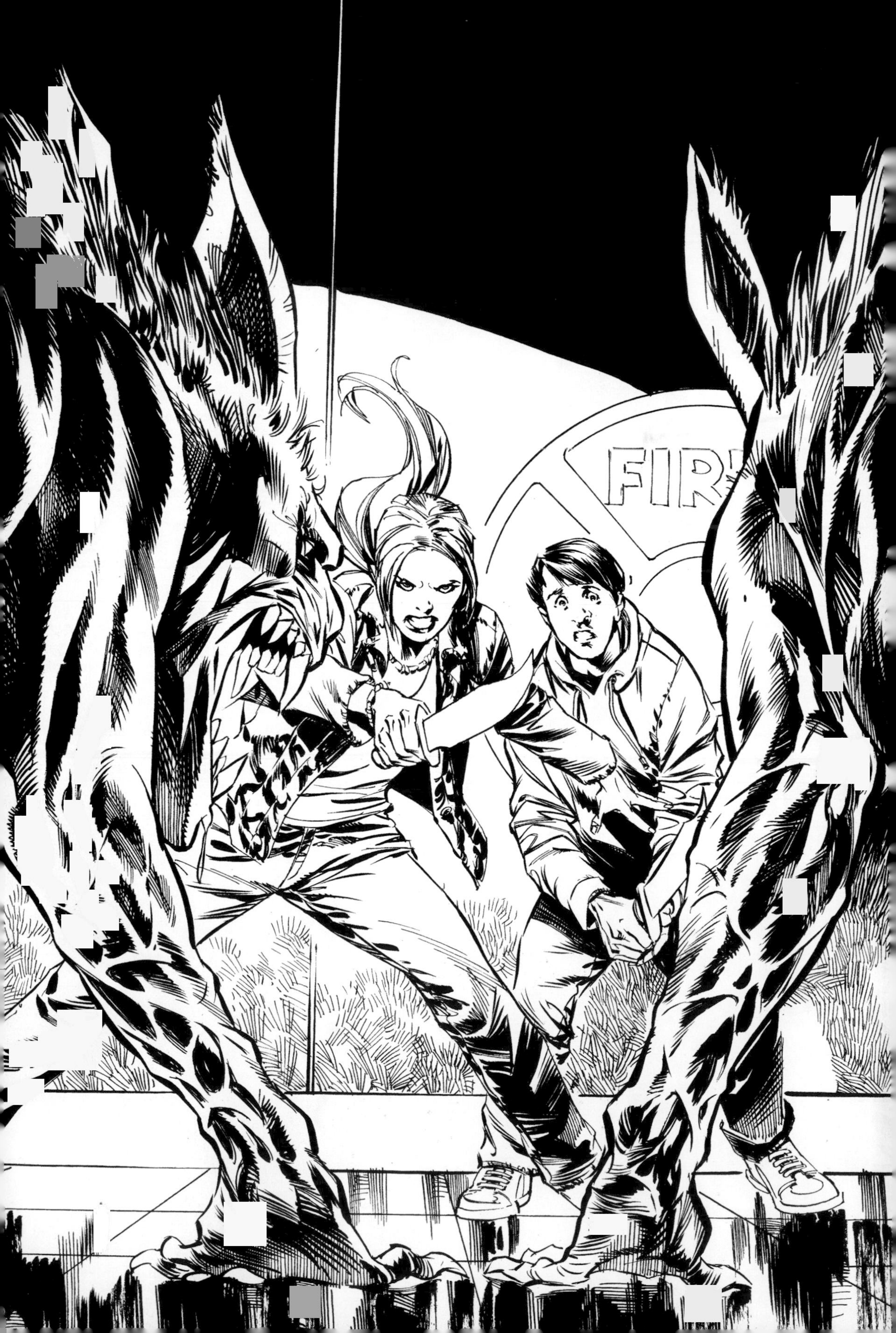

King's Road #3 front cover
colors by Douglas Sirois

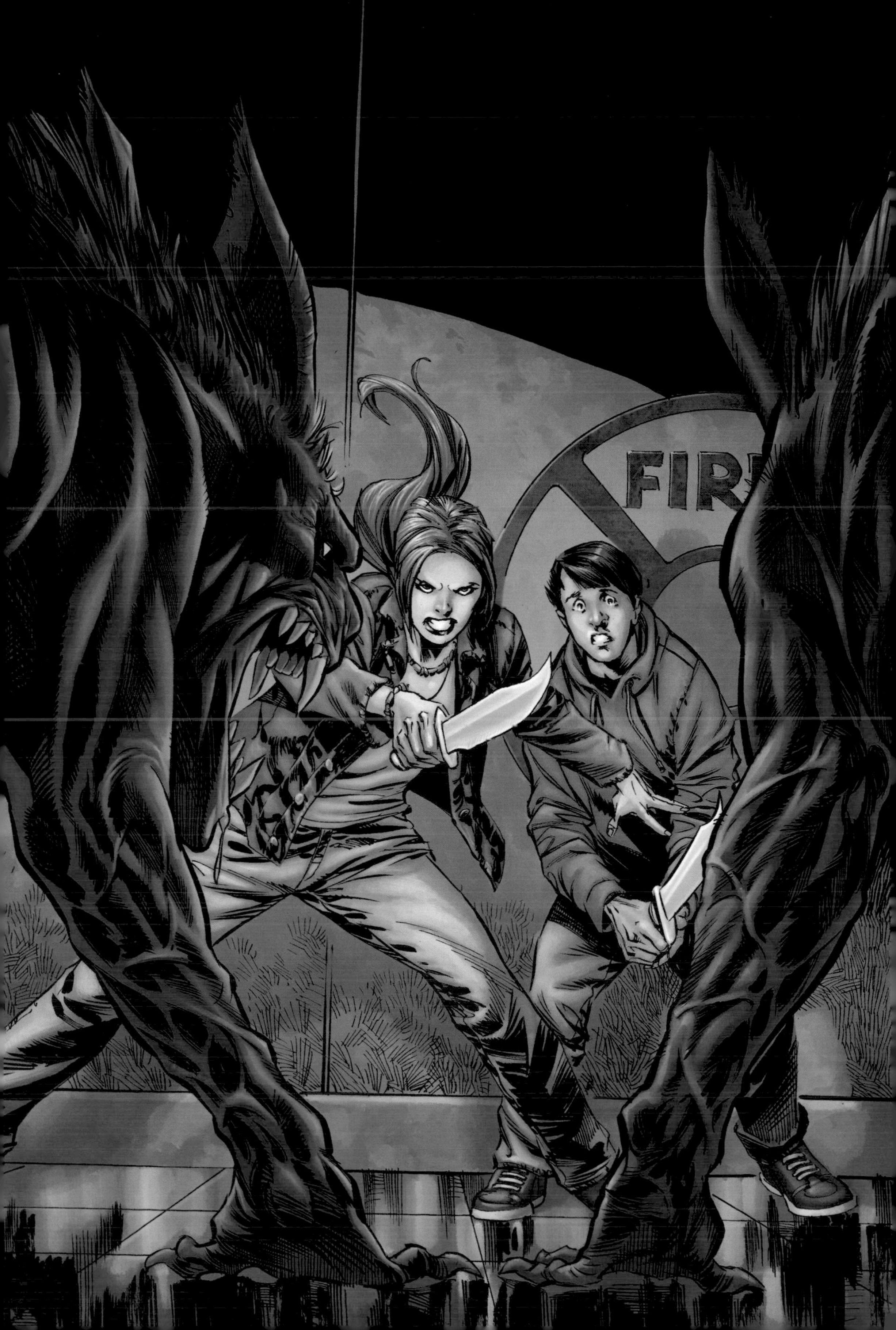
FIR

CREATIVE GIANTS!

GET YOUR FIX OF DARK HORSE BOOKS FROM THESE INSPIRED CREATORS!

MESMO DELIVERY SECOND EDITION

Rafael Grampá

Eisner Award–winning artist Rafael Grampá (*5*, *Hellblazer*) makes his full-length comics debut with the critically acclaimed graphic novel *Mesmo Delivery*—a kinetic, bloody romp starring Rufo, an ex-boxer; Sangrecco, an Elvis impersonator; and a ragtag crew of overly confident drunks who pick the wrong delivery men to mess with.

ISBN 978-1-61655-457-6 | $14.99

SIN TITULO

Cameron Stewart

Following the death of his grandfather, Alex Mackay discovers a mysterious photograph in the old man's belongings that sets him on an adventure like no other—where dreams and reality merge, family secrets are laid bare, and lives are irrevocably altered.

ISBN 978-1-61655-248-0 | $19.99

DE:TALES

Fábio Moon and Gabriel Bá

Brazilian twins Fábio Moon and Gabriel Bá's (*Daytripper*, *Pixu*) most personal work to date. Brimming with all the details of human life, their charming tales move from the urban reality of their home in São Paulo to the magical realism of their Latin American background.

ISBN 978-1-59582-557-5 | $19.99

THE TRUE LIVES OF THE FABULOUS KILLJOYS

Gerard Way, Shaun Simon, and Becky Cloonan

Years ago, the Killjoys fought against the tyrannical megacorporation Better Living Industries. Today, the followers of the original Killjoys languish in the desert and the fight for freedom fades. It's left to the Girl to take down BLI!

ISBN 978-1-59582-462-2 | $19.99

DEMO

Brian Wood and Becky Cloonan

It's hard enough being a teenager. Now try being a teenager with *powers*. A chronicle of the lives of young people on separate journeys to self-discovery in a world—just like our own—where being different is feared.

ISBN 978-1-61655-682-2 | $24.99

SABERTOOTH SWORDSMAN

Damon Gentry and Aaron Conley

When his village is enslaved and his wife kidnapped by the malevolent Mastodon Mathematician, a simple farmer must find his inner warrior—the Sabertooth Swordsman!

ISBN 978-1-61655-176-6 | $17.99

JAYBIRD

Jaakko and Lauri Ahonen

Disney meets Kafka in this beautiful, intense, original tale! A very small, very scared little bird lives an isolated life in a great big house with his infirm mother. He's never been outside the house, and he never will if his mother has anything to say about it.

ISBN 978-1-61655-469-9 | $19.99

MONSTERS! & OTHER STORIES

Gustavo Duarte

Newcomer Gustavo Duarte spins wordless tales inspired by Godzilla, King Kong, and Pixar, brimming with humor, charm, and delightfully twisted horror!

ISBN 978-1-61655-309-8 | $12.99

SACRIFICE

Sam Humphries and Dalton Rose

What happens when a troubled youth is plucked from modern society and thrust though time and space into the heart of the Aztec civilization—one of the most bloodthirsty times in human history?

ISBN 978-1-59582-985-6 | $19.99